A Fun Way To Enjoy FSX

TIPS
TRICKS
&
TRIPS

Adam Howe
Scott Slaughter

Abacus
www.abacuspub.com

D1241077

**THE INFORMATION IN THIS BOOK IS NOT INTENDED FOR REAL WORLD
NAVIGATION OR FLYING SITUATIONS**

Tips, Tricks & Trips Contents

Introduction

Thanks for buying and reading *Tricks, Tips & Trips*.

With the arrival of Microsoft Flight Simulator X, you now have an even more realistic way to fly with your personal computer. You can use a the phrase such as *"the sky is the limit"* to describe the potential of FSX and one way to strive towards the limit is to gain hands-on experience with the simulator's vast number of impressive features.

The goal of *Tricks, Tips & Trips* is reveal many of these features while keeping the experience an enjoyable one. Fly from lowly Death Valley to breathtaking Leadville; take a flight in the dark; try some nifty snaps and rolls; get there faster by slewing; introduce yourself to copter flying; make your own missions. As this book shows, there's plenty of fun and interesting things to do with FSX.

Here's a tip: Keep this book next to your PC as you fly with FSX and we think you'll be surprised how much fun it is to follow along.

Note About The Flights In *Tips, Tricks & Trips*

We've also included several flights you can try that accompany some of the chapters in *Tips, Tricks & Trips.*

To load these flights, start your FSX. Choose the **Free Flight** option from the main screen. Click the Load button above the Aircraft preview. You'll immediately see a list of pre-saved flights. After you've selected the flight, click the **Fly Now!** button to starts the flight.

Here's a list of the flights:

ttt_FurnaceCreek
    Accompanies the "Flying In The Great Outdoors" chapter

ttt_SignLanguage
    Accompanies the "Understanding Sign Language" chapter

ttt_FloridaFloatplane
    Accompanies the "Floatplanes & Feeling The Salt In Your Hair" chapter

ttt_Aerobatics
    Accompanies the "Rolling Over With Magical Aerobatics" chapter

ttt_DontBeAfraid
    Accompanies the "Don't Be Afraid Of The Dark" chapter

ttt_LostEngine
    Accompanies the "Uh Oh! You've Just Lost Your Engine — NOW WHAT?" chapter

Also, the Scenery Shortcut program (accompanies the "Managing New Scenery In FSX" chapter) is installed with the above flights. You'll have a shortcut to open the Scenery Shortcut on your Windows desktop.

A Note About The Videos

We'll mention in *Tips, Trips And Tricks* that the companion CD-ROM includes many videos and extras. All you need to view them is a media player such as Windows Media Player and make certain you have your speakers turned on.

The videos on companion CD-ROM include:

Aerobatics Video

Taxiway signs

Flying A Helicopter

Flying At Night

ILS Approach

Scenery Shortcut

We hope *Tips, Trips And Tricks* will help you enjoy your FSX experiences. Although we've checked everything in the book for accuracy, it you're an eagle-eyed reader, you may nevertheless find an error, misspellings or other problems; we apologize ahead of time if that is the case.

Recovering From Stalls & Spins

Most of us have spun our favorite Flight Sim aircraft into the ground on more than one occasion so perhaps it's not too surprising to learn that stall/spin accidents make up about 25% of all fatal general aviation accidents in the US according to the National Transportation Safety Board (NTSB). Therefore, understanding why your aircraft stalls or spins is important, but what is even more important is understanding how to recover from a spin or stall once you're in one.

So, we'll look in this chapter at these two similar situations that you don't want to experience while flying (unless you're doing them intentionally).

We'll first look at stalls and how to recover from the stall.

Stalls

A stall is a condition in which the angle of attack exceeds the wing's ability to produce lift. When moved through the air, the wing, by design will produce a great deal of lift if you're flying within the designed limits. The wing's forward speed must be above the stall speed for any given configuration and the angle of attack such that the air can flow smoothly over it. An aircraft will climb at high angle of attack and high airspeed and will maintain altitude as long as you use the right combination of power setting, speed and angle of attack. In real world flying, even without engine power lift is still possible thanks to prop wind milling and air speed just above stall speed.

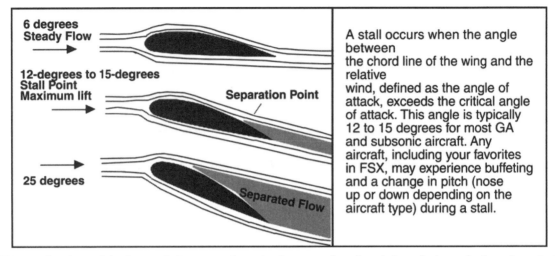

6 degrees Steady Flow

12-degrees to 15-degrees Stall Point Maximum lift

Separation Point

25 degrees

Separated Flow

A stall occurs when the angle between the chord line of the wing and the relative wind, defined as the angle of attack, exceeds the critical angle of attack. This angle is typically 12 to 15 degrees for most GA and subsonic aircraft. Any aircraft, including your favorites in FSX, may experience buffeting and a change in pitch (nose up or down depending on the aircraft type) during a stall.

The angle of attack is the angle between the wing's mean chord and the relative wind, or the wind moving past the airfoil as the airfoil moves through the air. The wind is called "relative" because the direction of the wind is relative to the altitude of the airfoil and is always parallel to the flight path of your aircraft. The velocity of the relative wind and the airspeed of the airplane are equal and opposite to each other.

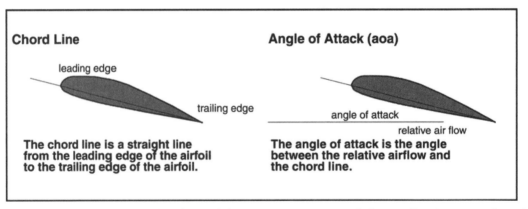

Chord Line

leading edge

trailing edge

The chord line is a straight line from the leading edge of the airfoil to the trailing edge of the airfoil.

Angle of Attack (aoa)

angle of attack

relative air flow

The angle of attack is the angle between the relative airflow and the chord line.

The stall occurs when the angle of attack becomes too great and the air flowing over the wing becomes turbulent. The low-pressure area above the wing begins to disappear as does lift. Always keep in mind that you can encounter a stall at any airspeed, any altitude and any amount of throttle. Stall speeds change with angle of bank, configuration and any changes in gross weight. Furthermore, an aircraft will stall at a higher speed with flaps retracted than with the flaps extended.

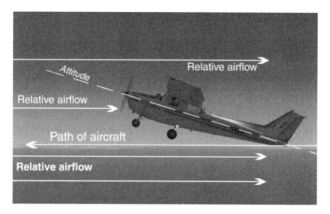

A diagram showing how the relative airflow is equal and opposite to the flight path of your aircraft.

Types Of Stalls

You may encounter one of three types of stalls while flying. The type of stall depends on different factors, including altitude, maneuvers and location.

Power-off stalls

Pilots practice power-off stalls (also called approach-to-landing stalls) to simulate normal approach-to-landing conditions and configuration. Many stall/spin accidents have occurred in these situations.

Power-on stalls

Pilots practice power-on stalls (also known as departure stalls) to simulate takeoff and climb-out conditions. As with the power-off stall, the power-on stalls have led to many accidents as well, especially during go-around procedures. One common factor these accidents share have been the failure of the pilot to maintain positive control due to a nose-high trim setting or retracting the flaps too early.

Accelerated stalls

You can experience accelerated stalls at higher-than-normal airspeeds due to applying abrupt or excessive controls to your aircraft (or both). Accelerated stalls may occur in steep turns, pullups or other abrupt changes in your flightpath.

Recognizing An Impending Stall

Understanding why an aircraft stalls, but more importantly, understanding how to recover from that stall are important in becoming a good pilot.

Fortunately you have four ways of recognizing that your aircraft is about to stall. You should become very familiar with these warning signs:

→ You experience less control over your aircraft as its airspeed is reduced. This is partly because the airflow over the flight control surfaces is reduced.

→ If you're flying a fixed-pitch propeller airplanes, you may detect a decrease in revolutions per minute (RPM) when approaching a stall while in power-on conditions.

➤ Your aircraft experiences buffeting, uncontrollable pitching or vibrations that begin just before the stall occurs.

➤ Many aircraft in Flight Sim use a stall indicator to alert you when the airflow over the wing(s) approaches a point that lift cannot be sustained. The stall indicator is part of your aircraft for a reason — don't ignore it!

Always keep an eye out for the STALL indicator in the lower right corner of your view screen in FSX.

You should consider these as warnings to take quick action by adding power to increase airspeed and/or lowering the nose and/or decreasing the angle of attack. Your reaction should be instinctive when you see one or more of these warnings.

You can also keep an eye on your airspeed indicator gauge. Although stalls depend more on angle of attack than airspeed, there is also an airspeed at which the wing's angle of attack will exceed the critical angle of attack for every weight of every aircraft. Therefore, airspeed in a given configuration is often used as an indirect indicator of approaching stall conditions. The airspeed indicator may indicate the VSO (the stalling speed or the minimum steady flight speed in the landing configuration) and VS speeds (the stalling speed or the minimum steady flight speed at which the airplane is controllable) of your aircraft. The VS0 is indicated by the bottom of the white arc on an airspeed indicator and VS is indicated by the bottom of the green arc.

Recovering From A Stall

Practicing stall recovery techniques not only increases your confidence as a pilot, but also provides you with a good feel for your aircraft at unusual airspeeds and altitudes that you may seldom experience. Keep in mind that the real goal when practicing stalls is not learning how to stall your aircraft but recognizing the first stages of an impending stall and taking quick action to recover from the stall.

Practice...Practice...Practice

The key factor in recovery from a stall is that you must regain positive control of your aircraft by reducing the angle of attack. At the first hint of a stall (see page 3), decrease the angle of attack of your aircraft so the wings can regain lift. Unfortunately, there is no preset amount of forward pressure anyone can give you because every aircraft requires a different amount of forward pressure to regain lift. Furthermore, applying too much forward pressure can impede recovery by imposing a negative load on the wing.

The next step in recovering from a stall is to increase power smoothly to increase airspeed and minimize the loss of altitude. As airspeed increases and you've completed the recovery, adjust power as needed to return to straight-and-level flight. Then maintain straight and level flight by using full coordinated use of the controls. Make certain the airspeed indicator never reaches its high-speed red lines at anytime during a practice stall.

You need to get it right the first time because if recovery from a stall is not made properly, the result may be a secondary stall or a spin. A secondary stall is caused by attempting to hasten the completion of a stall recovery before the aircraft has regained sufficient flying speed. When this stall occurs, the back elevator pressure should again be released just as in a normal stall recovery. When sufficient airspeed has been regained, the aircraft can then be returned to straight-and-level flight.

Practicing power-off stall recovery

We'll practice power-off stalls in the same configurations as you might have while making an approach to land at an airport. Stalls are safer to practice at high altitudes because at lower altitudes, you must perform your stall recovery quickly and properly.

→ Select an afternoon (preferably summer so you can have lots of sunlight).

→ Clear all weather so the sky is clear and the winds are calm (as you get more experience practicing stall recovery techniques, then by all means add some weather effects typical to the area where you fly the most often, especially winds).

→ Take off from your favorite airport.

→ Climb to 3000 feet AGL and fly a course of 360-degrees.

→ When you're flying straight and level at 3000 feet, make a 90 degree turn into the left and then repeat this to the right while at the same time looking for other aircraft in the area. This is the "clearing turn" and is a real world maneuver that signals other aircraft that you may be considering an unusual maneuver. Although it's a real world maneuver, it's also a good habit to develop in Flight Sim.

→ While still in level flight on a heading 360-degrees, pull the carburetor heat on (if required). Decrease the power to around 50% but keep your finger/hand on the throttle as much as possible to increase or decrease the throttle level while practicing stalls.

→ Maintain your altitude as long as possible by increasing the pitch attitude.

→ Don't panic when you see a decrease in the airspeed and when you see or hear the stall indicator. (Compare the airspeed in the following two images.)

Don't panic when you notice a change in your airspeed and if you hear/see the STALL warning.

✈ When you see or hear the stall indicator or feel an impending stall, lower the nose just below the horizon.

✈ Apply full power and make certain the carburetor heat is off.

✈ Raise the nose back to straight and level flight and adjust power.

→ Begin climbing back to 3000 feet and repeat as many times as you safely can.

→ Try recovering several times from a stall without applying power just to get the feel for your aircraft and what the wing is going through during the stall and recovery stages.

Remember to lower the nose first and break the stall before adding full power. Otherwise, if you were to add full power just as the stall occurred without decreasing the pitch attitude, you might have even more trouble coming your way. We'll talk about spins later in this article.

Pushing forward on the yolk excessively during the recover will result in a negative G-force. After you have decreased the pitch attitude, try not to pull back too much on the elevator until your aircraft has regained sufficient flying speed during the recovery or you may experience a "secondary stall."

Practicing power-on stall recovery

The power-on stall is also called the "take off and departure." What you're trying to do is to prevent a stall while flying low and slow, at a high power setting, similar to what you're experiencing taking off and climbing from an airport.

→ Select an afternoon (preferably summer so you can have lots of sunlight).

→ Clear all weather so the sky is clear and the winds are zero (as you get more experience practicing stall recovery techniques, then by all means add some weather effects typical to the area where you fly the most often, especially winds).

→ Take off from your favorite airport.

→ Climb to 3000 feet AGL and fly a course of 180-degrees this time.

→ Reduce throttle to about 80% and begin climbing.

The next step depends on the size of aircraft you're flying. If you're flying a smaller aircraft, consider practicing full power stalls but if your aircraft is larger, its engine(s) may overpower the aircraft in a full-power stall. If so, the ailerons may not be effective enough at slow airspeeds to counter the engine's torque. A spin may occur if the power is too great and the airspeed too low. Therefore, try using about an 80-90% power setting until you gain more experience in stall recoveries.

✈ At the first indication of an impending stall, and certainly when you see/hear the STALL warning, lower the nose (pitch attitude), apply full power and level off.

✈ If you think that nothing much happened, don't worry…you probably did everything right! Recovering from a power-on stall isn't real exciting when performed correctly. But that's not to say it's all easy because maintaining your heading throughout the stall is a challenge in itself. Apply a constant right rudder when necessary to counter the torque, p-factor and slipstream.

The stall speed will be less during a power on stall and the slower speed and higher pitch attitude means your aircraft controls will be less effective. Recovery will be quicker because at the same time you're applying more thrust, you're also lowering the pitch attitude. If one wing begins to drop as the aircraft stalls, immediately apply coordinated rudder and aileron to level the wings.

Practicing accelerated maneuver stall recovery

It's important not to attempt accelerated maneuver stalls in any aircraft that isn't certificated to do this type of maneuver. I'll repeat it here again, always check the owner's manual for limitations before assuming you can safely roll, loop, spin or even intentionally stall your aircraft.

The accelerated maneuver stall occurs during a high-speed dive when you apply full elevator and wait for the stall indicator to turn on.

Let's practice this type of stall.

✈ Select an afternoon (preferably summer so you can have lots of sunlight).

✈ Clear all weather so the sky is clear and the winds are zero (as you get more experience practicing stall recovery techniques, then apply some weather effects typical to the area where you fly the most often, especially winds).

✈ Take off from your favorite airport.

✈ Climb to 5000 feet AGL and flying a straight-and-level course, direction is at your discretion.

✈ Begin a shallow dive at about 20 knots above the unaccelerated stall speed.

✈ Pull back abruptly enough to hear or see the stall indicator come on. Don't hold back pressure more than a few seconds or you may be doing another power-on stall, loop or other unintentional maneuver.

✈ Never exceed the maneuvering speed for your aircraft while practicing accelerated stalls. In this case, the maneuvering speed is usually found in the airplane's owner's manual and is important when you are flying in severe turbulence.

✈ Perform one more accelerated stall by banking your aircraft 60 degrees to the left at cruise airspeed (stay below the maneuvering speed) maintaining altitude and applying just enough back pressure until the wing stalls. Reduce the power, if necessary. At the first indication of the stall, reduce the angle of attack, add full power and level the wings in a smooth, simultaneous move.

Then repeat these steps but this time to the right.

Make your stall recovery procedure prompt and not hurried and awkward… increase the throttle at a steady rate. Take your time, whether increasing power to climb, go-around or to recover from a stall. By practicing stall recoveries, you'll become a more confident pilot who won't panic under stress.

Keeping Clean By Understanding The Spin Cycle

A spin for a pilot is a special type of stall. It occurs when the aircraft descends rapidly and rotates in a helical direction, or a corkscrew path downward (it's also called autorotation), while it's at an angle of attack greater than the angle of maximum lift. Your airspeed indicator usually shows an extremely very low airspeed.

Spins will maintain a high angle of attack until you decrease the pitch altitude (as when recovering from any other stalled condition) and will continue until either the aircraft crashes or you take action to recover from the spin.

A spin will usually occur if you do not or cannot recover quickly and correctly from a stall. A stall on at least part of the wing precedes all spins, which is why it's important you understand stalls (see the section on stalls earlier in this article). A good pilot may be able to recover from a stall in less than 100 feet but recovering from a spin may require considerably more altitude once the aircraft begins to rollover in the direction of the spin.

Recovering from a spin may sound easy but without practicing the correct recovery, you'll go down very quickly and with very undesired results!

Because spins were little understood in the early years of aviation, proper recovery procedures were unknown; the pilot instinctively would pull back on the stick but that only made the spin worse. Therefore, spins were often fatal and earned a reputation as an unpredictable danger that might snatch an aviator's life at any time, and against which there was no defense.

Aerodynamic experts and a few brave pilots experimented with the concept of spins in the early 1900s. Lieutenant Wilfred Parke in August 1912 was the first known pilot to recover from an accidental spin when his Avro biplane entered a spin at 700 feet AGL in the traffic pattern at Larkhill. He attempted to recover from the spin by increasing engine speed, pulling back on the stick and turning into the spin but that action had no affect. His airplane continued to spin towards the ground. In an effort to neutralize the forces that had him pressed against the right side of the cockpit, Parke applied full right rudder and his aircraft soon leveled out five feet above the ground. With his aircraft now under control, Parke climbed, made another approach and landed safely.

Despite the "Parke's technique," as it became called, pilots were not taught spin recovery procedures until the start of World War I.

The first documented case of an intentional spin and recovery occurred in 1915. Squadron Leader J.C. Brooke recovered from an accidental spin but was convinced to repeat the spin. He then discovered that he could easily recover from a spin using Parke's technique.

In 1917, Frederick Lindemann, an English physicist, conducted a series of experiments that led to the first understanding of the aerodynamics of the spin.

Aircraft design can affect a spin

All aircraft in the real world must meet FAA certification standards for stalls but not all aircraft must meet be certificated for spin recovery requirements. So, even though manufacturers design their aircraft with spin resistance in mind, not all aircraft are approved for spins and may become unrecoverable if a spin is allowed to develop.

Many training aircraft are less likely to enter a spin; in fact, many light trainers can recover from a spin when the pilot simply takes his or her hands and feet off the controls. The result may be a high-speed dive but at least the aircraft isn't completely out of control.

On the other hand, some other aircraft spin very easily and require a quick recovery procedure to exit the spin. Unfortunately, many of the aircraft that do spin are not rated for this maneuver and may be very difficult to recover or may sustain structural damage if a spin is attempted. This has happened in the past with the Piper Tomahawk. It was initially certified for spins but the certification was revoked following several fatal accidents. Fortunately, we don't necessarily need to worry about spin certifications in Flight Sim.

Practicing A Spin

You should practice the spin recovery technique as often as you do with stall recovery so you react without thinking. As you prepare to practice spins, keep the following three points in mind:

1. Practice spins with sufficient altitude.

2. Practice only in clear airspace.

3. Make certain before practicing your aircraft is certificated for spins. Although this isn't really necessary in Flight Sim, it's another real world habit to develop.

Preflight Flight Sim Work

I recommend you completely read through this information before starting your spins. You don't want to read and spin at the same time! The information here refers primarily to the default FSX Cessna but you can use whatever aircraft you want.

Regardless of the aircraft you use, you must disable the auto-rudder because you will not use the ailerons to enter a spin or to recover from a spin; in fact, the ailerons should be neutral during the entire maneuver. To do this, select the **Aircraft | Realism Settings...** command. Look in the lower right of the dialog box for the "Flight controls" area. Make certain to remove the check next to the "Autorudder" checkbox (see following image).

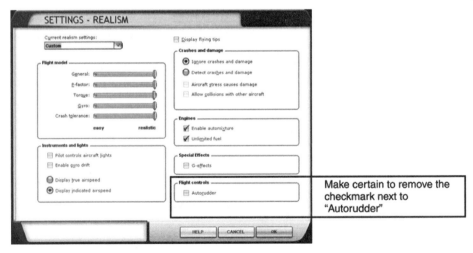

*Select the **Aircraft | Realism Settings...** command and disable Autorudder.*

Tips on takeoff and rudder control

If you've never flown an aircraft in Flight Sim with the auto-rudder off, this chapter may double as a quick lesson on rudder control, especially on takeoff. When you first apply full-power, you'll discover the rudder has very little directional control and you may need to apply a greater amount of the rudder to maintain a direction down the center of the runway.

As your speed increases, you'll find the rudder will become more effective in controlling your aircraft, which is important to remember as the speed increases on takeoff. You'll also probably discover your aircraft pulling to the left after you apply full power. Use enough right rudder to maintain, as much as possible, a takeoff roll down the center of the runway. Keep your wings level and heading straight by using a combination of aileron and rudder control. Use the trim and you can basically let your aircraft fly itself during the climb.

Let's practice a spin.

→ Select an afternoon (preferably summer so you can have lots of light).

→ Clear all weather so the sky is clear and the winds are zero (as you get more experience practicing stall recovery techniques, then by all means add some weather effects typical to the area where you fly the most often, especially winds).

→ Take off from your favorite airport.

→ Climb to 8000 feet AGL on whatever heading you want to fly but make certain you're flying straight-and-level. You should expect to lose about 500 feet of altitude for each three-second turn in most small GA aircraft.

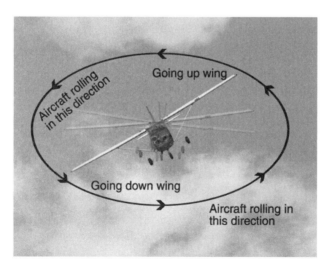

Example of how your aircraft begins a spin by rolling from a level flight to the right and eventually into a spin.

→ Reduce throttle close to idle (for example, around 1000-1300 rpm) and maintain your heading. You'll need to start slowing down your aircraft and go into a situation that allows a high angle of attack.

✈ Make certain to neutralize the ailerons and keep the pitch attitude just above the horizon. This will also increase your angle of attack to a point close to the critical angle.

✈ When your airspeed is about 50 knots, apply full back pressure on the controls. Don't panic when you notice the airspeed decreases to the point the STALL warning appears because this is what we want to do. What is happening here is that you're letting your aircraft stall one wing much more than the other wing.

✈ If everything is done correctly, your aircraft is rolling in the direction of the spin. You'll need to determine the direction of the spin and then apply full elevator and full rudder in the opposite direction of the spin. It's critical to hold the controls in this position until you have begun to recover from the spin.

An example of an aircraft entering a spin where it stalls, begins to roll and enter a spin.

✈ Although the ailerons are neutral, your aircraft will roll in the direction of the spin and may seem to go inverted as well as appearing to point straight to the ground.

✈ Check your airspeed. The airspeed indicator may read a very low airspeed but the instrument may be unreliable anyway because of the angle of attack. If it registers a high airspeed, you're probably in a spiral dive instead of a spin (see below).

✈ Maintain the spin by keeping the controls in the fully-back position and apply full rudder.

✈ Begin the recovery by reducing the throttle to idle. This will help the nose of the aircraft pitch down and give your aircraft a better chance to reduce the angle of attack.

 NOTE   Do not use the ailerons to stop a spin because doing so will increase — not decrease — the angle of attack on the down-going wing.

✈ Apply full opposite rudder until the spinning stops and relax the elevator slightly. As the turn stops, press ⑤ to neutralize the rudder.

✈ Although this should be enough to recover from some spins, you may be in a spiral dive. If so, use the controls to level the wings and gradually apply enough aft elevator pressure to return to ease out of the dive. Be careful here though that you don't pull back too far on the controls and enter into a second spin or stall.

✈ Easing forward on the controls and applying full rudder should be completed at the same time and held until you have stopped spinning.

It's possible that when you come out of a spin you're not on the same heading as before but at least you're out of the spin and spiral dive.

✈ Keep in mind that too much pressure on the elevators, rudder or ailerons during the recovery, or if you apply the pressure too quickly, can result in a secondary stall and possibly another spin.

Although when you're trying to recover from a spin, several seconds may seem like a long time, it really isn't much time to think. That's why you need to know what you're going to before you do it.

Continue practicing until you're confident you would have no trouble recovering from an unintentional spin in the future. This will prepare you for the unintentional spin you hope will never come your way.

Don't Be Afraid Of The Dark

Y ou may be intimidated by flying at night but there are many reasons that both flight sim and real world pilots find flying at night to be easier, if not more enjoyable, than daytime flying. One reason is that nighttime views can be very impressive, especially in areas around large cities, such as the brightly colored city lights of New York, Las Vegas and London (see below).

Night views can be impressive as you fly near large cities like Las Vegas, New York City and London.

The city lights help make metropolitan areas among the safest places to fly at night because those bright lights can make it easier to spot nearby terrain and obstacles, even on moonless nights.

If you use the FSX real weather feature, you may find that the air is usually smoother and cooler at night, which provides a more comfortable flight and improved aircraft performance. So, night is typically a better time to fly if you want to avoid turbulence. Severe thunderstorms are also less likely at night, which can add to your safety when flying in areas where thunderstorms are likely to occur.

Airport traffic, depending on your location, is usually less congested at night. (In the real world, less than 5% of GA flying is done at night). Also because of the less traffic, ATC will have more time to talk with you.

But we're by no means suggesting that nighttime flying is easy. The array of airport lights, city lights or the blackness of the countryside or water can distract even the most veteran FSX pilot.

Navigating by familiar objects on the ground during a night flight is not as easy as during the day. Stars, city lights, airport lights, taxiway lights, runway lights or a black void will likely replace your familiar visual daytime landmarks.

Locating a large controlled airport can be a challenge by visual references alone; and even radar vectors may not always help. In a very sparsely populated area the ground (or worse, water) can become a black void.

So, you're right...there are many reasons to be afraid of the dark while flying. But we hope this chapter will take away some of those fears. We'll start by talking about the lights inside and outside your aircraft and all those white, red, blue and green lights at the airport. Finally, we'll take a step-by-step nighttime flight to at least get you comfortable with the dark.

Aircraft Lights

You'll see many types and colors of lights on both the interior and exterior of your aircraft and you should understand the types of lights that your aircraft uses. We'll talk about two main types of aircraft lights...exterior lights and interior lights, primarily the instrument panel lights.

Instrument Panel Lights

The most important interior lights are those that illuminate your instrument panel. These lights are so important for real world pilots that their instrument panel must have at least two light sources, which are usually an overhead light as well as smaller lights within the instrument casings.

To view the instrument panel during a nighttime flight, look for the NAV light toggle switch. (You may need to select the **Views | Instrument Panel | Switches** command on some aircraft, for example the default Cessna 172 Garmin, to see the light switches.)

Move the switch to the ON position by clicking on it. As you'll see, when the NAV light switch is on, the instrument panel is illuminated. You might even notice a reddish tint to the panel. The red light is used by real world pilots because our eyes work more effectively at night under red lights without losing their dark adaptation. Therefore, the instrument panel in a real world aircraft is usually tinted red for night flights.

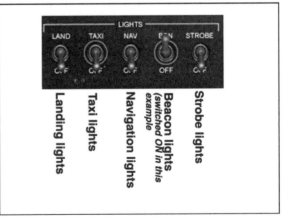

Example of how the instrument panel is illuminated at night. The instrument panel for real world pilots are usually reddish because our eyes function effectively at night without losing their dark adaptation under red lights.

Exterior aircraft lighting

Most aircraft use two types of exterior lighting — navigation lights and anti-collision lights. We'll first talk about the navigation lights since they are the most noticeable lights on your aircraft.

Navigation lights

The navigation lights include a red light on the left (port) wingtip, a green light on the right (starboard) wingtip and a white light is on the tail. See the following image for an example.

The exterior lighting consists of red (port), green (starboard) and white (tail) navigation lights.

These three lights are the most noticeable lights on the exterior of your aircraft and alert other pilots to both the location and flying direction of your aircraft.

To turn on the navigation lights, move the NAV lights switch up to the ON position. As mentioned above, if you know the locations and colors of the navigation lights of another aircraft, you can determine the direction that aircraft is flying by looking for those lights. (See the following diagram for more information.)

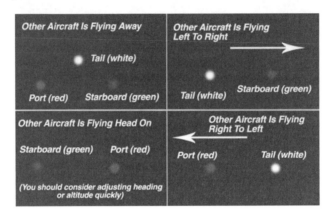

Anti-collision light

Another light located on the tail of your aircraft is a red rotating beacon anti-collision light. A good real world habit to follow is turning on the anti-collision beacon whenever your aircraft engine is operating. Real world pilots do this to warn anyone nearby to the danger of moving propeller blades or jet engine intakes.

To turn on the anti-collision light, move the BCN switch up to the ON position.

Strobe lights

One additional set of anti-collision lighting seen on many aircraft today are white strobe lights located on each wingtip and underside of the aircraft.

To turn on the strobe lights, move the STROBE switch up to the ON position.

Taxi and Landing lights

You also need to spot potential obstructions while taxing at airports and to move safely on the taxiway. Therefore, your aircraft should have a taxi light located either on the nose wheel strut/front empennage or on the port wing structure.

To turn on the taxi light, move the TAXI switch up to the ON position.

The landing light is located either near the taxi light or is part of the taxi light. Pilots use the landing light to illuminate the runway during landing.

To turn on the landing light, move the LAND switch up to the ON position.

Turn on the landing light as you approach the airport to help illuminate the runway during landing. The taxi lights have a similar affect when you're on the taxiways.

Take a look at the Flying At Night Video on the Companion CD-ROM for more information. See the Contents pages for more information about the Companion CD-ROM and all the videos.

Airport Lights

Although the white, red, green and blue lights of an airport at night may bewilder, confuse or intimidate you, there really is a good reason for these lights: They're designed to bring you to a safer touchdown or provide a safer takeoff.

Runway lighting

As you may have already discovered, runways are usually easy to spot from the air at night because they're marked by white lights that run their full length (with one minor but important exception mentioned below).

Take a look at the Flying At Night Video on the Companion CD-ROM for more information. See the Contents pages for more information about the Companion CD-ROM and all the videos.

White lights mark the sides of all runways (except runways using IAP where the last 2000 feet or half the runway length is marked by yellow lights).

The one exception to this may be on runways using instrument approach procedures. In this case, yellow lights mark the last 2000 feet or half the runway length (whichever is less) of these runways. These yellow lights are designed as a caution zone for landing by letting you know that available runway space is decreasing.

The runway centerline lights are white as you approach the runway until the last 3000 feet. Then out of those 3000 feet, the white lights alternate with red lights for 2000 feet and then all the centerline lights are red for the last 1000 feet.

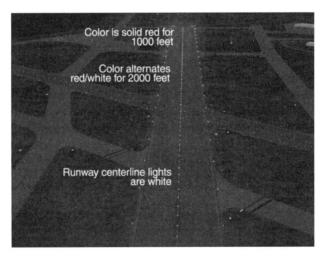

Notice how the runway centerline lights are white and then alternate white/red for 2000 feet and finally for the last 1000 feet are red (runway 14R at KORD). Note: This image doesn't represent how a runway necessarily should look as you're on approach.

Runway start and end lighting

A series of green lights marks the start of a runway, and as you probably guess, a series of red lights marks the end of the runway. Keep in mind these lights are green and red only in the same direction and on the same runway.

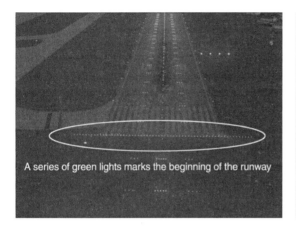
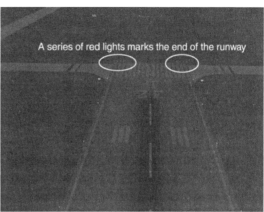

A series of green lights marks the start of a runway (highlighted left above) and a series of red lights marks the end of the runway (highlighted right above).

In other words, the lights marking the ends of the runway give off a red light towards the runway to a departing aircraft and give off a green light outward from the runway end to indicate the threshold to landing aircraft.

REIL (Runway End Identifier Lights)

Some airports use REIL (Runway End Identifier Lights) to highlight the approach end at a specific runway. REILs are usually two flashing lights on either side of the approach threshold and are either omni-directional or directed towards the approach path.

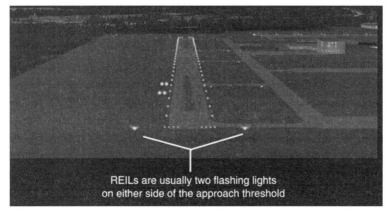

Some airports, such as Gerald R Ford International (KGRR), use REILs at some runways to highlight the approach end at a specific runway, it's runway 8L in this image at KGRR.

Holding point lighting

Larger and busier airports may use amber colored holding point lighting to increase awareness of holding points to a runway. These lights are typically embedded across the taxiway or as a setup of lights either side of the runway.

Note: These lights are not mandatory at airports so you may never see them used. Therefore, always look for the normal holding point lines regardless of the airport.

Approach Light Systems (ALS)

The ALS is a series of lights starting at the landing threshold and extending into the approach area a distance of 2400-3000 feet for precision instrument runways and 1400-1500 feet for nonprecision instrument runways. Some systems include sequenced flashing lights which appear to the pilot as a ball of light traveling towards the runway at high speed (twice a second).

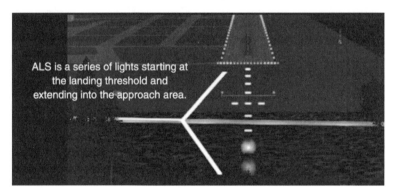

The ALS at runway 8R at Gerald R Ford International (KGRR) features sequenced flashing lights to direct you to the center of the runway.

Approach lighting

Many large, as well as many smaller airports, use approach lighting on specific runways. These lighting systems, also called visual glideslope indicators (VGI), are typically either PAPI (Precision Approach Path Indicator) or VASI (Visual Approach Slope Indicator) and serve as a visual aid to pilots attempting to fly a proper approach profile.

Visual Approach Slope Indicator (VASI)

VASI is an arrangement of lights that provides pilots with visual approach slope angle information while on final approach. Pilots can find the VASI system useful in both daytime flights and nighttime flights. VASI provides a color coded visual glidepath using a system of lights positioned alongside the runway but near the designated touchdown point.

VASI is particularly helpful if your approach is over water or featureless terrain where other sources of visual reference don't exist or can be misleading, and at night.

The VASI light units are arranged in bars. You're most likely to see VASI installations consisting of two bars (called the near bar and the far bar) but some VASI systems consist of three bars (near, middle and far) that provide an additional visual glide path to accommodate larger aircraft. Each light unit features a light that is white in the top half and red in the bottom half. Once you understand the principles and color code of the lighting system, flying the VASI is simply adjusting your aircraft's rate of descent based on the colors and staying on the visual glide slope.

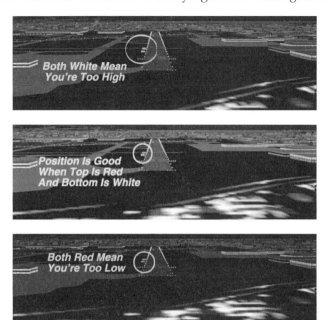

Using VASI on a landing approach

The VASI lights are arranged so that you'll see red lights if you're below the glide slope during the approach or all white lights if you're flying above the glideslope. When you're flying on the glide slope, you'll see all red lights and white lights.

So, if you're on a proper glidepath, you'll basically overshoot the downwind bars and undershoot the upwind bars.

Precision Approach Path Indicator Lights (PAPI)

The PAPI lights are designed to help you determine the appropriate approach path when landing. The lights are an important safety feature at large and medium size airports.

PAPI consists of four individual light units containing two lights each. These lights are located near the runway threshold.

You can determine the position of your glideslope by the color of the lights:

➤ 4 white means your glideslope is too high

➤ 2 red 2 white means your glideslope is correct

➤ 4 red means your glideslope is too low

See the following images for more information.

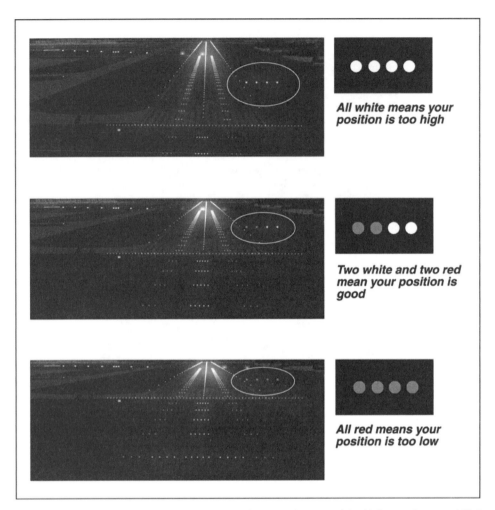

In this example of the Precision Approach Path Indicator, the two white lights and two red lights are showing the glideslope is good.

Taxiway lighting

Taxiway lights, which are always blue, mark the edges of the taxiway. Some airports in the real world don't light certain taxiways and perhaps you've seen this in Flight Sim, too. Therefore, avoid using these taxiways during night operations for obvious reasons.

Some airports — note this doesn't mean all airports — use green lights to mark the centerline of taxiways. These lights at real world airports are embedded into the taxiway surface so as to not impede the taxiing of the aircraft.

So, a rule to remember while taxiing at night is to taxi "between blue and over green." In other words, you're taxiing safely as long as you have blue lights on either side and the green lights, if available, in the middle.

Look for the blue lights while taxiing because they mark the edges of the taxiways. Some airports use green lights to mark the centerline of the taxiway.

It's not uncommon for real world pilots when taxiing at larger or unfamiliar airports to become lost in the maze of blue and green lights. Therefore, the control tower at some airports can turn off and isolate various taxiway lights in order to reduce confusion and assist the pilots in ground operations.

Airport beacons

In the "early" days before radar and navigational aids, pilots relied on a rotating beacon used at airports to distinguish the airport from the mass of lights that may surround them. This is the same basic idea as sailors relying on a lighthouse to guide them safely to port.

These beacons consist of either white or green/white lights and revolve or flash to display one color at a time. Today, beacons at nonmilitary airports flash green-white-green and those at military airports alternate green-white-white-green. Real world pilots can spot beacons from great distances but it's unusual for a pilot to be talking to ATC at the destination airport and line up on final at the wrong airport.

There are many other lights to indicate other boundaries and I've only be able to touch on a few here. So, for more information on airport lighting, check the FAA website (http://www.faa.gov/airports_airtraffic/air_traffic/publications/atpubs/aim/chap2toc.htm).

Preparing For A Nighttime Flight

You'll discover that preparing for a nighttime flight isn't much different than preparing for daytime flight. Nevertheless, you need to always remember that navigating by familiar objects on the ground in a nighttime flight is not as easy as a daytime flight. Furthermore, spotting other aircraft, either on the ground or in the air, may be more difficult at night.

Some of the preplanning decisions you need to make for a nighttime flight include the following:

- The type of flight: is this a cross-country flight or a local flight.

✈ Are you flying over water or mountains.

✈ Departure/Destination airports: is the flight between two big city airports or smaller rural airports.

✈ What maps and charts will you need (and are they handy so you won't lose control of your aircraft while you're trying to find them).

You must pay careful attention to some preparations for a nighttime flight that you won't worry about during the daytime. These preparations include the following (some of these apply more to real world pilots but it's also fun and realistic to follow these in FSX):

✈ Make certain you're familiar with any special procedures the airport(s) you're using might have for nighttime operations. For example, some airports enforce time restrictions on night flying or perhaps traffic patterns may be different at night.

✈ Check the weather in your flight area if you're using the real weather feature of FSX. To operate at night, the VMC conditions need to be slightly higher than those during the day. Even in Flight Sim, consider another night if there is a chance of a low cloud base or reduced visibility or use the FSX custom weather feature and change the weather.

✈ Always have an alternate airport in mind. You never know when your aircraft will develop mechanical problems, the weather will change or other unforeseen problems.

✈ Check the lights on your aircraft before takeoff (see information on "Startup" below). You can perform a "pilot walk-around" in Flight Sim by using the different FSX views to check the navigation lights (red, green and white) landing and taxi lights and the strobe lights.

Startup

The engine startup procedure for your aircraft is almost the same as you would follow if this were a daytime flight. However, because this is a nighttime flight, you need to add a couple items to the checklist.

For example, the lack of visual features at night might make it difficult to determine if your aircraft is moving while you're on the ground. So, make certain to set the parking brake (press the `Ctrl` + `.` key combination until you see "PARKING BRAKES" in the lower left screen). Setting the parking brake is especially important after you start the engine(s) because you might not realize that your aircraft is moving.

Although you won't have a worry in Flight Sim with people walking near your aircraft, a good real world habit nevertheless to develop is to switch on/off the landing or taxi lights before starting your engine. (This is a good habit regardless of whether you're flying at night or day.)

Refer to the recommended checklist for your aircraft when starting the engine(s). This is a nighttime flight and the risk of trouble is higher than a daytime flight so you'll need your aircraft to be airworthy. Then turn on all other necessary lights and radios. Make certain the rotating beacon, navigation lights and light lights are working properly. This will again alert anyone nearby to remain clear of your aircraft.

Before starting the engine, double-check that your parking brake is set. Then release the parking brake and move forward a little bit and apply the brakes to make certain they are functioning correctly.

Our Example Nighttime Flight

We'll use the Muskegon County Airport (KMKG) for this nighttime flight.

Start Flight Sim and select the **World | Go to Airport...** menu command. Select KMKG as the Airport ID (Make certain to have either "Any" or "United States" selected in the "Country/Region" option. Then select "6" in the "Runway/Starting position" option. Click the OK button to continue.

Select the **World | Time and Season...** menu command. Select "Night" for the "Time of day" and "Summer" as the "Season" option. Click the OK button. Select the **World | Weather...** menu command and click "Clear skies (clears all weather)" option. You can add clouds and weather later when you become more confident in your abilities and capabilities during nighttime operations. Click the OK button to continue.

Finally, select the aircraft you want to fly. I am flying one of the default Cessna 172SP aircraft.

Our Example Flight - Night Takeoff

We'll use the Muskegon County airport (KMGK) in this example. You can either download the flight from the companion CD-ROM or enter the following coordinates in the map view. This is an obvious statement but we have to say it anyway — a nighttime landing is different than a daytime landing. (The presaved flight uses the default FSX Cessna 172SP aircraft.)

- ✈ Double-check to make certain there are no inbound aircraft. You should do this regardless of whether you're at a uncontrolled or controlled airport and even if ATC has cleared you to "taxi into position" or "cleared for takeoff."

- ✈ Turn **ON** your STROBE lights as you come onto the runway. This alerts nearby aircraft that you've entered the active runway. Turn **OFF** the TAXI light and turn **ON** the LAND light (landing light) when you've aligned your aircraft with the runway centerline.

- ✈ Make certain to keep your aircraft aligned with the centerline of the runway, if it's available, otherwise line up midway between and parallel to the two rows of white edge lights.

Don't concentrate too much on the area illuminated by the landing light. Instead, scan the airspeed indicator, runway edge lights and other instruments.

✦ Push the throttle forward and when you've reached takeoff speed, ease back on the controls and maintain a safe climbing attitude. Adjust the pitch attitude as you would in any normal climb.

✦ Raise the landing gear only when you can no long use the runway for an emergency landing. Then follow the after-takeoff checklist for your aircraft.

That's it for the takeoff! Now you're flying at night.

Additional tips and suggestions for a safer takeoff

Make certain your aircraft continues in a positive climb and doesn't settle back to the runway. In other words, you're looking for a positive rate of climb so check the vertical speed indicator and the altimeter for an increase in altitude. So, as soon as your aircraft takes off, check the following instruments carefully:

✦ AI for aircraft attitude (the normal climb attitude for the Cessna 172 is about 8 degrees nose up).

✦ Vertical Speed Indicator (VSI) for a positive rate of climb.

✦ Heading Indicator to make certain you're maintaining the proper runway heading.

Keep an eye on these three gauges: Aircraft Indicator, VSI and Heading Indicator

Due to the lower lighting within the cockpit check each instrument carefully.

You probably used the natural horizon, weather permitting, for pitch reference during a daytime flight but at some airports at night, you may find the darkness below blending into the sky. The horizon may look creepy or unnatural but at least you can distinguish it. On the other hand, you may eventually takeoff from an airport, such as McCarran in Las Vegas, where the lights may make the horizon hard to distinguish.

So, when the visibility is limited for any reason, you will learn to rely on the attitude indicator.

You may encounter several combinations of conditions during a nighttime flight, especially during an extended flight. If so, you'll quickly discover that you're checking the instrument panel more frequently at night than you ever did during a daytime flight.

Flying A Pattern At Night

We're flying a pattern around KMKG, and specifically runway 6, with four *gentle* 90 degree turns at an altitude of 1400 feet. When you're turning to complete a pattern, limit your turns to a maximum of thirty degrees of bank to prevent becoming disorientated. Also, the flying times I mention are general flying times — so you don't have to worry about watching the clock...you should be concentrating on other things right now!

↣ Continue climbing until you're at about 1400 feet (or 700 feet AGL). This is the upwind leg.

↣ When you're at 1400 feet, begin a gentle left turn to 330 degrees. Continue climbing to 1400 feet. This is the crosswind leg. Make certain the airport is in view at all times.

When you're established on the crosswind leg of the circuit, you can take your eyes off the gauges for a moment and view the nighttime environment around your aircraft. Depending on where you're eventually flying, this could be city lights or nothing but blackness.

Fly the crosswind leg for about 30 seconds (depending on your aircraft and airspeed.) Keep an eye on your altitude and airspeed.

↣ Make another gentle left turn to 240 degrees, keeping the airport in view and fly the downwind leg. Remember in this flight you're flying VFR rules and therefore need to look outside as much as possible. You also need to view the runway throughout the circuit pattern so make sure you fly a nice rectangular pattern.

Again, try to limit turns to a maximum of thirty degrees of bank to prevent disorientation.

Also during the downwind leg, make sure you're flying a correct pattern. Check the instruments, especially heading indicator, compass, airspeed and altitude. This will help with problems later in the final approach.

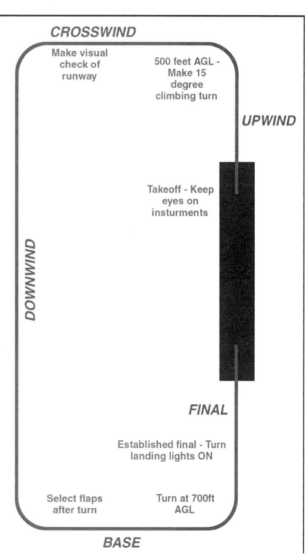

The airport diagram for KMKG with the taxiway route highlighted in yellow. The airport diagram was created using CoPilot V3.

Fly the downwind leg for about 60 seconds to a spot beyond the runway but don't lose sight of it. Keep an eye on your altitude and airspeed.

✈ Make a left turn to 150 degrees and look for runway 6. This is the base leg. Watch your airspeed at this point.

One important point to remember is that changing your aircraft configuration as you turn onto the base leg at night is seldom a good idea. One important reason is not to avoid becoming disoriented. At this point, you're much too busy checking instruments and the horizon to attempt to set the flaps. Therefore, wait until you're level or in your base leg to apply flaps.

✈ Be prepared before you begin your final approach (see below). To make this a gentle turn, anticipate and begin the turn earlier than would during a daytime flight. Start a left turn to heading 060 degrees to runway 6 for your final approach. Once you identify runway 6, don't lose sight of it.

Once you're established on final approach, turn ON the LAND light (landing light). This alerts other aircraft that may be on the runway or in the pattern with an intention to land. Plan a wider pattern and use power throughout the approach.

Additional tips and suggestions for a safer approach

Be prepared before you begin your approach; follow the landing checklist carefully for your aircraft.

✈ As with any daytime approach, use power to control the rate of descent and aircraft attitude to control airspeed. Apply power if you're getting low or raise the nose if you're going too fast. Use power and attitude together throughout your approach. Also, refer to your instruments often to make certain your airspeed is good and wings are level.

✈ As you come up to the final stages of the approach, you'll probably see your aircraft landing light begin illuminating the surface. At this point, you'll be tempted to follow the beam of the landing light to find the runway; however, this is a common mistake made by FS pilots (and too many real world pilots).

The reason to avoid staring down the light beam is that you may find that the runway suddenly appears out of the darkness and you're actually flying directly into the runway at a rather nose down attitude.

Therefore, ignore the landing light completely and concentrate on the runway lights instead. Use the landing light only to avoid obstacles that may appear on the runway, or later, the taxiway.

✈ The most difficult part of the landing phase is determining the time to flare and judging this time will come with experience flying at night. Transfer your focus from the start of the runway to the end of the runway in order to allow greater perspective. The side runway lights in your peripheral vision are your best measure to gauge height.

✈ The hardest part of a nighttime approach is judging the path to the runway. You must determine whether you're too high or too low and if you're aligned properly with the runway. Objects surrounding the runway, such as trees, buildings and the ground itself, will help during a daytime flight but these objects are difficult to spot at night because all you might see at night is the runway itself. Make sure your glidepath is high enough on your approach to stay well clear of obstacles (and not only the ones you see). Although you can spot obstructions near the airport, such as smokestacks and antenna, by their blinking red lights, it's nevertheless a good idea to keep your glidepath high and avoid a long low final approach.

It helps if you're landing on a runway that uses lighting systems such as PAPI and VASI but these aren't always available.

If this is the case for your runway, and assuming there is no crosswind, imagine a line extending from the center of the runway through to your aircraft. If the line divides the cockpit in half, you're on the centerline; otherwise, you'll need to change your path either left or right to compensate.

Our Example Flight - Night Landing

This is an obvious statement but we have to say it anyway — a nighttime landing is different than a daytime landing.

➤ Always look for other traffic when you're on final approach. This is obviously true regardless of the time you're flying but it's arguably more true for a nighttime flight.

➤ Follow the landing checklist carefully for your aircraft and take more time than in the daytime to avoid mistakes.

➤ Runway 6 uses PAPI lighting so you'll have help on your glideslope.

➤ Line up for landing at runway 6.

➤ Make certain your gear is down.

➤ Proceed with your approach to runway 6.

➤ As soon as you touchdown, apply normal braking because speed is hard to judge at night.

➤ Avoid locking the brakes suddenly when you spot the first taxiway. Although finding taxiway exits can be difficult at night, you'll find additional taxiways along the runway that you can use.

Further Flying At Night

Now that you have the basics involved in nighttime flying, you should be less afraid of the dark. Here's some additional suggestions you can follow to further your nighttime flying experiences:

➤ Make your first few nighttime flights from a familiar airport. Then practice from that airport until you become more confident and familiar with nighttime navigation.

➤ Start by moving around the taxiways and familiarizing yourself with the blue lights. Then as you gain confidence, try a few takeoffs and fly the basic flight pattern for a few full stop-and-go procedures. The experience of taxiing, taking off, flying the pattern and landing is a great start to becoming a veteran nighttime pilot.

➤ Next time fly out a few miles and remember the general direction back to the airport. Practice a few basic maneuvers such as slow flight, 360 degree turns and stalls. Then turn back to your departure airport and become experienced in locating it from a distance at night.

✈ Next plan a short flight to nearby but different size airports, such as an airport surrounded by city lights and then to an airport in the country surrounded by darkness.

✈ Practice climbs, descents, turns and straight-and-level flight.try climbs, descents, turns and straight-and-level flight.

✈ Practice takeoffs and landings without using the landing light.

When you feel like you're ready, start flying from airports all over the world. You'll be amazed at the lights and buildings of Las Vegas, Honk Kong, Paris, London, New York and others at night. So just turn off the room lights, load in Flight Sim and practice nighttime flying so you'll no longer be afraid of the dark.

Uh Oh! You've Just Lost Your Engine —
NOW WHAT?

A good pilot is always prepared for engine trouble (including partial or total power loss) at any time during the flight. How prepared are you to this emergency?

Your piloting skills will be tested when your aircraft suddenly becomes a glider and you need to land safely and quickly. To do so requires practice to ensure your procedures and skills are good enough to handle sudden engine failures. In this article we'll look at suggestions on how you can handle these situations in Flight Simulator during flight and immediately after departure.

Engine Failure During Flight

We'll first talk about what you should do if your engine fails during your flight. Then, so you can get some practical experience, we'll take you on a flight that may possibly include an engine failure.

The following are five general guidelines for you to follow in the event of an engine failure during flight. Keep in mind that these are only guidelines; you should refer to emergency checklists corresponding to your specific aircraft for detailed information.

A handy way to remember these guidelines is the SPELL mnemonic:

✦ Speed (Proper glide speed for your aircraft)

✦ Place (Find a suitable landing spot)

✦ Engine (Attempt engine restart)

✦ Location (Broadcast location — *simulate only in FS*)

✦ Land (Concentrate on landing)

Let's look more closely at these guidelines.

Speed (Proper glide speed for your aircraft)

Your aircraft will behave like a glider when its engine fails so you'll need to find a safe place to land quickly. No matter what else happens, you need to be in control of your aircraft whenever an emergency happens.

An engine failure quite likely will result in a critical low airspeed. If this happens, you *must* reestablish the proper glide speed immediately for your aircraft, even if it means losing more altitude.

Total Flight Simulator aircraft weight with full fuel	14,992 lbs

NOTE: To adjust fuel load, on the Aircraft menu, click Fuel and Load.

V_{MO} - Maximum Operating Speed	263 KIAS
M_{MO} - Maximum Operating Speed Mach	.58 Mach
Turbulent Air Penetration Speed	170 KIAS
V_{LE} - Maximum Gear Operating Speed	184 KIAS
V_{LO} - Maximum Gear Retraction Speed	166 KIAS
V_A - Maneuvering Speed	184 KIAS
V_{MC} - Minimum Control Speed	94 KIAS
V_X - Two-engine Best Angle-of-Climb	125 KIAS
V_Y - Two-engine Best Rate of Climb	140 KIAS
Best Glide Speed both engines inoperative	135 KIAS

Maximum Flap Placard Speeds

*You may be able to find the best glide speed for your aircraft listed in FSX under the reference section of the pilot's kneeboard (select the **Aircraft | Kneeboard | Reference...** command). Otherwise, you'll find the best glide speed for your aircraft in the pilot's operating manual.*

However, it's also possible that when the engine fails, your aircraft may be moving much faster than its best glide speed. This probably isn't an immediate concern, but the longer you take to establish the proper glide speed, the more energy will be lost to unnecessary parasite drag. (Parasite drag is, briefly, an unwanted resistance of the air to an object travelling through the air.) In this case, climb smoothly and try to convert airspeed to altitude.

Also, don't forget to use the trim controls. Besides trimming for the correct airspeed, you must properly configure other controls. In the "clean" configuration, your aircraft will glide much farther than if it is in the "dirty" configuration.

 NOTE

Glide approaches are simply a way of practicing flying your aircraft without using power to reach an aiming point. Nothing is written into the rulebook stating that you must touchdown with full flaps or that you must follow a prescribed path to the runway. So, use every means available to you so you can reach the runway safely.

Extend Or Retract Flaps

You should already know that extending flaps increases the amount of lift for your aircraft. However, what you may not realize is that extending flaps also increases the drag your aircraft experiences (and extending flaps probably increases drag more than any amount of lift they produce). The resulting large increase in drag not only increases your aircraft's rate of descent but also its angle of descent during a glide. A good rule to remember is that the more flaps you extend, the steeper angle of descent you'll experience.

You can extend flaps during the glide approach if you're careful. Extend the flaps if you're too high during the approach; this will increase your angle of descent. However, this is a one time decision because once the flaps have been extended, they cannot be retracted because you'll experience a corresponding loss of lift.

So the important rule to remember is to never use full flaps until you're established on the final leg and you're certain that you will reach your aiming point on the runway or landing area.

1 (Red) No flaps

2 (Blue) Apply flaps
increased drag = increased ROD and AOD

3 (Green) Apply full flaps
increased drag = increased ROD and AOD

Example On How Using Flaps Increases Your Rate of Descent (ROD) and Angle of

For example, if you start out at a higher altitude and need to glide a long distance, then you want to retract the flaps, retract the landing gear and set the propeller in the coarse pitch (low RPM) position (if possible on your aircraft).

Note that if your engine fails at low altitude, your primary attention should be finding a landing area and not worrying about the configuration.

NOTE You may read in your aircraft checklist that once the flaps are down, you should leave them down because at a low airspeed (below the bottom of the green arc) retracting the flaps can cause an immediate stall. Other experts, however, believe that if you need to glide a long distance, it's acceptable to retract the flaps but do it in a way so you won't stall.

Also, if you want to make a steep approach to a nearby field, you can glide with flaps extended, gear extended or both.

The time to extend the flaps is when you're finished gliding and you're ready to flare. You should do this so that you can touch down at the lowest possible speed. (See diagram above.)

Place (search for a suitable landing place)

Finding a safe place to land is obviously very important. If you're lucky, you might be able to glide to a nearby airport but you probably will need to find another suitable landing site. Here's some tips and techniques to help you find either an airport or other suitable landing site.

Nearby airports

Contact ATC by pressing the ⌐ key. Then ask for the "Nearest airport list" and pick the most suitable airport. The problem in finding airports using this method is that you have no idea of the course to the airport, only its distance away from you.

Fortunately, most aircraft in Flight Simulator now include a GPS gauge. The advantage of checking the GPS gauge is that it displays not only the names of the nearest airport(s), but also the bearing and distance from your present position to that airport.

Your GPS gauge (left image) may be invaluable when trying to find a nearby airport in an emergency. Push the button labeled NRST (or something similar) for a list nearby airport(s), along with the bearing and distance from your position to the airport (right image).

All you need to do is push the button labeled NRST (or something similar) to see the list of airports.

Roads/open fields

Unfortunately, you probably won't find an airport close enough to where you can glide. Your options in these situations may be limited to roads or open fields. To determine which fields are within gliding range, begin by looking down at a 45 degree angle or even straight down. If an open field is immediately below you, it's probably within gliding range.

Note when selecting a road as a landing spot, make certain you can avoid power/telephone poles, towers and other obstacles, especially in a crosswind.

When selecting a country road as an emergency landing field, make certain you can avoid telephone poles and other obstacles. The trees in this example may be a problem but the road is level and straight.

Ground slope

You may unfortunately find yourself without power over hilly terrain and this will make your job of finding a suitable landing site much more difficult. You can hope for a downslope landing but the choices are usually difficult at best and most likely, impossible.

A landing on a moderate upslope is possible but you must perform the pre-touchdown flare almost perfectly. There is a much greater change in the flight path during the flare, for example if the upslope has a one in six gradient (about 15°) and the aircraft's glide slope is 10° then the flight path has to be altered by 25° so that the aircraft is flying parallel to the upslope surface before final touchdown. A higher approach speed is needed because the increased wing loading during the flare (a turn in the vertical plane) increases stall speed. If the wind is upslope, then a crosswind landing may be possible.

Wind strength and direction

Also, don't forget the wind! If you're flying in windy conditions, the area of possible landing sites obviously changes. For example, if you're gliding at 60 knots (airspeed) into a 30-knot headwind, your groundspeed has been decreased by 50% so your glide will be twice as steep compared to similar situations with zero wind.

NOTE

To find the wind speed and direction in Flight Sim, press the (Shift) + (z) key combination. The information will appear near the top of the screen.

Ground obstructions after landing

Your aircraft will need some stopping distance after you land so check for obstructions such as trees, buildings, rolling terrain, etc. If you see obstructions, make certain that you can steer clear of them after landing.

Approach obstructions

Your final approach may require some diversion around or over trees, under or over power lines and other obstacles. You also need to be able to handle turns near the ground safely. Make certain there is a safety margin for misjudgement and miscalculations, wind gusts and any other unknown problem.

Also, avoid a final approach into a low sun if possible.

Water landing

An emergency landing on water presents its own problems. However, the approach and landing procedures remain basically the same except that you'll want the gear up in most aircraft if you're preparing for an emergency water landing.

Don't fly hoping for a better area in the distance

Keep in mind that in most forced-landing situations, your glide path is likely to be quite steep. For example, the lift-to-drag ratio in best-glide configuration of an average Skyhawk or Cherokee is about 10-to-1, which corresponds to an angle of six degrees. This is about two times as steep as a typical power-on approach and even slightly steeper than the typical "power off" approach.

You should also know how far your aircraft can glide. For example, if you're about 5000 feet when your engine fails, you can probably glide about ten miles (although this doesn't consider any wind factors). If, however, you find a nearby field, use it — don't glide ten miles simply because you think you can while hoping for a better field in the distance.

In other words, don't select a field that is at the limit of the gliding ability of your aircraft because you'll probably end up short if anything more goes wrong. Also, remember, you may lose altitude by circling, adjusting the length of the base leg, extending flaps, slipping, etc. In short, now is not the time to take anymore unnecessary risks — select a field that is much closer than your glide limit.

Engine - Determine Failure/ Attempt Restart

If you believe the engine has failed due to fuel problems, switch tanks and turn on the boost pump, if available, as appropriate. Also, turn on the carburetor heat because it's only effective while the engine is still warm.

 To try and restart your engines, press the [Shift] + [e] key combination. Double-check everything before taking too much time on one particular item unless you're certain you know what the problem is

Then double-check the gauges on the instrument panel. Make sure the primer is in and locked. Check if the engine runs better on the left magneto, right magneto or both. Also check if it's better with a leaner or richer mixture. The propeller may keep spinning even when the engine quits but this is due to momentum and possibly the wind — if it stops, use the starter to get it going again. Double-check everything before spending too much time on one particular item unless you're certain you know what the problem is.

Location

Unfortunately, you cannot declare an emergency in FSX to the air traffic controllers. However, you can switch to the international distress frequency (121.5 MHz) on your COMM1 if you want to simulate what a real world pilot would do in an emergency. Also, to simulate a real world emergency, switch the transponder to the emergency code (7700). Again, this won't signal an emergency in FSX but it's a good habit to start because perhaps the next version of Flight Sim will include emergency frequencies.

Landing (Focus on landing)

You'll be surprised how easy it is to overlook the importance of the details in emergency landing procedures. It could ruin your flying experience to make an impressive power-off approach to an ideal field but forget to extend the landing gear.

At 100 feet AGL, make sure you pull the throttle and mixture to idle cut-off. Do this to prevent the engine from roaring back to life just after touchdown. The reason a real world pilot would do this at 100 feet AGL is to give the engine a chance to cool down and thereby reducing the risk of a fire after the crash.

You're not alone if you're skeptical about shutting off the engine at this point. After all, you've spent the last several minutes in an emergency situation trying to restart the engine but now you're supposed to shut it off at 100 AGL.

What's next after selecting an emergency field

You now have what you hope is the best area in mind in which to land. As you approach the field, strategic turns are important early; use flaps later on the short final. The types of turns you make, too, are important because S-turns on final are seldom the best way to descend in this situation. Also, small-angle turns have little effect and large turns not only take too long to complete but also take your selected field temporarily out of sight. Furthermore, after two turns (one to the left and one to the right) you'll be back on your original heading, but offset laterally; you need to make two more turns to get back on course. And, quite frankly, if you have time and altitude to do all that, you need to be doing something else more important.

Example Of An Emergency Landing Pattern

Use this pattern for simulated engine failure (glide approaches), engine failure or other engine problems or any precautionary emergency landing situations.

1. DESCENT
Check your airspeed or glidespeed is appropriate for your aircraft (select the Aircraft I Kneeboard command and then the Reference icon in FS 2004). Make certain your gear is up and that flaps are up.

2. 1500 AGL (High Key)
Check airspeed...should be about 90 KIAS but depends on your aircraft. Begin turn to low key (step 3). Lower gear, if necessary on your aircraft, for prepared surfaces or gear up for water or unprepared surfaces. Prepare to decrease speed to 85 KIAS.

3. 1000 feet AGL (Low Key)
Decrease airspeed to 80KIAS if gear down or 90KIAS if gear is up. Check abeam for runway threshold for intended landing point.

4. 500-600 feet AGL (90-degree Turn)
Complete landing checklist. Be careful when setting flaps at this point

5 Final
You should be 200 AGL and 800 feet straightaway.

If you're on long final and can keep the field a constant angle below the horizon by using flaps, you're probably in good shape. You should be able to glide straight in for a successful landing.

If you're on long final with excess energy, or if you're approaching the field from a substantial angle relative to the intended direction of landing, don't aim directly for the field but instead aim for the *base key point* (the point where the base leg begins).

You have several options when you reach the base key point. If you arrive with the ideal amount of energy, you can fly a nice base leg and then turn final. If you arrive with slightly more or less energy than that, you can angle the base leg away from or toward the field. Fly along the base leg until the desired destination is the appropriate angle below the horizon and then turn on final.

One more point to consider is using the full *width* of the landing field to your advantage. You may not be used to landing this way since we're accustomed to landing as close as possible to the centerline of the runway. However, this is not a typical landing situation.

Finally, don't plan your final approach to take you to the threshold of the landing field. Regardless of the length of the field, aim for a point one third of the way along the field. Keep in mind that many things could take energy from your glide, and you *really* don't want to land short.

Engine Failure Soon After Departure

In this section we'll talk about engine failure shortly after departure. You may be like many FS pilots who are tempted to turn back to the airport. However, as you'll read in this section, this is not always the right choice.

What you should do depends on many factors, including:

+ Wind

+ Runway length

+ Aircraft capabilities

+ Whether partial power is still available

+ Your capabilities as pilot

Because every situation is different, we can't discuss each in great detail. It's up to you to plan in advance. Know and recognize your options. Make sure you have a backup plan appropriate to the situation in each phase of your flight and always be ready to carry out that plan at anytime.

When a total or near total engine failure occurs after takeoff, the important rule to follow is to continue flying the aircraft. At first this means quickly getting your aircraft into the right glide attitude and waiting until your airspeed reaches the appropriate glide speed for your aircraft and then fine trimming. (Keep in mind that when going from climb to glide attitude, you must push the nose down through several degrees, which might feel excessive particularly if the aircraft was not trimmed to the climb speed.)

Unfortunately, simply continuing to fly your aircraft at this point won't be easy. Keep in mind that during the climb out, your aircraft is at a high angle-of-attack, which produces high drag and when the engine fails, airspeed drops very quickly— even more so if the aircraft is a "naturally draggy" type. You may need a second or two to react and push the control column forward and therefore your aircraft needs a few more seconds to regain a safe maneuvering speed.

Meanwhile, your aircraft will be sinking and if height and airspeed are insufficient you're heading for an unpleasant landing.

Landing On The Departure Runway

One advantage about taking off on a long runway is that if you do have engine problems, you might be able to land straight ahead on the same runway. For example, if you're taking off from a long runway, you might be able to climb several hundred feet, lose engine power and still land straight ahead on the same runway with plenty of runway remaining.

Runway 31L at JFK is good for this exercise

This is easy to setup and practice because all you need to do is select an airport with a long runway. I have usually used runway 31L at Kennedy International (KJFK) for this practice exercise. Takeoff as normal but when you're at, say, 100 feet, cut the throttle. Even at that altitude you should have enough runway directly ahead on which to glide to a safe landing.

Landing On An On-field Site

If you experience engine failure immediately after liftoff, your best option is probably to keep the wings level and try to land straight ahead. This may not be a problem if the airfield area ahead is clear and the runway is long enough (see above).

Avoid obvious problems such as your wingtip striking an airfield marker or other obstruction or getting caught in long grass and causing the aircraft to cartwheel or wheelbarrow.

Avoid obvious problems such as your wingtip striking an airfield marker, sheds or other obstruction.

Airspeed is likely to be low so keep the nose down and the wings level during the descent. Use the rudder carefully and change direction only if necessary. It's OK in this case to lower the flaps to full but be ready for the sudden change in attitude.

Try to get your aircraft down (but not nosewheel first) and use whatever reasonable means is available to slow to a stop. Gentle "S" turns will help slow the aircraft but if necessary, groundloop it to avoid major obstructions by applying full rudder (and brake) on the side to which you want to swing. This action in the real world would probably damage the wing, undercarriage or propeller damage but that is repairable.

Landing On An Off-field site

When your engine fails after departure and an on-field landing is not possible, your only choice then is an off-field landing. You obviously need to look for somewhere to land and you must do so quickly.

Consider your altitude, airspeed and the turn possibilities available at your current altitude, for example:

→ Can you safely turn through 10°, 20° or even 30° using only very moderate bank angles and still make it to a suitable landing site?

→ Is the wind going to help or hurt you?

You have only a few seconds to make these decisions and plan the approach. If you hesitate or have any doubts whatsoever on what to do, simply go "straight ahead" and hope.

You need to look for somewhere to land quickly if one or more of your engines fail right after takeoff and your only choice then is an off-field landing.

We mentioned this before but it's worth repeating here. Because this information is impossible to assess in the few seconds you have available, it's important to be familiar with the airport area and have an emergency procedure for any situation that may happen.

Don't hope for a better landing site in the distance. A closer landing site is better because you can use your current altitude advantage for maneuvering your aircraft into the best approach position.

Remember, you don't have power available so you need to maintain an adequate height margin to allow for your miscalculations, adverse wind shifts, sinking air, vertical gusts and other unforeseen events – and you can dump excess height quickly by sideslipping.

Turning Back To The Airport

The cardinal rule here is a simple one: Do not turn back unless you're absolutely sure you can make it — and you *won't* make it back in most situations. As an example, consider a fully loaded Cessna 152. It has a power-off glide ratio of ten to one. Unfortunately, in no wind conditions the climb gradient is *less* than ten to one. Therefore, even if the aircraft could turn sharply, at every point on the return trip the aircraft would be below where it had been on the outbound trip. Then if you consider the altitude lost while getting the aircraft turned around, it's easy to see why the aircraft cannot possibly return to the point where it left the ground.

Under these conditions, the farther you have flown on the departure leg, the more options you have for an off-airport landing and the more impossible the turn around becomes.

An important point to remember is that a quick 180 degree turn is not enough to return you to the departure runway. Your aircraft will travel a considerable distance *sideways* during the turn. You won't need to do a full procedure turn, but you will need to do some additional maneuvering that makes an already-bad situation worse.

If the runway is long enough, you might be able to return to a point on the runway closer to the departure end — which is good enough because you're still safely on the runway.

You can try this yourself. Select JFK in Flight Sim and runway 31. Then climb while maintaining the runway heading and cut the throttle when just beyond the departure end of the runway. Your altitude should be about 1000 feet by this time and should now be able to reverse course and make a downwind landing near the beginning of runway 13R (although you could not glide back at the point of takeoff).

It's possible, under some conditions, to land at the takeoff spot of the departure runway.

A modest headwind on departure may seem to be a big advantage because it helps keep your aircraft near the airport during the outbound leg, and will quicken your route back to the airport during the return trip. You might believe the wind increases the possibility that you can glide back safely to the runway. The trouble is that (whether you make it back to the airport) you must handle a downwind landing and even a modest tailwind (say 15 knots) can greatly affect a downwind landing.

Simply consider the math in an example. If your aircraft is touching down at 55 knots and consider the 15 knot wind, you have an actual groundspeed of 40 knots (55-15=40). However, if you land downwind you have a groundspeed of 70 knots (55+15=70).

You might not realize how important this is. Because runway usage depends on the *square* of the groundspeed, the downwind landing in this example requires *three times* as much runway: $(70/40)^2$ = 3.06. If this situation resulted in a real world collision, the amount of damage and injury would be typically proportional to the square of the groundspeed — so if you turn downwind and *don't* manage to land on the runway you are in very big trouble indeed.

Landing On Another Runway

You may have another option if your airport has a second runway running crosswise to the active runway. If your engine fails somewhere over the cross runway, you might be able to turn 90 degrees and land on that runway.

This is especially true in windy conditions because even in less ideal circumstances, it's quite likely that a crosswind landing on a different runway (or even a taxiway) is easier and safer than a downwind landing on the departure runway.

If you're concerned about engine failure during the departure climb, and the airport is the only safe area to land, consider beginning a slow turn almost immediately after takeoff. Then if your engine fails, you're closer to the airport and you probably have a more favorable (and possibly safe) heading.

However, you probably should attempt this type of maneuver at small, slower airports because *possible* engine failure is not your only consideration. You need to worry about causing a mid-air collision in the pattern. A turning departure climb toward the traffic-pattern side of the runway would cause you to enter the downwind leg from below at just about the point where inbound traffic is entering from the 45 degree leg. Therefore, be careful when using this type of maneuver.

Another possibility is landing on a second runway running crosswise to your departure runway (in this image, we're taking off on runway 31 at JFK and attempting to return to runway 13L.

Practice - Practice - Practice

Now that you've read the information and are at least somewhat familiar with procedures, let's put your skills to the test. We'll start by practicing glide approaches and then we'll fly a route which might just give us some engine trouble!

Glide Approaches

Now finally, one more skill you should practice: glide approaches. Practicing and understanding glide approaches is one of the best ways to handle engine failures. If you're not familiar with the term, a glide approach is a maneuver in which you learn to control your aircraft's flight path and configuration as you try to land on a specific part of runway. But, this isn't nearly as simple as it sounds because, as the name "glide" suggests, this is done without aircraft power.

So, let's practice by cutting the throttle at an altitude of about 2000 feet or so and perform a glide approach to an airport. This may seem simple (if not fun) but seldom is because remember, if this was a real emergency situation, you probably have only one chance to get it right.

We'll practice glide approaches on runway 27 at Grand Haven Memorial (3GM - 3746 feet, asphalt surface, elevation 604 feet) but you can practice at any of your favorite airports. We recommend you set wind conditions for this exercise to at 10-knots directly down the runway.

Approaching 3GM from the west, the runway is to the left in this image.

Remember, the glide approach starts like any other practice circuit until you're mid downwind on the active runway (runway 27 in this exercise).

Quick steps

Practicing glide approaches can be a lot of fun but make certain you check for air traffic first. We've listed basic steps below and will talk about them in greater detail on the next few pages.

→   Abeam (or aligned with) the runway number, cut the power and apply carb heat. Pitch for best glide angle.

→   Start a slow, gentle turn to the threshold and carefully watch your aiming point and its position.

→   If you're getting too close (and, therefore, too high), reduce your turn rate to "increase" your descent path to the runway.

➤ If you think your approach is becoming too low to reach the aiming point (in other words, you realize you'll be too short of the runway), increase throttle enough and, if necessary, change course. When you're confident, you can cut throttle again for a final glide approach once you are back in range.

➤ A perfect result in this maneuver is if you can be a little bit high and close to the runway, and then drop full flaps for a steeper, but more stable approach.

A glide approach is helpful in that it gives you a greater awareness of just how fast your aircraft descends during the glide and how you can control the flight path to arrive at your aiming point safely.

➤ If at any point during the glide approach you're even a little bit uncertain that you'll make it, increase the throttle and go around and try it again.

➤ Make sure you are aligned with the runway centerline well before you begin your flare.

Determining an aiming point

As you fly parallel to the runway, you'll need to determine your aiming point for the approach. This is normally about a third of the way down a normal runway (or the corresponding distance on a larger runway or field). One main reason to aim for this spot is for a little extra safety margin.

The aiming point should be about one-third of the way down the runway to provide for an extra margin of safety.

Keep in mind as you plan your glide slope that it has a longer base leg and much shorter final leg than a regular approach. This is so you won't stray far away from the runway or field during the approach.

Turning point onto base

When lined up with the threshold of the runway, start turning onto the base leg of the approach. During this turn, reduce the power all the way to idle. Note that if you're operating an aircraft with carburettor heat, this needs to be applied to prevent any ice buildup at the lower power setting. As you become more comfortable with glide approaches, try shutting the engine completely off and continuing with the approach.

When you're in line (abeam) with the threshold of the runway, start turning onto the base leg of the approach.

Base leg

The base leg is where you set up your aircraft in terms of configuration and flight path in order to achieve your target touchdown point. The most important consideration is to immediately check your glide speed. This is 68 knots in the Cessna 172 but heck your operator's handbook for your aircraft). Maintain this speed through your approach by controlling the nose attitude.

Another important consideration is altitude and determining the correct altitude to reach the touchdown point. The simple answer is to refer to the aiming point that should be set at a 45-degree downward angle from your aircraft. Because you obviously don't have time to measure this accurately, refer to how high or low your aiming point is in relation to parts of your aircraft.

If you're high on the approach, deploy a stage of flaps to increase your angle of descent. But do so in stages. When the first stage of flaps has been lowered, deploy the second stage if you're still too high. However, don't deploy all the flaps yet; otherwise, you may find yourself crashing short of the field and with no room to maneuver. So, DO NOT pull full flaps down until you're on the final leg.

Note On Being Too High Or Too Low

Too high
If you have the maximum amount of flaps extended and are still high, then extend your approach out more from the airport along the base leg. However, keep in mind this increases your final leg, so be careful not to go too far, otherwise you may run out of room when you turn onto final approach, especially if you're turning into direct headwind.

Too low

If, however, you're too low on the approach, begin to cut the corner and make a more direct route towards the runway and your aiming point. Remember, you don't have any power available to halt your descent. Also make certain you're maintaining the best glide speed and avoid using flaps at this stage because doing so will increase your angle of decent.

Final approach

At this point, if all goes well, you should find yourself on a very short final leg. Also, be prepared if you're turning into a direct headwind because the angle of your descent will increase considerably.

Once you're certain that you'll reach the aiming point, deploy the last section of flaps. Although this increases the angle (and rate of descent even more), you can now move the aiming point nearer to the threshold of the runway.

Maintain the flare speed and resist the temptation to raise the nose in order to gain every bit of altitude, because that will not work and you'll likely stall.

Landing is similar to a normal landing except you need to have a more pronounced round out to counteract and arrest the high rate and angle of descent. So, when you reach the flare height, overexaggerate the round out phase, but be careful not overdo it because performing a loop at 15 feet is usually not a good idea.

A successful glide approach is complete when you touch down within your landing area with enough distance to come to a stop.

A Flight With An Engine Failure

Now that you have successfully practiced glide approaches and have read the other information about what to do when an engine fails, you're ready for the next step. You may not be aware that Flight Simulator can let you simulate unexpected situations and emergencies. For example, FSX can create failures that occur immediately, randomly or within a specified period of time affecting instruments, system, radio and engine (or engines if you're flying a multi-engine aircraft).

One important piece of equipment to have with you, although it's often overlooked, is an emergency checklist for your type of aircraft. You should read it often and review it right before each flight. Don't wait until your engine quits at 5000 feet to find out what is explained in the emergency checklist.

Setting a random engine failure

Although it can be fun to experiment with this feature, it also has its serious side. Conscientious pilots in both FSX and the real world always consider that someday they may have to handle real emergencies in the cockpit.

Route information

This flight takes place from Grand Rapids (KGRR) to Traverse City (KTVC) in Michigan. Its approximate distance is 111nm under excellent weather conditions.

Keep in mind that you set up *random* engine failures; therefore, it's possible you won't experience any problems on the flight. But if you do, follow what you have learned in this article and continue practicing!

✈ Select your favorite single-engine aircraft that you want to fly on this flight.

✈ Select the **World | Go To Airport...** command and make certain United States is selected for the Country/Region and Any for the State/Province. Type in KGRR for the Airport and select 8R for the Runway.

✈ Select the **World | Time and Season...** command and set clock to 1400 and Season to Fall.

✈ Select the **World | Weather...** command and select the "Fair Weather" option in the Weather Themes (you can change the weather settings once you're more experienced).

✈ Select the **Aircraft | Failures...** command and then the ENGINES tab. Select the "Random engine failures" button. Set 1 for the "Fail engines" option.

✈ Select the number in the left box corresponding to the "Failures begin after:" option. Type the minimum number of minutes you want to pass before the failure occurs, for example "5".

✈ Select the number in the right box corresponding to the "Failures end after:" option and type the maximum number of minutes you want to pass before the failure occurs, for example "15".

✈ Click (OK) to close the dialog box.

✈ Dial in the Traverse City (TVC) VOR 114.60 on Nav1.

✈ Take off from runway 8R and make a right climbing turn to 3500 feet, heading 005 degrees.

✈ Begin tracking the TVC VOR.

✈ 15nm out of the TVC VOR begin descent to 2500.

✈ On top of TVC, turn left heading 344 degrees and proceed with visual approach to runway 34.

✈ Check gear down if necessary and proceed with the approach.

✈ Land and taxi to parking or the hangar. Make any necessary repairs.

Understanding Sign Language

Too many FS pilots believe their flight begins by starting from the "active runway" and ends with a successful landing and don't care about the ground portion of their flights. The reasons for this attitude are many but seem to mostly be either they don't know how to taxi on the ground or more unfortunately, don't care. However, FSX has increased the realism of flight more than ever before and designers have created excellent airport scenery, we're seeing many real world visual indicators in our FSX flight experience. So, the more you know about your airports, the more skilled you'll become as a pilot. Therefore, we'll look at airport signage and markings in this article.

Runway And Pavement Markings

Let's first consider runway markings. They help you determine information during your takeoff and landing transitions and as you taxi the airport grounds.

We can divide pavement markings into four categories: Runway Markings, Taxiway Markings, Hold and Position Markings and Other Markings.

Runway markings

Runway markings are categorized in three groups. The runway markings identify whether the runway is for *Precision Approaches*, for *Non-precision Instrument Approaches* (IFR) or only acceptable for *Visual Approaches* (VFR). All runway markings are white, except for areas that are designated as unusable for landing, takeoff, or taxiing, which are generally indicated by yellow chevrons (see image below). White arrows designate displaced threshold areas, which are considered usable for taxiing.

Yellow Chevron Markings

Yellow chevron markings on runways indicate areas that are designated as unusable for landing, takeoff, or taxiing

Let's see how those three types of runways are different:

→ Precision runways
Precision runways are equipped with an ILS approach, or with another type of precision approach method. Precision Runways also contain additional markings on the surface of the runway and taxiway, such as touchdown zone marking, ILS Hold signs, and yellow ILS hold lines.

→ Non-Precision Instrument Approach runway
A Non-Precision Instrument Approach runway services either a VOR or ADF instrument approach that is published with the approval of the FAA. Non-precision instrument runways are very similar in appearance to VFR runways but have threshold markers.

→ VFR Runway
A VFR runway has no Instrument Approach Procedure. VFR runways most typically contain a runway number and an aiming point marker on each side. It may also contain threshold markings and fixed distance markers for jet aircraft.

Runways also show some rather obvious markings, including centerlines, side stripes, shoulder markings and large numbers to indicate the runway number. The runway number may also have an additional letter added ("R" or "L" or "C") to indicate whether the runway is right, left or center if an airport has multiple runways at the same direction.

Example of threshold markings

Runway areas such as displaced thresholds, which are designated as usable for taxiing, are marked in white. This image of runway 6R at KLAX also shows the threshold markings of 12 stripes, which indicate the runway is 150 feet wide.

Threshold markings

Threshold markings are longitudinal stripes located at the threshold end of the runway. They identify the beginning of the runway surface suitable for landing and are displayed in two different configurations. One common configuration consists of eight stripes located on either side the centerline. Alternatively, they can indicate the width of the runway by the number of stripes using the following stripe configurations:

✈ 4 stripes = 60 feet   ✈ 6 stripes = 75 feet

✈ 8 stripes = 100 feet   ✈ 12 stripes = 150 feet

✈ 16 stripes = 200 feet

If the threshold area is displaced or preceded by another area of pavement, that area is available for taxi, run-up or takeoff but you should not use the area when landing.

Runway Aiming Point Markers

Many real world pilots use different techniques for capturing the right runway perspective in relationship to landing their aircraft. A pilot may, for example, align the top of the panel eyebrow 5 - 7 fingers below the horizon or view the runway length from a certain angle or try to "hit the numbers." Although these techniques are not easy to duplicate in FSX, the runways in FSX do have Aiming Point Markers for you to establish a visual aiming point for landing your aircraft. The Aiming Point Markers appear as two solid wide stripes, each one on either side of the runway centerline and located approximately 1000 feet from the threshold (see following image).

Example of aiming point markers

Aiming point markers appear as two solid wide stripes on either side of the runway centerline. They're located about 1000 feet from the threshold (image is of Runway 4R at JFK).

Runway Touchdown Zone Markers

The purpose of touchdown zone markers is to identify the area for landing operations by providing distance information in 500-foot increments. The markings consist of one to three stripes spaced 500 feet apart down the runway. The grouped bars are symmetrically placed on each side of the runway centerline (see following image).

Touchdown zone markers

Touchdown zone markings consist of one to three stripes spaced 500 feet apart down the runway (image is from Runway 6R at KLAX).

Surface Painted Signs

You may have already discovered that not all airports contain free standing and night-lighted taxiway signs but instead have the directional signage painted on the surface of the taxiway. Taxiway direction signs are black characters painted on a yellow background. They indicate the direction of the adjacent or intersecting taxiway. Taxiway location signs, on the other hand, are painted just the reverse — black backgrounds with yellow characters. Surface painted signage may also have intersecting runway information that feature red backgrounds and white characters.

Always keep in mind when on the taxiways that the taxiway markings are yellow for a reason: to suggest *caution*. Therefore, always treat all ground operations with caution.

Taxiway edge markings

You should already know that taxiways allow you to exit and approach runways and areas of ground transition safely while operating your aircraft. Unfortunately, the different versions of Microsoft Flight Sim haven't always provided a realistic viewpoint from the cockpit while on the ground and this therefore can make taxiway transitions occasionally more difficult.

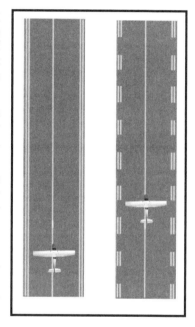

Taxiway edge markings are either a continuous running double yellow line about six (as you can see in the image on the right) or they are sometimes dashed double lines of the same size and location as the continuous running double lines.

Continuous running lines indicate there is an adjacent surface outside of the lines *that is not intended for you to use*. Dashed or noncontinuous yellow lines define the edge of the taxiway, where the adjoining pavement or apron is available for taxi operations.

Hold and position lines

Hold lines are usually placed right before where the taxiway intersects the runway, but can be on the runway where land and hold short operations frequently occur. Their meaning is rather straightforward: Hold or stop! Therefore, never cross this line unless given permission by the ATC. In non-tower-controlled environments, make sure that the area is clear, and that you announce your intentions before you move across the hold lines. Hold lines consist of two solid lines proceeding two dashed yellow lines and extend across the width of the taxiway. (Or in the case as previously noted runway operations, they extend across the runway.)

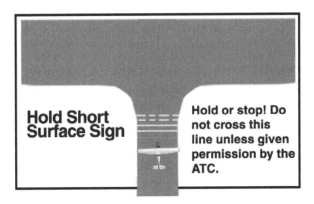

Hold lines consist of two solid lines proceeding two dashed yellow lines and extend across the width of the taxiway and mean hold or stop until ATC gives you permission or the area is clear.

ILS or "ILS Critical Area" holding lines

Because these lines are meant to protect the inbound pilots who are on instrument approach, you should never cross them unless given permission from ATC. Aircraft beyond this point may interfere with the ILS signal to approaching aircraft. The ILS hold line consists of 2 solid yellow lines spaced 2 feet apart across the width of the taxiway. It's connected by pairs of solid lines spaced 10 feet apart. You may also see another sign beside the lines to the outer edge of the taxiway that validates the markings as an ILS critical area hold line.

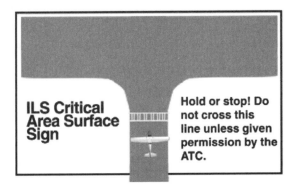

You should never cross the ILS Critical Area marking unless given permission from ATC.

Other Markings

Some airports may use other markings that are unfamiliar to you or are specific for the adjoining facilities or other operations. An example could be a closed runway, which can be defined by large yellows X's, or crosses, that are painted at each end of the runway and additionally at 1000 foot spacing on the runway.

Airport Signs & How To Get From Here To There

Y ou'll see signs everywhere at airports. They'll not only tell you what to do but sometimes how and where to do it. It's important to understand the color codes and meaning of the four main categories of signs when taxiing at your FSX airports.

Location Signs

These are used to advise or identify taxiways or runways on which the aircraft is located. They're designed with a black background and yellow character (exceptions include runway boundary and ILS critical area signs, which have a yellow background and black character). An easy way to remember these signs is with the saying *"Black square, You're there."*

Taxiway location signs

You'll find these signs alongside taxiways, adjacent to direction signs or runway signs.

Runway location signs

Runway location signs are located near connecting runways, or ones that are in close proximity, to help alleviate confusion to the pilot and validate magnetic compass information.

Runway boundary signs

Runway Boundary Signs are used by a pilot exiting a runway onto the taxiway. The sign provides a "heads ups" to the pilot, and the aircraft is considered clear of the runway after it has taxied beyond this sign.

ILS Critical Boundary Signs

ILS Critical Boundary Signs as noted before, are similar to the mandatory sign, but in this instance informs the pilot that he is clear of the ILS critical area.

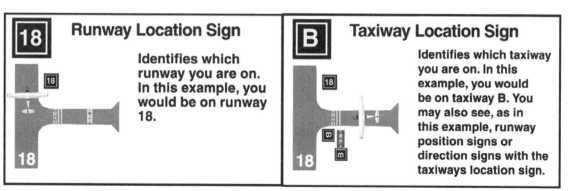

Runway Location Sign

Identifies which runway you are on. In this example, you would be on runway 18.

Taxiway Location Sign

Identifies which taxiway you are on. In this example, you would be on taxiway B. You may also see, as in this example, runway position signs or direction signs with the taxiways location sign.

Airports use location signs such as these to identify taxiways or runways on which the aircraft is located. An easy way to remember these signs is with the saying "Black square, You're there."

Mandatory Instruction Signs

These signs are designed with red backgrounds and white characters. They alert you to intersections to a runway or critical area or areas where aircraft are prohibited from entering.

An example of a mandatory instruction sign are *runway holding position signs* that are used on taxiways that intersect runways at a point other than at the runway end (see diagram below). You may also see these signs located at the yellow hold line on the taxiway at the end of the respective runway. It may be necessary to hold aircraft at a position on the taxiway other than at the runway end. These holding points prevent interference with landing or departing aircraft.

Another example are *ILS Critical Area Signs* that are used to hold departing aircraft farther from the ILS runway when instrument landings are in progress.

One final example are *No Entry Signs* that are used on taxiways with "one-way" traffic only or at intersections with roadways that could be confused for a taxiway.

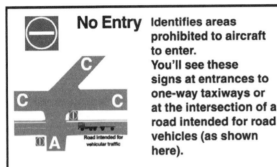

No Entry Identifies areas prohibited to aircraft to enter. You'll see these signs at entrances to one-way taxiways or at the intersection of a road intended for road vehicles (as shown here).

ILS Critical Area ATC may tell you to stop (hold) at this sign when the ILS is being used at the airport. It's possible that aircraft taxiing beyond this point in real world situations may interfere with the ILS signal to approaching aircraft.

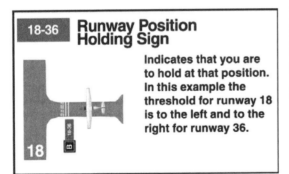

Runway Position Holding Sign Indicates that you are to hold at that position. In this example the threshold for runway 18 is to the left and to the right for runway 36.

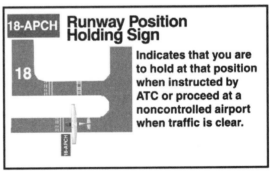

Runway Position Holding Sign Indicates that you are to hold at that position when instructed by ATC or proceed at a noncontrolled airport when traffic is clear.

Mandatory instruction signs, designed with red backgrounds and white characters, alert you to intersections to a runway or critical area(s) where aircraft are prohibited from entering.

Destination signs

These signs, which also have a yellow background with a black character, usually show an arrow pointing to the destination. They're used to help assist and guide you to your destination on the airport. Destination Signs commonly used at apron areas, terminals, FBOs military areas, cargo areas, parking, etc.

Destination sign

Indicates a destination at the airport. The arrow points in the direction you need to travel for the destination. In this example, the FBO is to your left on taxiway C.

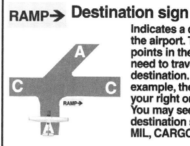

Destination sign

Indicates a destination at the airport. The arrow points in the direction you need to travel for the destination. In this example, the RAMP is to your right on taxiway C. You may see other destination signs such as MIL, CARGO or TERM

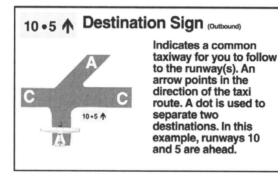

Destination Sign (Outbound)

Indicates a common taxiway for you to follow to the runway(s). An arrow points in the direction of the taxi route. A dot is used to separate two destinations. In this example, runways 10 and 5 are ahead.

Destination signs, which have a yellow background with a black character, usually show an arrow pointing to a specified destination.

Other types of signs

Information Signs

These signs, which have a yellow background with black character, provide information to you about noise abatement issues, radio frequencies, etc. You probably won't see these too often in FSX.

NOISE ABATEMENT
PROCEDURES IN EFFECT
2300-0500

Runway Distance Remaining Signs

Runway Distance Remaining Signs have a black background with a white number character. They're usually located along one or possibly both sides of the runway. The numbers are rounded off to the first number for thousands of feet. For example, number "7" would be used for the 7,000 foot marker and "12" would be used for the 12,000 ft.

Sign Arrays

You may see several direction signs appear in a group, especially at large airports. Although they may look confusing with their arrows pointing in every direction, there is a logical order to it (see following diagram).

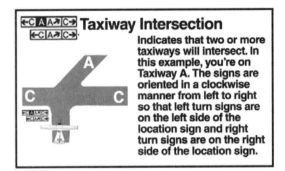

Taxiway Intersection

Indicates that two or more taxiways will intersect. In this example, you're on Taxiway A. The signs are oriented in a clockwise manner from left to right so that left turn signs are on the left side of the location sign and right turn signs are on the right side of the location sign.

The orientation of the signs starts from the left and goes right in a clockwise manner. The left turn signs are on the left of the location sign and right turn signs are on the right side of the location sign. You may see other sign arrays too such as Holding Position/Location signs or Direction/Location signs:

Understanding Sign Language With A Practice Flight

Let's do some practice to see how well you understand airport signs. We'll operate from Muskegon County airport (KMKG - see the airport map on the following page). We'll start at GA parking and we want to taxi to runway 32. Select the **World I Go to Airport...** menu command. Select KMKG as the Airport ID (Make certain to have either "Any" or "United States" selected in the "Country/Region" option. Then select "PARKING 2 -- RAMP GA SMALL" in the "Runway/ Starting position" option. Click the OK button to continue.

Select the **World I Time and Season...** menu command. Select "Day" for the "Time of day" and "Summer" as the "Season" option. Click the OK button. Select the **World I Weather...** menu command and click "Clear skies (clears all weather)" option.

Finally, select the aircraft you want to fly. I am flying one of the default Cessna 172SP aircraft.

Take a look at the Taxiway Signs Video on the Companion CD-ROM for more information. See the Contents pages for more information about the Companion CD-ROM and all the videos.

The following map shows the route you need to take to runway 32. It may seem, well, long and crazy, but it's an actual assigned procedure. We'll need to taxi on taxiway D-E-A-B (Delta-Echo-Alpha-Bravo). Keep in mind this is just to test your knowledge of airport sign language so we won't be using ATC.

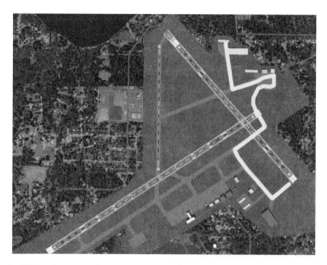

It looks like a long taxi to runway 32 but it will be a good test for you!

I suggest you read the following flight information *before* you take to the sky because this will help give you an idea of the flight plan before you attempt flying. The type of aircraft you're flying may determine your altitude, speed and the time you take in the turns.

If you're ready, let's start:

➤ Before beginning to taxi, turn on your TAXI , NAV and BCN (if available) lights as you should do when taxiing. To avoid hitting the building, press the (Shift) + (P) key for a pushback (or the key combination you have assigned to this function). Once you see the yellow lines, you can press the (Shift) + (P) key combination again to stop the pushback.

➤ Release the parking brake and *gently* apply enough power to move forward but keep in mind that you may be moving faster than you think.

➤ Make certain to follow the yellow taxi lines as you taxi through the GA ramp area. It may be tempting to "cut across" to the taxiway but that is a dangerous habit to develop.

✈ Keep following the yellow line until you see the <-D-> taxiway marker (see the following image). Taxi slowly in the direction of the marker but keep between the yellow boundary lines (and therefore on the taxiway).

✈ This is a direction sign. You need to turn left but keep on the yellow taxi line to ensure a proper path on the taxiway. Continue on taxiway D until you see the next group of buildings and a GA ramp/parking area. You'll need to slow down as you approach this area because you'll be taking a quick right turn (see following image)

✈ Continue on taxiway D up to runway 24. It's important to stop here because this is a runway position holding sign. Also notice the lines painted on the surface of the taxiway indicating a Hold Position.

✈ Notice the sign here tells you that you're on taxiway D and at runway 24. When you've verified the traffic is clear (or when cleared by ATC if you're using ATC) , taxi over runway 24 and then hold again at runway 32 for the same reason.

→ When you've verified the traffic is clear (or when cleared by ATC if you're using ATC), taxi over runway 32 and proceed with your taxi on taxiway E.

→ Continue your taxi and watch for the destination signs so you know you're on the right path. Notice the next direction sign shows taxiway B is to the left so you'll need to turn left onto taxiway b>

→ You should pass the control tower on the right and the water tower should be ahead. Notice the B<-B sign. We need to turn left here to the runway.

✈ Continue on taxiway B up to runway 32. Notice this is another position hold sign. Also notice the lines painted on the surface of the taxiway indicating a Hold Position.

✈ Congratulations, you've arrived at the correct runway and awaiting additional ATC instructions.

This should give you an idea of reading and understanding sign language at your favorite airports.

Flying In The Great Outdoors

Welcome to a fun and relaxing flight in the great outdoors over the southwestern United States. This flight will be a scenic flight for you and perhaps a different kind of flight, too, because you're starting in the lowest point in North America (Death Valley, California) and fly to the highest airport in the US (Leadville, Colorado). We'll mention interesting facts and scenery along the way but don't worry... we'll provide airport and runway information, VORs and other navaids enroute and additional information for you to reach Leadville.

Background Information

Before we talk about the flight, you should read and understand the following information. Most importantly, keep in mind the information in this chapter is for entertainment purposes only and should not be used as an aviation, technical or historic reference.

1. We used Microsoft FSX for this flight but you can use Microsoft FS 2004 as well.

2. We suggest you read the flight information before you take to the sky because this will help give you an idea of the flight plan before you attempt flying. The type of aircraft you're flying may determine the altitude at which you fly.

3. We're primarily using VOR navigation in the flight but feel free to deviate if you spot some scenery that you want to investigate or check out more closely. Simply return to the original VOR or GPS heading.

4. We're starting the flight in mid-morning but consider flying the adventure at different times of the day because the scenery may look quite different in the early morning or early evening when the canyons, mountains, etc., cast different shadows. In addition, try these flights during different seasons. The mountains and cliffs are impressive when covered with frost or snow.

5. Always keep in mind that you're flying over and around mountains, plateaus, deserts, lakes and more so don't forget to check all views from your airplane. In other words, what appears directly ahead may be an unimpressive looking desert but a series of canyons or mountains may be to the right or to the left (minimize the instrument panel when necessary to improve your view).

 Text continues on page 70

Death Valley Background Information

Death Valley National Park features over 3.3 million acres of spectacular desert scenery, interesting and rare desert wildlife, complex geology, undisturbed wilderness and sites of historical and cultural interest. Its border to the west is the 11,049-foot Telescope Peak in the Panamint Range and to the east is 5,475-foot Dante's View. Badwater is the lowest point (-282 feet) in the Western Hemisphere.

The National Park Service first noticed Death Valley's outstanding natural beauty and scientific importance in the 1920s. President Hoover designated it a national monument in February 1933. Congress passed the Desert Protection Act of 1994, which not only designated Death Valley as a national park but added over a million acres to its size. This makes Death Valley one of our newest national parks.

Although its name suggests a forbidding and gloomy area, you can find spectacular wildflower displays, snow covered peaks, beautiful sand dunes and abandoned mines. However, most visitors believe Death Valley is named correctly; it's the hottest place in North America and much of it is below sea level.

Death Valley is usually sunny, dry and clear year-round. The winters are mild but winter storms are not unusual. However, summers are extremely hot and dry with temperatures commonly running above 120 degrees Fahrenheit. Comfortable clothing providing sun protection and a broad brimmed hat are recommended in summer. Winter requires warmer clothing and light to medium jackets. Sturdy walking shoes are important year round

A geologist named G.K. Gilbert, who worked in the area in the 1870s, was the first to note the impressive rock formations. These rock layers constitute an almost perfect record of the earth's past except that the record is out of sequence. The reason is that the rock layers forming the mountains are very ancient but only rising in recent geologic time.

Erosion began wearing the mountains down even as they rose. Occasional streams, resulting primarily from the infrequent but strong rain storms, rush down the steep canyons and scours boulders, soil and other debris before carrying the debris mass with it. It then deposits it on the valley floor at the mouth of the canyon.

The valley floor usually shimmers silently in the heat. The air is so clear that distances are "telescoped." The sky is a deep blue except for an occasional light cloud. The main weather

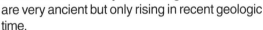

feature is heat. Oppressive heat dominates the area for six months of the year and even more brutal heat dominates for the other six months. The mountains protect the area from getting significant rain. Nevertheless, the little rain that does fall in the valley provides enough water for the wildflowers that transform this desert into a vast garden.

Despite the harshness and severity of the environment, over 900 types of plants live within Death Valley National Park. The plants living on the valley floor have obviously adapted well to the desert climate. Some of these plants have roots that extend sixty feet into the ground searching for water. However, not all plants have such deep root systems because the root system of other plants extends several feet horizontally in all directions but just below the surface. Other plants have skins that allow very little water to evaporate. Moisture levels increase with height, too, so that juniper, mountain-mahogany, pinyon and other pines appear on high peaks.

Different types of wildlife have also adapted to the desert heat. These animals are mainly nocturnal. The air is so dry in Death Valley that the air temperature can drop quickly after sunset. Therefore, small animals thrive in the cool dark night air on the desert floor. Larger animals, such as the desert bighorn, live in the cooler, higher elevations. The higher peaks surrounding Death Valley are often snow-covered.

So, Death Valley is an active world of exciting contrasts and wonders and quite the opposite of its name.

Leadville Background Information

As you've probably guessed by its name, Leadville has a rich gold and silver mining history. Countless people through the years have made and lost fortunes in this frontier mountain area. Most of these people have unfamiliar names and are now lost to history but other people with more familiar names such as Carnegie, Guggenheim, Susan B. Anthony, the "Unsinkable" Molly Brown, Doc Holliday and Oscar Wilde fill Leadville's past.

Ever since Abe Lee discovered gold in the California Gulch, thousands of hopeful prospectors came looking for immediate fortunes. Leadville is home to the National Mining Hall of Fame & Museum, the only federally chartered mining museum in the country. But Leadville is more than just a mining area. It's designated as a National Historic Landmark District because of its original seventy square blocks of Victorian-style architecture. The main street in Leadville, Harrison Avenue, features over fifty magnificent 19th century buildings, filled with charming shops, memorable restaurants, abundant accommodations and splendid museums.

6. We're not using ATC information in this flight so if you want to use ATC, you might be given different information, depending on the weather and time of your flight as you're flying the routes.

Selecting an aircraft

It's always important to know and understand your aircraft. You should probably select a larger general aviation aircraft for this route because of the distance (about 600nm) and altitude (over 15,000 feet in some areas).

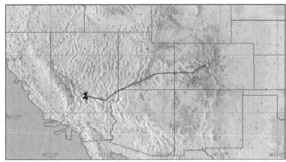

Map of our route from Death Valley to Leadville

If you're flying a new or unfamiliar aircraft, study it thoroughly and know its systems and limitations before flying in the mountains. A great way to do this is to "test fly" the aircraft at a small airport in a level area (for example, GH3 (Grand Haven Memorial)).

You may also want to consider the *USA Extreme Landscapes* package from Abacus to enhance the impressive scenery of the route.

Preparing for the flight

Death Valley National Park has two airports and both have very forbidding sounding names: Furnace Creek and Stove Pipe Wells. However, these names fit in well with the surroundings of this large and impressive area.

We're going to start our flight on runway 15 at Furnace Creek (L06). You can use whatever aircraft you want to fly (see above); I'm flying the FSX default Beechcraft King Air 350.

To set up the flight, make the following settings in FSX:

1. Set the time for 10:00 and the Season for summer by selecting the **World | Time & Season...** command.

2. Set the weather for "Fair Weather" by selecting the **World | Weather...** command (or set the weather at your discretion or select real world weather option).

We're flying the route mainly by a combination of GPS and VOR navigation so you'll need to refer to your GPS gauge occasionally. This will especially be true on the approach to Leadville and in the mountains and valleys. The entire route with navaids is shown on the following page, alongwith a map showing the route.

You can either enter the route as listed on the following page in your FSX Flight Planner or you can download the route from the companion CD-ROM. The flight name is FURNACECREEK.

Microsoft Flight Simulator Flight Plan
Furnace Creek -> Lake Co
Distance: 564.1 nm
Estimated fuel burn: 207.9 gal / 1392.6 lb
Estimated time en route: 1:52

Waypoints	Route	Alt (ft)	Hdg	Distance	GS (kts)	Fuel (gal/lb)	Time off
				Leg		537.0	0:00
L06				Rem	Est	Est	ETE
				564.1	Act	Act	ATE
LAS (116.90) (VOR)	-D->	17500	092	86.5	300	31.9 / 213.8	0:17
				477.6		/	
MMM (114.30) (VOR)	V394	17500	033	59.4	300	21.9 / 146.7	0:11
				418.2		/	
PHYLI (waypoint)	V8	17500	046	22.1	300	8.1 / 54.4	0:04
				396.1		/	
JEZOB (waypoint)	V8	17500	046	25.7	300	9.5 / 63.5	0:05
				370.4		/	
LOISS (waypoint)	V8	17500	047	6.2	300	2.3 / 15.2	0:01
				364.2		/	
MATZO (waypoint)	V8	17500	047	2.1	300	0.8 / 5.2	0:00
				362.1		/	
BCE (112.80) (VOR)	V8	17500	047	53.1	300	19.6 / 131.2	0:10
				309.0		/	
HVE (115.90) (VOR)	V8	17500	047	87.4	300	32.3 / 216.1	0:17
				221.5		/	
PIGSE (waypoint)	V244	17500	075	33.9	300	12.5 / 83.6	0:06
				187.6		/	
ANIUM (waypoint)	V244	17500	076	9.6	300	3.5 / 23.5	0:01
				178.1		/	
PAROX (waypoint)	V244	17500	076	43.2	300	15.9 / 106.7	0:08
				134.9		/	
HERRM (waypoint)	V244	17500	077	11.3	300	4.2 / 27.8	0:02
				123.6		/	
NADIN (waypoint)	V244	17500	077	15.2	300	5.6 / 37.5	0:03
				108.4		/	
MTJ (117.10) (VOR)	V244	17500	077	18.5	300	6.8 / 45.5	0:03
				89.9		/	
MEYRS (waypoint)	V26	17500	084	20.6	300	7.6 / 50.7	0:04
				69.3		/	
KLXV (airport)	-D->	9928	040	69.3	300	25.6 / 171.2	0:13
				0.0		/	

Not For Operational Use

Furnace Creek (L06)
Airport Diagram

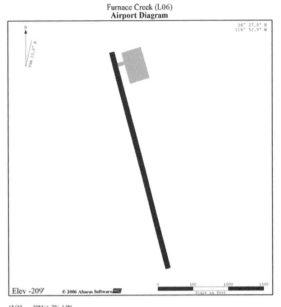

Elev -209'　　© 2006 Abacus Software

15/33　3064'× 70' LIRL
15:
33:

Lake Co (KLXV)
Airport Diagram

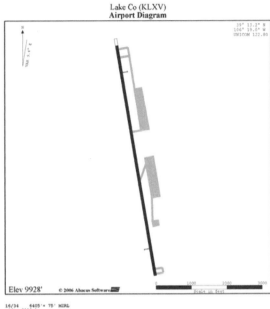

Elev 9928'　　© 2006 Abacus Software

16/34　6405'× 75' MIRL
16:　PAPI-L
34:　PAPI-L

Altitude at Furnace Creek (left image) is a bit over 205 BELOW sea level (-205) while the altitude at our destination airport, Lake County (right image), is a bit over 9,932 feet (9932.4).

Let's Takeoff

✈ Make certain your radios and flight plans are set (LAS – 116.90 on NAV1 and MMM – 114.30 on NAV2). Instead of flying directly to LAS, we'll take in a bit of Death Valley scenery by first flying to the other airport in the national park: Stove Pipe Wells. See the airport maps on page 71.

✈ Takeoff from runway 15 and make a right climbing turn to 10,000 feet on a heading of 290 degrees to make a flyover of Stove Pipe (L09) airport. This will give you good views of Death Valley. Make certain to look out both windows because you'll see that only a part of Death Valley is below sea level. It also has many high mountains, peaks and other areas (and some with very interesting names). Also, make certain to check altitude and rate of climb as you approach Stove Pipe Wells.

✈ Once on top Stove Pipe (or near – feel free to fly around and explore Death Valley some more if the mood hits), turn heading 090 degrees and begin tracking the LAS VOR.

✈ The first VOR waypoint is at McCarran Field in Las Vegas. You'll probably spot Mount Charleston when you're 80nm out from (to) LAS so be careful of the terrain when approaching Las Vegas. Climb to 15,000 feet if necessary or adjust heading to avoid Mount Charleston.

✈ When you're over the mountains you should be able to spot Lake Mead in the distance. And Las Vegas should be approaching soon as well (perhaps you can see why the city is called Las Vegas, which means "Meadows" in Spanish). Once you're safely past the peaks, you can descend to 10,000 feet again.

✈ On top LAS, turn heading 031 and track the MMM VOR. You should notice Lake Mead out the right window at this point. If you want to explore Lake Mead, feel free to do so and just pick up the MMM VOR when you're ready to resume to flight to Leadville.

✈ Enroute MMM VOR, make certain to dial in the BCE VOR (112.8) on NAV1.

✈ On top MMM, turn heading 045 and track the BCE VOR.

✈ Enroute BCE dial in the Hanksville VOR (HVE – 115.90) on NAV2.

✈ Notice how the terrain changes when you're about 40nm out from (to) BCE. This is the area near Bryce Canyon National Park. Also be a good time to climb to 13,000 feet.

✈ On top BCE, turn heading 045 and track the HVE VOR. Unless you deviated from the course to check out some scenery, this should not be much of a course change.

✈ About 70nm from HVE, climb to 15,000 feet.

✈ Enroute to HVE, dial in the Montrose VOR (MTJ – 117.10) on Nav 1.

✈ On top HVE, turn heading 073 and track the MTJ VOR.

✈ About 105nm out from MTJ you're over a major portion of Canyonlands National Park.

✈ Watch terrain in this area – climb if necessary!

✈ On top MTJ, it's time to turn on the GPS gauge if you have not already done so. Turn slightly left heading 084 and fly to the MEYRS intersection. This is about an 20nm flight but you can track the distance away from the MTJ VOR.

Flying over Canyonlands national park

→ 12nm out from (away) KLXV descend to 10,000 feet when terrain allows and check airspeed. Look for the airport in the upper left when coming over the terrain. You may want to circle around the airport for a safer landing on runway 34 (see diagram below).

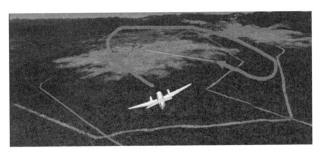

Consider circling around the airport if the descent is too steep for runway 34

→ Make certain your gear is down.

→ Proceed with your visual approach to runway 34 (see airport diagram on page 71).

→ Land KLXV and proceed to parking.

→ Announce you're clear of the runway and check your fuel level(s).

Welcome to Leadville Colorado!

You can view a slideshow presentation of this flight by viewing the FURNACECREEK video on the Companion CD-ROM. We used TV Slide Show Studio from Abacus to produce the slideshow. See the Contents pages for more information about the Companion CD-ROM and all the videos.

Are You Under The Weather?

A huge lightning flash appeared directly in the ominous dark cloud in front of me. I could hear the crackling of thunder over the engines as they strained against the fierce wind. The gauges on the instrument panel were moving in many directions, left/right, up/down. I was afraid that at any moment FSX would flash the dreaded "AIRCRAFT OVERSTRESSED" message on my monitor as my aircraft broke up from the tremendous turbulence. I was still 15 miles from my destination and definitely not enjoying the white knuckle excitement of this flight.

Flying in perfect weather conditions or even "Fair" weather conditions can become less interesting after a few flights. So, did you know that you can change the weather conditions in FSX at your destination airport or at any point during your flight?

Weather is an important but often overlooked addition to FSX. We'll talk about the weather conditions in this chapter and even set up a flight to show how easy it is to change the weather at a destination airport. After all, you want to simulate real world flying experiences, don't you?

Controlling Your FSX Weather

One thing we all have in common in the real world, regardless of who and where we are, is that we cannot control the weather. However, this isn't true in FSX where you have two ways of controlling or at least influencing the weather conditions:

1. Download real-world weather (although this requires an active Internet connection).

2. Create your own weather conditions.

Start controlling the weather by selecting the **World | Weather...** command in the FSX main menu. (If you're running FSX in full screen mode, access the main menu by pressing Alt on your keyboard.) This opens the following Weather dialog box.

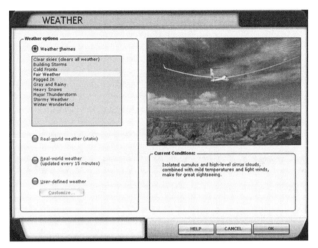

Real World Weather

Update weather automatically

Perhaps the easiest way to set weather conditions is for the Internet take care of it for you. In other words, you can download real-world weather from the nearest weather reporting station. An advantage of using this option is that the weather is updated automatically . To select this option, click the "Real-world weather (updated every 15 minutes)" option in "Weather options" and click the [OK] button. A disadvantage of using this option is that it not only requires an active Internet connection but also can slow your frame rate.

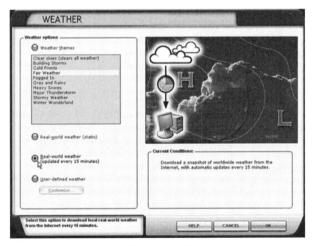

After you click the [OK] button, you'll see the "Weather Download" screen that shows the conditions at the nearest (local) weather station. Click the [OK] button to start or continue your flight.

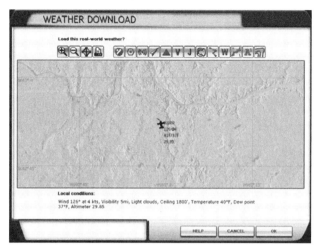

Real-world but static

If you're concerned about frame rates, you can still use real-world weather without FSX updating it every 15 minutes. Although this option still requires an Internet connection, the frame rate would not be affected as much because the weather is not updated regularly.

This might be a better choice if you don't have a fast Internet connection or aren't flying a long distance. (Consider downloading the real-world weather again before reaching your destination airport.)

To use this option, select the "Real-world weather (static)" option click the (OK) button. This opens the following screen which, like the screen above, shows the conditions at the nearest (local) weather station.

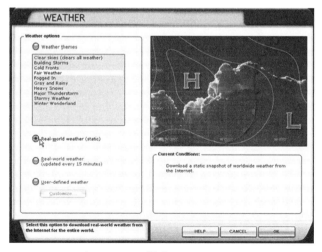

Click the (OK) button to start or continue your flight.

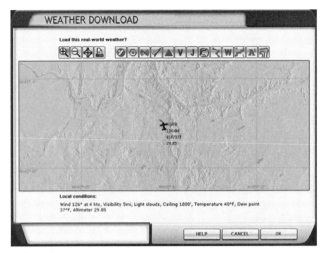

Create Your Own Weather

You can also set create specific weather conditions by selecting the "User-defined weather" option. This can be fun if, for example, it's nice and sunny where you're at now but you want to fly in wintery or storm conditions at another location.

Click the [Customize...] button to open the following screen:

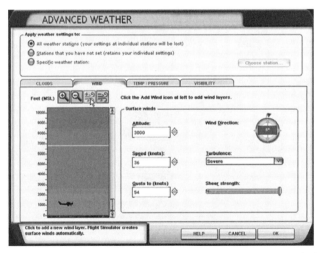

Use the sliders on the right to set values for the clouds, precipitation, visibility and wind speed.

NOTE

To activate the Precipitation slider, you must set Clouds to a value other than Clear. Also, be careful using cumulus clouds or thunderstorms because they tend to decrease frame rates on slower machines.

Setting values in Precipitation depends on both your current location in FSX and on the Seasons settings; you'll either see snow or rain outside the cockpit. (Don't expect to see snow accumulating on the runway, however). If you want to see the most realistic snow, set Precipitation to Very High.

Be careful with Visibility if frame rate is a concern. Visibility set to UNLIMITED may dramatically decrease the frame rates on some PCs. If frame rate is a concern, set this value to 30 miles or less.

You can create foggy conditions by setting Visibility below a ½ mile. Visibility settings might only have an affect below the lowest cloud layer. So, if you climb above the clouds you may suddenly notice that the fog has disappeared, and you'll see the ground clearly, unless you descend below the lowest cloud layer again.

Set the Wind speed to any strength you wish to try. To set the Wind Direction, click the triangle and move it to the desired direction. With 0 degrees represents northerly winds, 90 degrees is easterly winds, 180 degrees represents southerly winds and 270 degrees represents westerly winds.

These are just some basic weather settings to get you started. When you're set, click either the [OK] button to continue or the [Cancel] button to close the Weather screen without saving any settings.

Setting Advanced Weather Conditions

You can also set more advanced weather settings by clicking the [Advanced Weather...] button in the WEATHER window. This opens the Advanced Weather window:

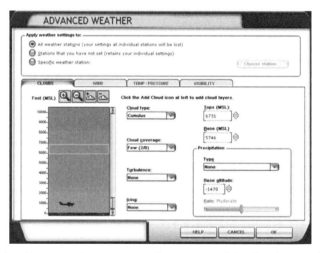

Notice the aircraft in the diagram...it represents the current altitude of your aircraft and, to the left, the altitude scale. Use the plus or minus button on top of the diagram to zoom in/out.

Advanced Clouds settings

Click the CLOUDS tab to set values for the clouds (this should be the default opening screen, also shown above). You'll use these options to set the cloud type, coverage and more. Again, avoid low frame rates by being careful with the clouds settings: Using cumulus clouds or thunderstorms will decrease frame rates on some PCs.

Advanced Wind settings

Click the WIND tab to set values for the winds. You should first create a surface wind level and set the Altitude by either typing the desired value into the digit box or using the up and down arrows to change the value. You may also click the vertical blue line right to the scale, hold the left mouse button and move the line to the desired altitude.

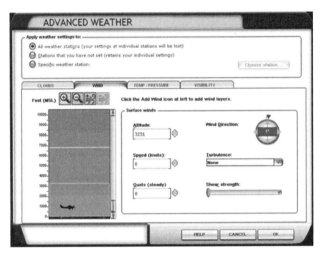

Set wind Speed for the surface layer.

Set Gusts to (knots) at a higher value than Speed.

Use the sliders to set the value for Shear strength. By increasing wind shear (moving the slider to the right) will tend to make your landing more difficult.

Set values for Turbulence from None to Severe.

To set the Wind Direction, click the triangle and move it to the desired direction. With 0 degrees represents northerly winds, 90 degrees is easterly winds, 180 degrees represents southerly winds and 270 degrees represents westerly winds.

You can add multiple wind layers by clicking the + (cloud symbol) button on top of the scale window. To create realistic settings you should set the wind speed to a higher value than in surface winds. Wind direction should be a bit different from the surface winds value, too. Add as many wind layers as you like. To access higher altitudes, use the slider on the right side of the scale window. To delete a layer, press the cloud symbol button on top of the scale window.

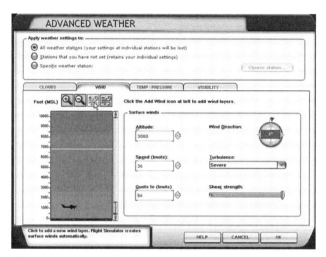

Click the TEMP/PRESSURE tab at the top to adjust the temperature or pressure.

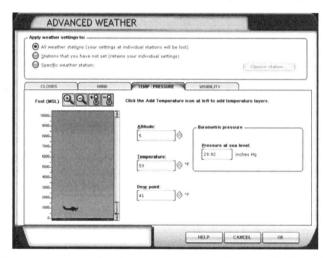

Setting the Barometric pressure is quite simple — type a value into the box, just try to use realistic values between 950 millibars (very low pressure) and 1050 millibars (very high pressure). Normal pressure is 1013 millibars. Low pressures in real world weather usually indicate storms and high pressures indicate good weather.

Setting the Temperature is also easy. First create some temperature layers by clicking the + (temperature scale symbol) button on top of the scale window. Then click the vertical blue lines in the scale window, drag them to the desired altitude of the temperature layer or type a value into the altitude digit box.

The value for the Dew point is typically lower than the daytime temperature.

You may create as many temperature layers as you like but if you want realistic layers, set the temperatures to decreasing values at increasing altitudes.

Click the VISIBILITY tab at the top to adjust the visibility.

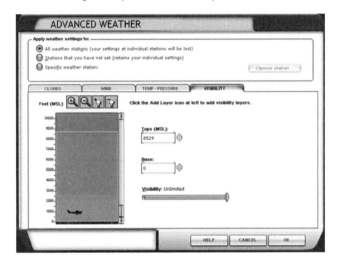

Type a value into the Tops and Base boxes or use the arrows to change the values. You'll only see your visibility settings between these two values. Be careful with the settings of visibility.

Use the slider to change visibility from 1/16 miles to Unlimited. Unlimited visibility may decrease frame rates on come PCs. A good setting with better frame rates will be anything below 30 miles.

When you're set, click the [OK] button or the [Cancel] button to close the Weather screen without saving any settings.

Flying Through Changing Weather Patterns

This route starts in downtown Toronto at Toronto City Centre airport (CYTZ). You'll see the Toronto Skydome (now called the Rogers Centre) and the CN Tower directly to the left. We're flying to the Greater Rochester International airport (KROC) across Lake Ontario. Also, to keep with the theme of this chapter – there may be a definite change in the weather between Toronto and Rochester!

We won't give any landing instructions or information for this flight because I want only to talk about how simple it is to change the weather pattern along your right or at your destination airport.

> ✦ Select your favorite airplane that you want to fly on this flight. I am using the default Beech King Air 350.

> ✦ Select the **World | Time and Season...** command and set clock to 1100 and Season to Summer.

> ✦ Select the **World | Go To Airport...** command and make certain Canada is selected for the Country/Region and type in CYTZ for the Airport and select 08 for the Runway.

> ✦ Select the **World | Weather...** command. Then select the "Fair" option in the Weather Themes. We've been told there is rain and fog across Lake Ontario at Rochester.

✈ Dial in the Rochester (ROC) VOR frequency 110.00 on your NAV2 radio.

✈ Because this is an exercise in weather settings, we won't be as concerned about ATC here or even in landing at Rochester. Our intention is to show you how easy it can be to change the weather pattern either along your route or at your destination airport.

✈ Take off from runway 08 and make a right climbing turn to 8000 feet on a heading of 123 degrees.

✈ At about 60nm from KROC, select the **World | Weather...** command so you can set the weather for the Rochester area. Select the "User-defined weather" option and then click the ⟨Customize ...⟩ button. Select the "Specific weather station:" option and click the ⟨Choose station...⟩ option.

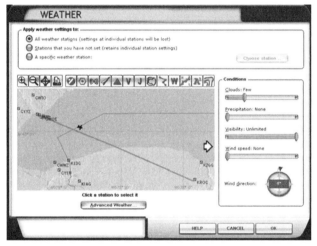

Use the arrow keys or the zoom in / zoom out icons to change the map view so that KROC appears on the map.

Move the mouse pointer over the airport name and click one time. Make certain that the airport name appears in the "Nearest station" line. If so, click the [OK] button and set the following weather conditions:

```
Set Clouds to Overcast
Precipitation to Very high
Visibility to 2 miles
Wind speed to moderate and the direction is your choice.
```

The screen should look similar to the following:

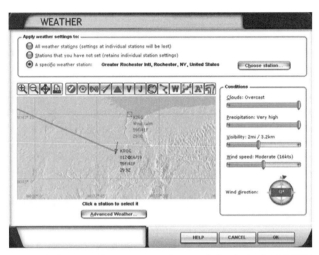

✈   When you are set with the weather pattern for KROC, click the [OK] button to continue your flight.

✈   When you're about 25 miles out from KROC, descend to 2500. Reduce speed to below 200.

✈   Dial in the KROC ATIS 124.82 for the latest weather information and verify if the weather reports reflect the changes you entered into FSX.

✈   You can continue with your approach to KROC at this point if you wish.

This is a quick example of how you can set weather during your flight.

Rolling Over With Magical Aerobatics

If you've ever attended an airshow, you must have marveled at the aerobatic artisans as they perform their aerobatic maneuvers. I know that I was impressed and amazed last July at the Air Venture show in Oshkosh watching pilots such as Sean D Tucker, Patty Wagstaff and others fly beautiful, precise aerial routines.

Unfortunately, there's little chance I could tolerate the G-forces the maneuvers would place on me. These G forces are real and definitely affect the performance and ability of every pilot.

Therefore, I get my aerobatics thrills in Flight Sim. Perhaps it's the excitement of attempting the same maneuvers flown by airshow performers before cheering crowds or it's completing an impressive aerobatic routine. But I think it's mostly because performing aerobatics in FSX is just plain fun.

Preparing To Fly

As you can well imagine, you cannot simply jump into your favorite FSX aircraft and begin your aerobatic tricks. As with any flight, you must prepare first.

Selecting an airport

An important but often overlooked consideration when performing aerobatics is selecting the right airport. You might want a big backdrop, such as the skyline of a large city or busy airport, to have in your maneuvers, however, keep in mind that all that extra scenery will slow down your PC and perhaps at a time when you really don't want it to slow down! Therefore, you should select a small, uncongested airport in level terrain, at least while learning your maneuvers.

I started at the Grand Haven, Michigan Municipal Airport (3GM). It's a small airport with Lake Michigan to the west and a long and straight north-south road runs west of the airport and parallel to Lake Michigan for reference. (This is US31 in case you're interested!)

Selecting your aircraft

Keep in mind that you don't necessarily need to fly a propeller aircraft to perform aerobatic maneuvers. Many jets, especially in FSX, make excellent aerobatic aircraft but keep in mind we're not necessarily referring to military jets. Although military fighters, like the F-15, offer supersonic speeds and maneuverability, even these impressive aircraft cannot perform some of the maneuvers that a propeller-driven aircraft can do. Then again, military jets aren't designed for aerobatics, just as the Extra 300S isn't designed to provide air cover for soldiers in Iraq and Afghanistan (at least not to the best of my knowledge).

Although you can do aerobatics in some jet aircraft, we're only talking about piston-powered aerobatic aircraft in this chapter, specifically the Extra 300S. The reasons that aerobatic performers fly piston powered aircraft is that slipstream, p-factor and torque all play an extremely important role in aerobatics, (including FSX) and jet aircraft have none of those advantages.

Also, you're not just limited to the Extra 300 that comes with FSX because many other aerobatic aircraft are available on the Internet and many of these aircraft are free. Aerobatic aircraft to look for on the Internet include Sukhoi, Pitts and Stearman.

Setting the FS Views

You should consider turning on smoke when you try your aerobatic maneuvers (do this by pressing the ⊡ key). The smoke gives the best reference of your performance and flight path. Otherwise, a flat spin is not impressive when viewed from the outside.

It's better to fly aerobatics from an outside view such as the tower mode. Also, try either the Spot or Tower view when performing your aerobatics. Tower might be better because it's fixed either on the ground or in the air and doesn't move with your aircraft like spot view.

The cockpit mode is a good mode as well, especially for accuracy of competition style maneuvers that require crispness in banks and rolls.

If you do chose to use an external view mode, press (Shift)+(Z) three times to display speed, g-factor and altitude. These three settings are all you really need for freestyle flying, but for competition style flying, it is best to be in the cockpit and flying in the aerobatic box.

We're only talking about a few aerobatic maneuvers in this article and there are many more you can try...tailslide, hammerhead and others.

Then when you're really confident about your ability, use the Flight Video feature in FSX to record your aerobatic maneuvers and prove your abilities to your friends.

Loading your aircraft

You'll need to load in the Extra 300S in your version of Flight Simulator. Select the **Aircraft | Select Aircraft...** command in the menu bar. Then select the "Extra" from the "Aircraft Manufacturers" list. FSX may display more than one variation of the Extra 300S so make certain to select "Extra 300S Patty Wagstaff" in "Variation" if you have more than one Extra 300S aircraft.

 For more information on Patty Wagstaff, please visit her website: **www.pattywagstaff.com**.

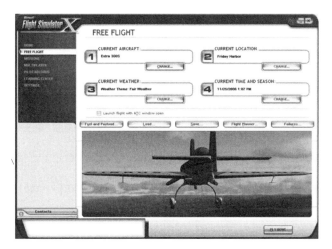

Selecting the Extra 300S in FSX

Before performing aerobatics, make certain you're familiar with the Extra 300S, especially with the joystick as controller. Until you're comfortable and recognize how the Extra reacts to your stick (and how the joystick reacts to the Extra), practice by watching from the one of the Outside Views.

Select a favorite airport and runway. Then takeoff in the Extra 300S. Climb to at least 3000 feet above ground level (a few maneuvers require an even higher minimum altitude). Then do some loops, climbs, etc., and remember how the Extra reacts to how you move the joystick. Don't worry about doing anything fancy at this point but avoid crashing!

Practice aerobatics by watching your maneuvers in Spot view until you're comfortable and recognize how the Extra reacts to your instructions.

Setting up options and final things to check

After you've decided on the aircraft, you should set up the realism options. Select the **Aircraft |
Realism Settings...** command in the menu bar.

You may want to consider making these changes in FSX to get the most out of your aerobatic flying.
In the "Flight model" area, move all the sliders to the right. Also, make sure that Autorudder (in the
lower right of the window) is unchecked.

I would also recommend leaving "Detect Crash and damage" off until you're more confident about
your aerobatic talents. If you crash or when the aircraft suffers too much stress, the flight restarts,
which can require too much as FSX reloads scenery and other files. But if you ignore crash and
damage and if you're unlucky enough to hit the ground, your aircraft will be back at 1000 feet AGL
immediately.

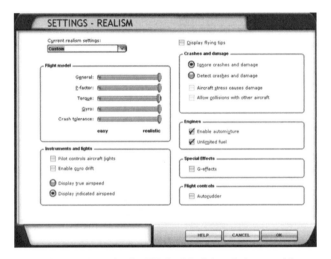

Setting options in the Flight Model and Autorudder

The other realism settings and options are your choice.

Before performing any aerobatic maneuver, make certain to check fuel quantity and fuel tank
selector (unless you've set fuel to unlimited). Also, double-check your engine instruments all read
normal. In particular, you'll need to keep an eye on the following four gauges when performing
aerobatics in the Extra 300:

Pay particular attention to the G-meter (1), Airspeed Indicator (2), Attitude Indicator (3) and Altimeter (4) when performing your aerobatics.

As an important reminder, be at least 3000 feet above ground level before beginning a maneuver. Please note this is *above ground level* (AGL) and not above sea level. Also, some maneuvers may require an even higher minimum altitude.

Also, don't forget to press (Shift)+(Z) to toggle the flight information on the main window. You can find this to be extremely useful.

The following pages describe several maneuvers. I suggest you first read the information before attempting any aerobatic maneuver. A good way to understand how the maneuver looks is to study the accompanying diagram.

Loops

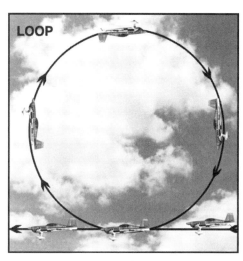

The first maneuver we'll do is a loop. The advantage of learning loops first is that it helps you become familiar with different attitudes, airspeeds and G-forces. These can change very rapidly as you perform a loop. Although flying a loop seems simple and is a basic maneuver, it's not always easy to fly well. You may believe that all there is to do is to get your aircraft at the proper airspeed and pull back on the stick. Although this will take your aircraft through a 360-degree loop, you won't win many aerobatic competitions flying that way. Instead, you're more likely to stall at the start of the maneuver or lose enough airspeed that you'll fall out of the loop (or worse).

As you can see in the diagram, the loop must be perfectly round and not oval or egg-shaped. Also, the entry into the loop and the exit from the loop must be at the same altitude.

A good way to perform your first loop is to line your loop up with a road or very long runway. I used the Grand Haven, Michigan Municipal Airport (3GM) as my starting point. A long and straight north-south road runs west of the airport and parallel to Lake Michigan.

Try lining up with a road or long runway before beginning a loop to help you judge direction (the view used here is "Tail View").

Keep an eye on your airspeed. Adjust your speed so you're flying at about 140 knots in level flight. Then start a smooth consistent pullback on the stick. Watch the G-meter on the panel because you need about 4 Gs to do perform a good loop.

The loop starts with a pull up of 3 to 4 G. Look over the left wing and make certain it creates, or draws, a circle on the horizon (see image to the right). This is very important to completing a successful loop. Adjust the amount of backpressure to keep the wing tip moving in that circle. The reason to look over the left wing is that you won't see anything but sky by looking over the nose at this point of the loop and you need something to reference to complete the loop.

*Make certain your left wing forms a
circle on the horizon as you execute a loop.*

When you're past the vertical, slowly relax the backpressure on the elevator so you're almost "floating" over the top of the loop. This will help round off the loop. Otherwise, if you hold full backpressure on the stick, your loop will be egg shaped and you're likely to stall at the top.

*When you're past the vertical, slowly relax the backpressure on the elevator so you're almost
"floating" over the top of the loop.*

When you've reached the top of the loop, slowly increase the backpressure again throughout the backside until you're flight becomes horizontal. Check airspeed and power throughout the backside because you may need to reduce the throttle. Look over the nose to stay aligned with the reference point (the road in this case), but don't forget to look over the left wing often to see if it's still tracing a perfect circle.

Slowly increase the backpressure throughout the backside until you're flight becomes horizontal.

Make certain the wings remain at right angles to the flight path. Look back over the tail as you pass through the vertical to make sure the wings stay level with the horizon. Use the rudder to maintain the plane of the figure and use the ailerons to maintain the orientation of the wings. Maintain backpressure as the nose comes back to the horizon.

Look behind as you pass through the vertical to make sure the wings stay level with the horizon.

You should pull about 4 Gs at the bottom of a normal loop.

Use the rudder and the ailerons to maintain the orientation of the wings. Maintain backpressure as the nose comes back to the horizon.

Try this to test your skill

Once you're familiar with the basics of the loop maneuver and want an additional challenge, increase the wind setting and then try a loop maneuver. (If you're flying in competition, it helps to watch what your competitors are doing so you can judge the effects of the wind when it comes your turn to fly.)

Aileron Roll

An aileron roll involves a four-step maneuver and is easy to accomplish. You'll rotate your aircraft 360 degrees around its longitudinal axis. However, to do this successfully you must keep the nose following a tight circle around a point on the horizon. Thanks to the brisk roll rate of the Extra 300S, the aileron roll one is an easy aerobatic maneuver to accomplish. As with many aerobatics in the Extra 300S, performing an aileron roll occurs very quickly (its roll rate exceeds 400 degrees per second). The following is the diagram of the roll:

Start by selecting a reference point on the horizon, such as a smokestack, road, building or even a cloud. In this example, I'm using an antenna/smokestack.

Select a reference point on the horizon, such as a smokestack, road, building, etc. I'm using the smokestacks here.

Maintain a level flight and airspeed of about 140 knots. Bring the stick back slowly so you're raising the nose smoothly to 20 – 30 degrees above the horizon. This neutralizes the elevator and deflects the aileron fully in the direction of the roll. Remember, pulling the nose up too much or too little at the start of the maneuver results in a bad roll.

Look to the left and make certain you've set the correct pitch attitude. Otherwise, by increasing backpressure after you've established the correct pitch attitude may force you from the reference point (the smokestacks in this example) or may drop the nose too much when you've started inverted flight.

Most aerobatic professionals believe it's easier to start with rolls to the left. Therefore, hold backpressure on the stick and move it quickly, but smoothly, all the way to one side.

Most aerobatic professionals believe it's easier to start with rolls to the left.

Maintain controls in that position until you complete the roll. Center the stick as the wings become level with the horizon. After the roll is completed the nose is usually 20 - 30 degrees below the horizon.

Maintain controls in that position until you complete the roll and center the stick as the wings become level with the horizon.

More you can try to test your skill: Slow rolls and snap rolls

Other types of rolls you can try include *slow rolls* and *snap rolls* (called *flick rolls* in Europe). Most slow rolls must be flown normally on a straight line. Maintain a constant rate for the roll and the longitudinal axis of the aircraft must be straight. To fly this type of roll successfully means that you must constantly change rudder and elevator control inputs throughout the roll.

A snap roll also must be flown normally on a straight line. A snap roll is an autorotation with one wing stalled. You must intentionally stall your aircraft by applying positive G-forces and in an outside snap, you need to stall your aircraft by applying negative G-forces. The rudder is then used in either case to start autorotation as in a spin.

The Immelmann

The Immelmann turn is a simple yet very effective maneuver under the proper technical circumstances. Many historians credit World War I German ace Max Immelmann with creating this maneuver. However, the version of the maneuver with which most of us are familiar today from aerobatics is not the maneuver that Max Immelmann found so successful.

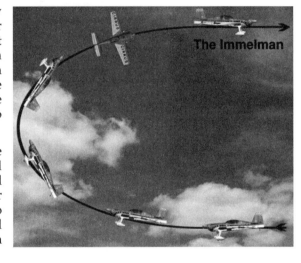

The Immelman

The following diagram shows that the Immelmann starts with a half loop to inverted flight. A half roll then results in horizontal upright flight. Although no one can say for certain whether Immelmann was the first to perform this maneuver, it was nevertheless used in World War I to reverse direction and gain altitude to "shake" an attacker.

As with the loop, a good way to perform your first Immelmann is to line your loop up with a road or very long runway. I'm using the Grand Haven (Michigan) airport again as my starting point with the long road running near the airport. Start the Immelmann by lining up with the road and flying level at between 150-160 knots.

Watch the G-meter on your instrument panel because you need about 3-4 Gs to start an Immelmann. Then start a smooth and consistent pull on the stick to start a steep climb. Apply full power as the nose reaches the vertical. Maintain this climb until your aircraft passes through the vertical and completes a half loop. Look to the side to check your flight path.

Look to the side to check your flight path.

Your aircraft should be inverted when you reach the top of the loop.

*Your aircraft should be inverted
when you reach the top of the loop.*

Then roll the aircraft back into the upright position. Look back and as you see the horizon, move the stick to the side to start a roll. Maintain back pressure until the nose reaches the horizon and center the stick as you return to upright level flight. You should now not only be at a higher altitude but changed directions 180 degrees.

Split-S

The Split-S, as with the Immelmann, was a maneuver used in World War 1. English pilots called the maneuver the *Split-arse* to describe the effect of the maneuver on the anatomy of the pilot. It was also a popular evasive maneuver of the Nazi pilots in World War II.

Although the Split-S looks like a simple maneuver, even experienced aerobatic pilots can have trouble successfully completing it. Because airspeed builds rapidly during the descending half loop, a sloppy roll technique can lead to a dangerous steep spiral. Therefore, make certain you understand loops and aileron rolls before attempting a Split-S.

The Split-S

The Split-S starts with a half roll to inverted followed by the second half of a loop downward. (Use the rudder to same side as roll to increase the roll rate significantly). This is another maneuver to reverse direction. This one, like the Immelmann, does not preserve speed and altitude but trades altitude for speed.

Altitude is important to completing a Split-S so the starting altitude should not be less than 3000 feet (maybe even higher until you're more experienced with the maneuver). Start by lining your loop up with a road or very long runway. I used the Grand Haven (Michigan) airport as my starting point and the long and straight road that runs north/south along the westside of the airport.

Keep an eye on your airspeed. Unlike other maneuvers we talk about here, you'll start this maneuver at a slower airspeed. Therefore, adjust your speed so you're flying at about 90 knots in level flight. (To decrease your speed, drop flaps and/or landing gear if necessary. This will allow you to perform a tighter curl). Then start a half aileron roll (see above for information on aileron rolls) and ease the throttle all the way back.·

Look over the nose and make certain the wings are level at the inverted position.

Take a look at the Aerobatics Video on the Companion CD-ROM for more information on many of these maneuvers. See the Contents pages for more information about the Companion CD-ROM and all the videos.

*Look over the nose and make certain
the wings are level at the inverted position.*

Then start a smooth consistent pull on the stick and start a half-loop. Do not let the nose move around the pitch axis. This can be prevented by maintaining enough back pressure on the stick. Keep an eye on your airspeed because you don't want the airspeed building too quickly.

*Start a smooth consistent pull on the stick and start a half-loop but do not let the nose move around
the pitch axis. Keep an eye on your airspeed because you don't want the airspeed building too quickly.*

Finally, recover to straight and level flight. Adjust airspeed as the nose returns to the horizon. You should now not only be at a lower altitude but changed directions 180 degrees.

Hammerhead

The hammerhead is one of the more thrilling aerobatic maneuvers performed at airshows. The hammerhead is also sometimes called a stall turn but this is really incorrect because your aircraft never should stall in this maneuver.

Although you can attempt a hammerhead in any aircraft left or right, it's best flown to the left with a clockwise rotating prop, and to the right with an counterclockwise rotating prop due to propeller torque/gyroscopic effects.

It starts with a quart loop (pull or push) into a vertical climb. As your momentum and airspeed decrease, apply the rudder. When your aircraft stops its climb, it will pivot around its vertical, or yaw, axis (which is now horizontal). The nose moves in a vertical circle from pointing up through the horizon to pointing down to the ground. You'll need a momentary pause here to draw the vertical down line After moving vertically down to pick up speed again, the maneuver is finished with the last quarter of a loop to horizontal flight. The quarter loop is flown just like the first part of a loop. As your aircraft becomes vertical, completely release elevator backpressure.

HAMMERHEAD

During the vertical line up, you'll probably need to add some right aileron and right rudder to maintain the vertical attitude because of the engine torque and p-factor. When your aircraft has slowed enough (typically immediately before it comes to a complete stop), apply full ruder to begin the turnaround. The hammerhead is performed when your aircraft decelerates through about 20 – 30 knots of airspeed, depending which aircraft you're flying.

The cartwheel portion of the hammerhead is performed with full rudder and full opposite aileron. At this point, your propeller will produce a pitching and rolling moment during the rapid rate of yaw so you'll probably need to add a bit of forward stick to keep the aircraft from coming off-line over the top. The yaw is stopped with opposite rudder while the ailerons and elevator remain in position, then once the yaw is stopped and your aircraft is pointed straight down, all controls are returned to neutral together.

The pivot is stopped with opposite rudder when the nose points straight down. When you complete the pivot, you'll also have neutralized the ailerons and ruder. Keep applying elevator and rudder to keep the nose pointing straight down. The pivot must be completed within one wingspan.

Keep in mind to perform rolls on the downline requires only aileron input if your aircraft is trimmed correctly. As you get more experienced with the hammerhead, try embellishing it by adding rolls on both the upline and the downline.

Controlling FSX With Its Menus

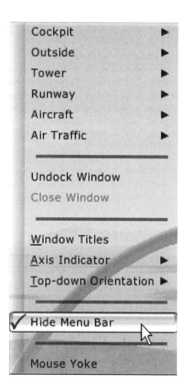

The menus in FSX allow you to control just about every aspect of the Flight Sim environment from changing airports and aircraft to adjusting image quality and screen resolution.

Typically a program will have the menus listed at the top of the screen starting in the top left. In some cases, especially in games, the program may be running in Full Screen Mode and won't show the menus. If you open FSX and don't see any menus available, press the [Alt] key on the keyboard one time. This will show the menus at the top of the FSX program. You can also right click on the FSX screen, but not on the panel area, and choose Hide Menu Bar from the pop-up menu to uncheck the selection (see image on the right for more information).

When a menu is opened and an item from the drop-down list is selected, either the option chosen will be invoked or a new window will open. When this happens, the menu at the top may disappear. Note that menu items that have a period of ellipse (...) after them will open a new window.

To start understanding what FSX can do, we'll go through the menus one at a time and explain what each option will do. Some of the menus will be described in detail in other chapters in this book. To begin, we'll press the [Alt] key on your keyboard if you don't already see the menus and click the Flights menu at the top of the screen.

Flights Menu

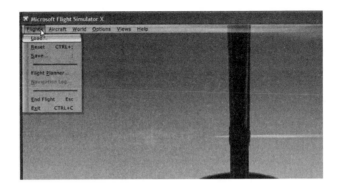

Load

The Load option in the Flights menu will open a new window that allows you to select a pre-saved flight. A Pre-saved flight or situation is saved using the Save option also found under the Flights menu. The saved flight is a file that contains virtually all conditions of a flight. For example, say you like to practice landings at a certain airport, but it takes quite a while to set up the flight (select the plane, select the airport, position your aircraft by either flying or slewing and so on). You can set up this flight one time, then save it. To fly the flight again, you can load FSX and use the Flight | Load menu to start you right where you saved it every time.

Reset

Choosing Reset from the Flights menu will reset the flight to the last loaded situation. Using our practice landing example, let's say you load the flight, fly in but miss the approach. You can either obviously fly a go-around, or you can choose Flight | Reset or the keyboard shortcut of Ctrl + ; (semicolon) and FSX will automatically reset the loaded flight. If you have not loaded a flight and choose Reset, FSX will reset the flight back to when you loaded FSX, to when you last switched aircraft or last switched airports or runways.

Save

The Save menu will open a dialog allowing you to select a name for the flight as well as a description. It also gives you the option of allowing you to make the flight you are saving the default flight. The default flight is the flight that FSX loads when it opens. By default FSX loads the AirCreation Trike Ultralight aircraft currently in flight over Friday Harbor north of Seattle.

Flight Planner

Choose Flight Planner from the Flights menu will open the FSX Flight planner. The Flight Planner allows you to select a departure and destination airport and the type of flight plan using instruments (IFR) or visual flight (VFR) and if the flight will be direct, VOR to VOR, Low Altitude Airways or High Altitude Airways and save them for future use. You can also load a previously saved flight plan and even print out flight plans called the Navigation Log.

Navigation Log

The Navigation Log is a view of the loaded flight plan that can be printed. This Navigation Log can also be accessed through the Flight Planner menu also found in the Flights menu.

End Flight

The End Flight option will give you three options:

- End Flight
  Closes the current flight and returns you to the FSX's opening screen.
- Continue Flying
  Closes the dialog box and returns you to your flight.
- View Flight Analysis
  Opens an overhead map view that shows you where you have flown and allows you to play back the flight showing you the aircraft's altitude and location as you flew complete with controls to speed up the playback if desired.

The End Flight menu can also be opened by pressing the Esc key at any time during flight.

Exit

Choosing Exit from the menu will close FSX back to your desktop after giving a confirmation screen first. FSX can also be closed by pressing Ctrl + C.

Aircraft Menu

Select Aircraft

The Select Aircraft menu will open a window showing you all of the aircraft available to fly in FSX. You can sort the aircraft by Manufacturer, Publisher and Engine Type.

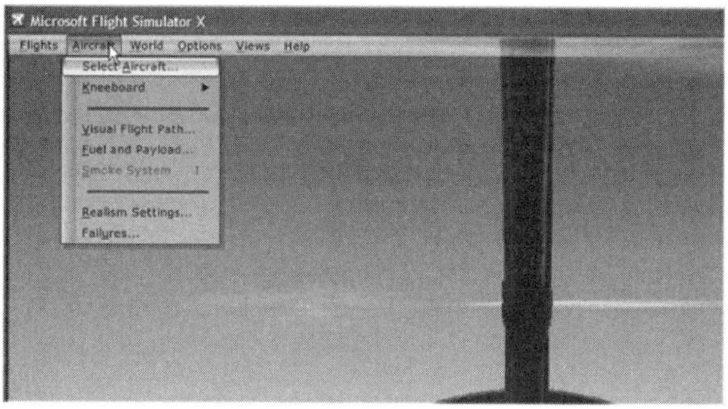

When a aircraft is selected, you can click a Details button to show you information about the aircraft. It's important to note that many of the aircraft in FSX have multiple variations, but by default the aircraft selection window only shows one variation. To see all the variations, click the Show All Variations checkbox on the Select Aircraft screen.

Kneeboard

The kneeboard in FSX is a window that will open up over top of the Flight Sim window. This window will have multiple tabs, one tab for each submenu as shown below.

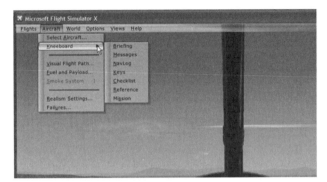

A kneeboard is used by many pilots to hold important information about the pilot's flight. It's called a kneeboard because pilots usually strap or fasten the information to their knee for quick reference.

You have several ways of opening the Kneeboard:

→ Selecting the desired kneeboard view from the **Aircraft | Kneeboard** submenu

→ By pressing (Shift) + (F10) on your keyboard (hold the (Shift) key and tap the (F10) key). Pressing the (Shift) + (F10) key combination multiple times will cycle the kneeboard

→ By clicking the checkmark icon on the aircraft's instrument panel. Clicking Messages will open the Kneeboard directly to the Messages screen:

Briefing Tab

The Briefing tab will show a general overview of the active mission. If you are not in a mission, this screen will be blank.

Messages Tab

The Messages tab will show all of the ATC (Air traffic Control) communication as well as information heard in a mission.

Nav Log Tab

The Nav Log is an overview of the loaded flight plan including waypoints (airports and/or VORs), headings, distance and estimated flying times between waypoints. If no flight plan is loaded, there will obviously be no information displayed.

Keys Tab

The Keys tab shows a list of all of the keyboard shortcuts available to FSX.

Checklist Tab

A Checklist is a list of things a pilot must go over before a flight. For real pilots, this typically includes visual inspection of the exterior of the plane, then continues into the cockpit. It's used to prevent oversights and to make sure every instrument and moving parts on an aircraft is functioning properly before it takes to the air.

The Checklist tab covers all the of the things to check inside the cockpit of the loaded aircraft before flight.

Reference Tab

The Reference tab shows you all the important information about the aircraft including stall speeds, cruise and max speeds for the loaded aircraft.

Mission Tab

The Mission tab shows a list of all of the mission objectives of the currently loaded mission. If no mission is loaded, this tab will be blank.

Clicking the checklist icon on the panel will open the kneeboard to the Briefing tab. Clicking it again will cycle the kneeboard to the Messages tab and so on. When the final tab, the Mission tab is active and the checklist icon is clicked again, the kneeboard will close. The same will happen by pressing the [Shift] + [F10] keys.

Visual Flight Path...

The Visual Flight Path is a guide used to practice ILS approaches. When activated, a series of red boxes, circles or the like will appear that will extend from the runway up and out. They will represent the proper glideslope required to land on the runway. Keeping the aircraft in the boxes or circles will assure a proper landing.

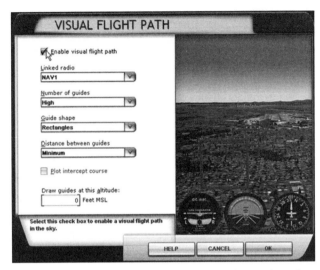

To activate the Visual Approach Path, set the parameters similar to that shown above being sure to click the Enable Visual Flight Path box. Then, tune the NAV1 radio (or NAV2 radio is selected in the settings) on the aircraft's radio stack to the desired runways ILS Frequency. You can refer to the Practicing ILS Approaches chapter in this book for more information and an example to practice.

Fuel and Payload...

The Fuel and Payload option will open a window showing you the current weights of the aircraft and maximum weights as well as current fuel load and maximum fuel loads. You can also adjust the amount of fuel and the weights of the payload stations assigned to the aircraft. Adjusting these settings can affect how the aircraft performs in flight.

Smoke System

The smoke system is commonly used on acrobatic aircraft. The smoke is assigned to an aircraft in the aircraft.cfg file. The smoke system is either on or off.

Realism and Settings

The Realism and Settings menu allows you to adjust how realistic the aircraft will perform in Flight Sim. The Flight Model section adjusts how the aircraft will respond in flight to things like the engine torque as well as how sensitive the aircraft is to detecting a crash, each ranging from Easy to Realistic.

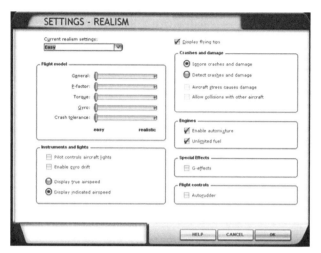

The Instruments and Lights section allows you to choose if the instruments will drift, if the pilot controls the aircraft lighting or if it is left up to the pilot (yourself) and if the airspeed is displayed as indicated airspeed or the true airspeed.

The Crashes and Damage portion allows you to turn on or off crash detection. If off, the aircraft will not crash in any situation – it will simply rest itself to level flight a couple thousand feet above the ground in most cases. You can also choose to allow the stress on the aircraft to cause damage and allow collisions with other aircraft.

The Engines section allows you to enable the auto-mixture thus taking the responsibility away from the pilot and choose to have unlimited fuel. Unlimited fuel allows you to fly a Cessna from Seattle to London nonstop if so desired.

The Special Effects portion allows you to experience the effects from G-forces. With these enabled the screen will go red representing the blood rushing to the pilots head or black representing a blackout state when insufficient blood is present. It can be difficult to get these effects in an ultra light or small aircraft. Military aircraft however can typically produce these effects easily.

The Flight Controls lets you enable or disable the autorudder. I personally choose to have this turned off. When the autorudder is on, you will be unable to 'slip' the aircraft on approach or really use the rudder much at all.

Failures

The Failures menu allows you to assign system failures or instrument failures.

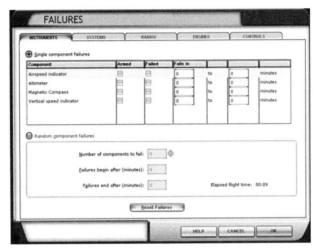

You can specify if a specific system is armed or failed and a range of time after setting up the failure it will occur. You can also set FSX to have random instrument or system failures including how many will fail and how long before they fail and when they end. There are tabs across the Failures window allowing you to select which components will fail including Instruments, Systems, Radios, Engines and/or Controls.

World Menu

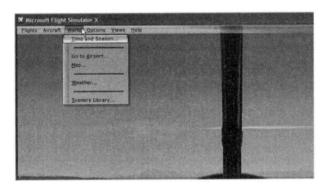

Time and Season...

The Time and Season lets you set the time of day in general terms including Dawn, Day, Dusk and Night, or manually set the specific time.

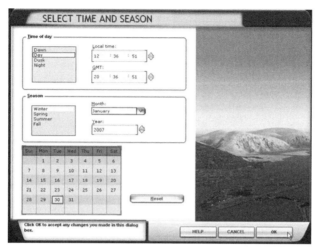

You can also choose the season, the month and even the year. Feel free to go back in time and see what changes! After changing any of these settings, the FSX will need to reload the scenery.

Go To Airport..

Select Go To Airports to set your aircraft at any airport in the FSX world. You can enter the name of the airport, the airport ID or the city where the airport is located if you know it. As you type text into these fields, the Search Results window narrows down the list of airports matching the text you enter.

If you're not certain of the exact airport name, airport ID or the city you are looking for, you can select the country or region and/or the state or province. Once the airport is selected, you can select the runway you wish to take off from and if available you can choose a parking area, gate or ramp to start from.

Map...

The Map menu shows you an overhead map view of the earth with the aircraft's position in the center.

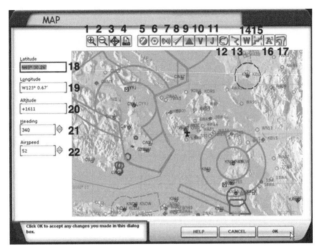

The icons along the top of the map view will alter the items displayed on the map or control the map's appearance.

1. Zoom In
2. Zoom Out
3. Center the Map and on aircraft
4. Print map
5. Display Airports
6. Display VORs
7. Display NDBs
8. Display ILS Markers
9. Display Intersections
10. Display Vector Airways
11. Display Jetways
12. Display Airspace Boundaries
13. Display Flight History (path shown on the map where you've flown recently)
14. Display Weather Stations
15. Display Weather Fronts
16. Display Data Tags (airport IDs for example)
17. Display Terrain Shading

18. Aircraft's current latitude

19. Aircraft's current longitude

20. Aircraft's current altitude

21. Aircraft's current Heading

22. Aircraft's current Airspeed

The left side of the Map (18-21) shows you the aircraft's current Latitude, Longitude, Altitude, Heading and Airspeed. Each of these can be adjusted by typing in new information. When changed, click the (OK) button to accept the changes and reposition the aircraft. FSX will have to reload the scenery.

You can also scroll the map by placing the mouse at the edges of the map view. The mouse pointer will turn into a large arrow. When you click the left mouse button with this large arrow, the map will scroll in that direction. To move at an angle, place the mouse pointer in the corner of the map.

Weather...

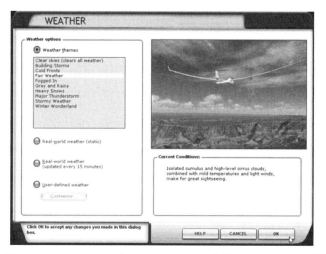

The Weather menu allows you to control every aspect of the weather in FSX. For general, local weather, you can simply select from the list of predefined weather conditions ranging from clear or partly cloudy skies to major thunder storms and winter snow storms. If you are connected to the Internet, you can turn on Real-World Weather, which will download the current weather for your aircraft's location and will keep those weather conditions as long as you are flying in that area. You can also choose to have the weather automatically updated every 15 minutes.

Choosing the User-Defined Weather option allows you to customize every aspect of the weather in the area or areas you wish to fly.

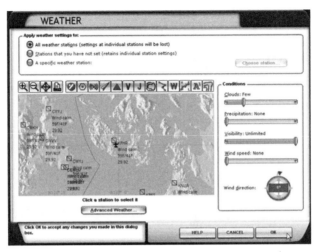

You'll notice a map view with all the controls of the World | Map menu. On this screen you can choose the specific weather station and adjust every aspect of the weather including cloud cover, cloud type, cloud ceiling, wind speed and direction, precipitation, visibility and more.

 For more information on setting the weather, be sure to read through the Are You Under The Weather chapter starting on page 75.

The Scenery Library

The Scenery Library is a list of the scenery areas that FSX loads and in the order that they are loaded. From the image you can see that Addon Scenery is on top of the list with a priority of 1.

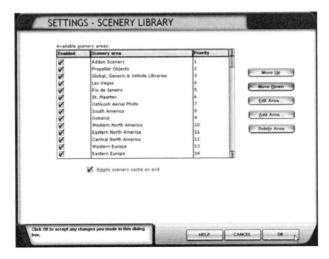

This means that FSX will load all the scenery on this list from the bottom up. If you scroll down to the bottom of this list, we'd see that FSX will load the Default Terrain, which is a basic ground base for the entire terrain, then the Default Scenery followed by the Base scenery files which contain the detailed ground terrain and the airport information. Next are scenery files for the major country regions like Africa, Asia, Australia, Eastern Europe, Western Europe and so on. Loaded next are high-detail areas such as cities including St. Maarten, Rio de Janeiro and Las Vegas. On top of that are the Global, Generic and Vehicle Libraries and Propeller Objects. These libraries include the buildings and such that are visible in most cities and at airports across the world. Last on the list is the Addon Scenery area. This is typically where scenery that is downloaded from the Internet or scenery that you created can be placed to get it to appear in FSX quickly and easily.

If you have downloaded new scenery and have installed it into the FSX but it does not appear, your best bet is that the folder the scenery files are in is not added to the Scenery Library, or is not added properly.

To add a new area to the Scenery Library, you simply click the Add Area button, then browse to the new folder containing the scenery files. It's important to note that all scenery files (BGL files) must be in a folder called Scenery.

The Move Up and Move Down buttons allow you to move a selected area up and down in the list. This will change the scenery areas priority and change how FSX will load the scenery in that area.

Clicking Edit Area allows you to change details about the scenery area including the title that appears in the Scenery Area list.

The Delete Area allows you to permanently remove a scenery area from the list. Note that certain areas cannot be removed because they are required for FSX to run.

The Check marks next to the scenery areas tell you that the scenery are is enabled or disabled. When checked, FSX will load the scenery in that area. When unchecked, FSX will not load the scenery in that area.

The information in the Scenery Library is saved in a text or configuration file called Scenery.cfg. You can manually edit the scenery.cfg file. This is covered in the book in the "Managing New Scenery In FSX" on page 239.

Any change made to the Scenery Library will result in FSX rebuilding the database.

Options Menu

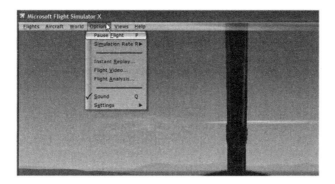

Pause Flight

Selecting Pause from the Options menu will pause the flight simulator. Repeat these steps to unpause FSX. Pause mode can also be turned on and off by pressing the P key on the keyboard.

Simulation Rate

The Simulation Rate has a submenu allowing you to select the speed at which FSX will run. The options range from Slowest which is one fourth of the normal speed, up to the fastest which is 128 times normal speed. The Simulation rate can also be invoked by pressing the R key on the keyboard, then pressing the plus (+) or minus (-) keys along the top of the keyboard.

Adjusting the simulation rate is a good way to speed up long and tedious flights like intercontinental flights or to slow down difficult approaches.

Instant Replay...

Ever make a miraculous landing that you wish everyone could see? Well, the Instant Reply option lets you play back that last few minutes of your flight so you can catch that awesome landing. Unfortunately, the replay cannot be saved and loaded later on though — so if you want to show off, make sure someone is around to see it!

You can specify the number of seconds you want replayed as well as the speed of the replay and even repeat the flight continuously. Once the replay is complete, the simulation will be paused.

Flight Video...

The Flight Video is a like a video recorder. You start the Flight Video, then you fly your flight and it will be saved so you can play it back at a later time. Going back to your miraculous landing, if you start the Flight Video, then fly the approach and save the video, you can easily play it again for your friends!

To record a flight video, first select the recording interval. Be default this is set to 1 second. If you are recording long flights with few altitude changes for long periods of time, you can increase this to a few seconds. Once the time interval is set, click the Record New Clip button, then proceed with the flight like normal. If Flight Sim becomes paused, press the Ⓟ button your keyboard to resume flight.

While flying you will see a message along the bottom of the screen reading:

```
Video Recording Rate: 1 Second - ESC to stop
```

This is telling you that Flight Sim is recording the video and the rate it is being recorded.

To stop the recording, press the (Esc) key on your keyboard. This will open another screen to save the video.

Enter a name for the video in the Video Title line and if desired, a short description of the flight. You can either click Review Video to watch the flight again, click Resume Recording to continue with the flight and add to the video, or click (OK) to save the video and return to Flight Sim.

To play a video back at a later time, click the Options | Flight Video menu. Then, select the flight from the Save Video Clips list. Click the (Play Clip) button to watch the flight.

Flight Analysis...

The Flight Analysis screen includes a map view and all the controls available to the map view. The Flight Analysis screen does not let you change the aircraft location or altitude, but it does show you a break down of the flight. Move the slider at the bottom by clicking it and dragging it with the mouse. As the slider moves, it will retrace the path you flew on the map view.

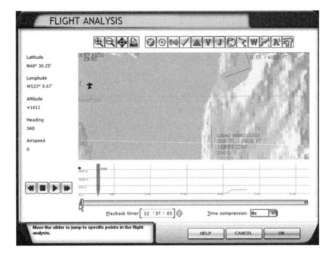

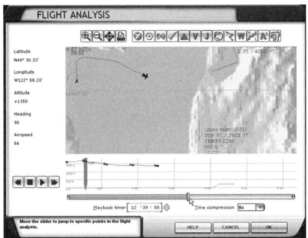

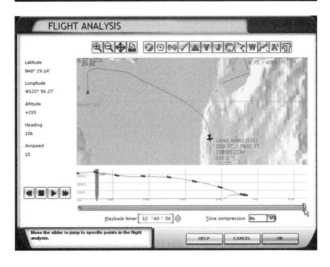

As the slider moves and the plane with it, notice the latitude, longitude, altitude, heading and airspeed on the left side of the window. This will show you the coordinates of the plane at the current point in the flight as well as the altitude, heading and airspeed.

The bottom of the window shows a chart with a side profile of the flight showing the altitude of the aircraft along the left side and the distance traveled along the bottom. The red line shows the altitude of the aircraft through out the flight.

The line along the bottom of the chart shows the ground elevation. The examples above show the ground elevation or sea level for the first 4 miles of flight, then rising up a bit when the aircraft crossed over onto land.

The controls in the bottom left of the window allow you to rewind, stop, play and fast forward the flight respectively. The Time Compression drop-down box sets the speed at which the flight is played back. This ranges from 0.25 or ¼ speed to 64 times regular speed.

Sound

The Sound option will turn on or off all sound to the speakers from the Flight Simulator. When checked, you will hear sounds. When Sound is not checked, Flight Sim will be muted and you will hear no engine sounds or stall warnings and so on.

Settings

The Settings menu contains submenus that allow you to adjust most of the Flight Simulator environment.

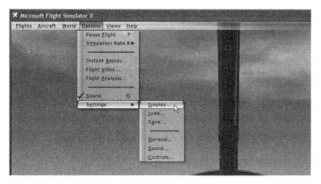

Settings | Display menu

The Display menu had 5 different tabs; Graphics, Aircraft, Scenery, Weather and Traffic. Each tab contains settings that change how FSX will perform. Each of the tabs will have a Global setting that ranges from minimal to ultrahigh. Choosing one of these from the drop-down list will automatically set the sliders and options on the tab. Manually adjusting the options on the tabs will set the Global Settings to Custom.

Graphics Tab

The Graphics tab allows you to change the screen resolution of FSX, set the target frame rate and set the type of filtering and if FSX will use anti-aliasing to render the textures. The left side of the Graphics tab lets you set the Global Texture Resolution, choose if the camera position will show a lens flare and light bloom from the sun and if the FSX will render advanced animations. You can also set if the text that is displayed on the screen will be continuous or displayed on a single line.

Aircraft Tab

The Cockpit settings on the Aircraft tab let you set if the aircraft you load will start in the 2-D panel view or the 3-D panel view (virtual cockpit). When you use Free Flight for example and click [Fly Now] to start the flight, the plane will be loaded with the 2-D panel visible.

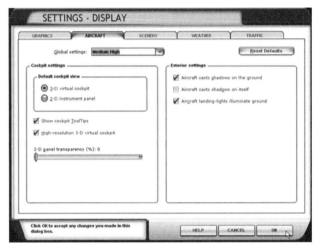

With the cockpit ToolTips box checked, the FSX will show a small pop-up box when your mouse if placed over top of a gauge.

The High-resolution 3-D Virtual Cockpit option tells FSX to draw the virtual cockpit in high resolution or a lower resolution.

The 2-D Panel Transparency slider allows FSX to draw the 2D panel, but makes it see-through. This allows you to see both the instruments and the scenery behind the panel.

The Exterior Settings options let you choose if the aircraft casts a shadow on the ground, on itself and if the lights on the aircraft will light up the ground.

Scenery Tab

The Scenery tab controls how FSX will draw the scenery. Your options include how far away from the plane FSX will show detailed scenery on the Level Of Detail slider.

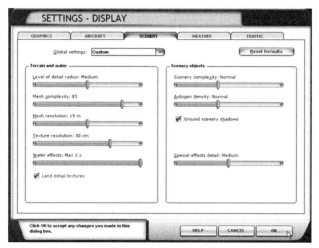

The Mesh Complexity sets how accurate FSX will draw the terrain. A high setting forces FSX to draw the terrain with high accuracy. With a lower setting, you may find areas where FSX will not be drawing all the elevation points with 100% accuracy.

The Mesh resolution ranges from 305 meters down to 1 meter. The scenery files FSX loads to draw the terrain are created at a certain resolution, typically 38 or 76 meters. This means that there are 38 or 76 meters between elevation points. Some areas are at a higher resolution, like 19 meters or 10 meters. This slider can tell FSX to lower the resolution. For example if you have scenery installed that was created at 38 meters and you set the slider to 76 meters, FSX will draw the terrain at 76. This can help to increase performance in FSX. If you have scenery installed that is 38 meters and you set the slider to 1 meter, you will not see any change in the scenery. FSX cannot invent elevation points that do not exist in the scenery files.

The texture resolution sets how clear the textures on the terrain will appear. The slider ranges from 10 meters to 7 centimeters. Obviously 7 centimeters requires more processing power for FSX to achieve.

The water effects range from none to max. A settings of none will produce flat blue water. A high setting will produce realistic water complete with wave effects and reflections.

The Land Detail Textures box allows FSX to draw detailed textures on the terrain when available.

The Scenery Objects section lets you adjust how much scenery objects are drawn.

The Scenery Complexity slider ranges from Very Sparse to Extremely Dense and controls how much scenery will be displayed. The scenery objects affected by this slider are the buildings and objects that are always in place such as the Empire State Building, Statue of Liberty, Space Needle in Seattle and all other objects that always will appear in the same place every time FSX is running. A very sparse setting will not reveal very many objects at all. This is a good way to increase frame rate especially when flying at busy or complex airports or in major cities. Setting the slider to Extremely Dense can seriously slow down the FSX performance, but will provide a much more realistic view of the scenery.

The Autogen Density ranges from None to Extremely Dense. Autogen scenery includes the trees that are visible when flying in the mountains or in city outlying areas as well as the buildings that are scattered around in cities and the countryside. These objects are randomly placed so trees and buildings may appear in slightly different areas when revisiting an area in FSX. Similar to the Scenery Complexity, a low setting on the slider will result in fewer objects being displayed and a higher setting will have FSX draw more of the objects.

Weather Tab

Unlike the World | Weather menu, the Weather tab here controls how FSX will display the weather.

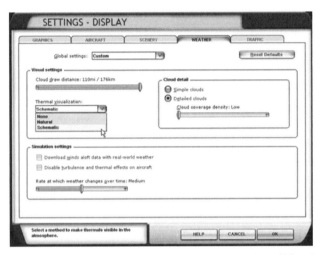

This tab allows you to set how far away from the aircraft the clouds will be drawn and if the clouds will be simple or detailed and if detailed, how dense the coverage will be. You can also turn on Thermal Visualizations. This will visualize the thermals in FSX.

It's hard to see transparent green spirals, but with the Schematic options set in the Thermal Visualization drop down box, they will be visible typically near mountains.

The Simulations Settings on the Weather tab allow you to download winds aloft while updating real-world weather and to disable the turbulence and thermal effects on aircraft. You can also set the rate at which the FSX allows the weather to change.

Traffic Tab

The Traffic tab controls how much Artificial Intelligence or AI FSX will draw. AI traffic are moving vehicles within FSX that can be seen during flight. Each type of vehicle has it's own slider including:

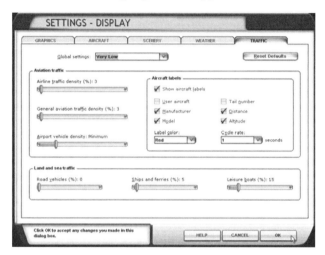

+ Airliners
  Heavy airliners like Boeing 747s and Airbus aircraft

+ General Aviation aircraft
  Smaller aircraft like Cessna 172's and Piper aircraft

+ Airport Vehicles
  Fuel trucks and baggage vehicles

+ Road Vehicles
  Cars and trucks

+ Ships and Ferries
  Ferry boats, oil tankers or the likes

+ Leisure Boats
  Sail boats and yachts

The sliders control the percentage. These sliders can make one of the largest impacts on the performance of FSX. The higher the percentage, the more vehicles FSX will draw.

The Aircraft Labels section lets you turn on information about the AI aircraft or your own aircraft. With the labels on, you will see information about the planes appear above the aircraft while under the control of FSX. The information displayed can include the aircraft manufacturer, the aircraft model, the aircraft's tail number, how far away the aircraft is from your aircraft and the AI aircraft's altitude. Since showing all of this information on the screen at once can be confusing on the screen,

FSX cycles the information every second. This rate can be adjusted from 1 second to 5 seconds by adjusting the Cycle Rate drop-down box.

Load and Save Menu

FSX allows you to save your current settings and load them again at a later time. This can come in handy if you want to use different settings. I

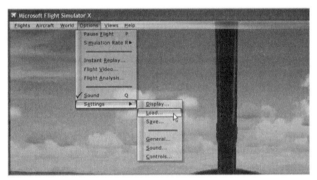

If you want to practice air traffic control approaches with a lot of AI traffic, you can set the Traffic tab in the Options | Settings | Display menu to include high traffic, then save it as a configuration file using the Options | Settings | Save menu. You can also create another set up with low traffic, but high scenery and terrain settings for mountain flying and save it to another configuration file. Later on, you can simply load the desired configuration file instead of manually setting each option every time.

General

The General menu under the Options | Settings menu contains some basic settings for FSX including.

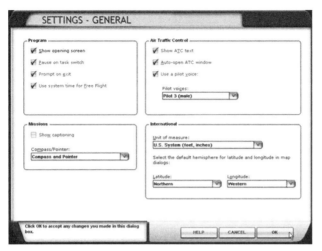

Show the Opening Screen
    When checked, this will load FSX to the default screen allowing you to choose to select a
    Mission, Free Flight, Multiplayer, Pilot Center and so on. When unchecked, FSX will load
    directly into the simulation by loading the default flight.

Pause On Task Switch
    When checked, FSX will pause when minimized for example. When this is not checked, FSX will
    remain running and not paused.

Prompt on Exit
    With the Prompt On Exit box checked, FSX will ask you if you are sure you want to close FSX.
    When not checked, FSX will just close.

Use System Time For Free Flight
    When you choose Free Flight from the FSX's opening screen, the time of the flight will be set to
    your computers current time. If you are on Eastern Time and start with the default flight which
    near Seattle, which is on Pacific Time, the time of the flight will be three hours later than the time
    on your system.

✈ Show ATC Text
    This will show you the text of the Air Traffic Control (ATC) communication.

✈ Auto-open ATC window
    This will automatically open the ATC window when an a message is intended for you.

✈ Use A Pilot Voice
    When checked you will hear the ATC. When not checked, you will only see the ATC text
    displayed. You can choose from 10 different voices for your pilot including male or female
    voices.

You can also choose to have all the units of measure be based on the U.S. System, all units set to the
Metric System or a Hybrid of both. You can also set the default hemisphere for the Latitude and
Longitude in the map dialogs.

The Missions section of the General settings allows you to show or not to show text versions of the dialog heard during the missions. You can also choose to have the Compass and Pointer, the Compass only or neither visible during a mission.

Sound

The Options | Settings | Sound menu holds the individual volume levels for the different FSX sound sources including the aircraft engines, the cockpit noises, the environment including the wind and the voices heard in missions and in ATC communication.

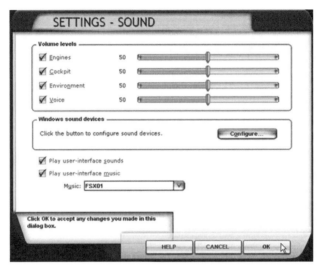

Clicking the Configure button will open the standard Windows Sound and Audio Devices Properties window.

The Play User-Interface Sounds being checked will play a small click sounds when a button is clicked on any FSX window. The Play User-Interface Music option allows you to turn on and off the music that is heard on the FSX opening screen. You can also choose the type of music that is heard.

Controls

The Controls menu lets you enable controllers like a joystick or game pad and calibrate them as well as all adjust the sensitivities of the controller and alter how the controller functions by assigning the controller buttons to certain FSX functions.

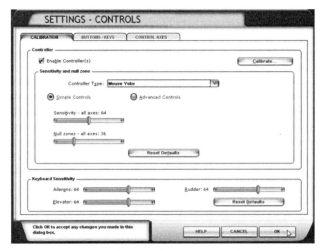

 The Buttons / Keys tab allows you to change the controller button functions and if desired, the functions of the keyboard keys. For example, you want to create a new assignment on your controller to the raising and lowering the tail-hook, you can do so in this menu.

Views Menu

As discussed in the Working With Views chapter, the View menu in FSX allows you to change the current view or open a new view or camera position.

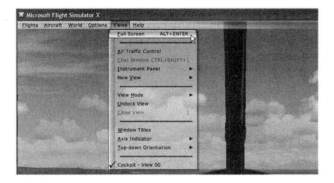

Full Screen

Choosing Full Screen from the View menu will toggle FSX between a 'windowed' mode and Full Screen mode. The Windowed mode is a regular Windows-type window with the blue bar at the top and the menus visible at the top. Full Screen mode will literally take up the computer monitors full screen. Typically you will not have the menus at the top of the FSX screen. The FSX screen will typically go black or flash while switching between views.

You can also switch between full screen and windowed mode by pressing the Alt and Enter keys. Hold the Alt key, tap the Enter key and release.

Chat Window

The Chat Window can be opened and closed by choosing Chat Window from the Views menu or by pressing the Ctrl, Shift and]. Hold down the Ctrl and Shift keys and tap the right bracket key ( ]) and release all. The Chat window is only available in Multiplayer.

Instrument Panel

The Instrument Panel menu contains a list of available pop-up panel windows for the current aircraft. This will typically include the main panel, the GPS, Radio Stack and Throttle Quadrant, but will be different for each aircraft.

Clicking these will open the pop-up window the same way clicking the icons on the panel, or pressing the Shift + 1, Shift + 2, Shift + 3 and so on. To close the windows once opened, you can click the window in the View | Instrument Panel menu again, click the icon on the panel or right-click the window and choose Close Window from the pop-up menu.

New View

The New View menu allows you to open a new view, which will appear in the top, left corner of the screen. You can open any view of the aircraft including virtual cockpit views, outside aircraft views, views or nearby AI aircraft and tower views.

To close the new view, right-click in the new view and choose Close Window from the pop-up window.

View Mode

Unlike the New View, which opens a new window, the View Mode menu option changes the main view. As discussed in the Working With Views chapter, you can change the views in FSX by pressing the ⑤ key to cycle between Cockpit, Outside, Tower, Aircraft and Runway view categories, then use the ⓐ key to cycle specific views within each category. These views can be selected directly from the Views | View Mode menu. When a view is selected, FSX will jump from the current view to the newly selected view.

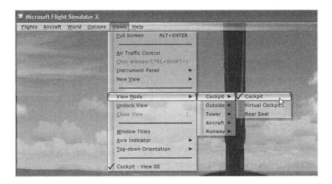

Undock View

Choosing Undock View places the current view in a separate window. This window can be moved around the screen and closed by clicking the X in the top right corner of the window.

Close View

When a new view is opened, it can be closed three different ways:

1. Select Close View from the Views menu

2. Right-click the new view and choose Close Window from the pop-up menu

3. Press the right bracket key on the keyboard ([ ]).

Window Titles

The Window Titles option will show the title of the window at the top of the screen. To turn it off, simply choose Window Titles from the View menu again.

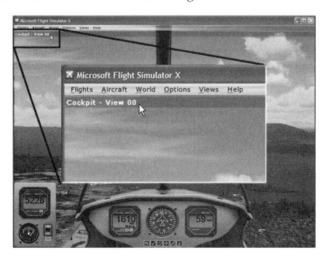

Axis Indicator

The Axis Indicator will place a mark in the center of the screen that represents the axis. You can choose between 4 dots, a small V or a large V. This can be very handy flying in foggy weather to make sure you are flying level.

The Axis Indicator will not be visible in front of the 2-D panel views. For best results, use the Axis Indicator with the main 2-D panel window closed and perhaps only the Minipanel open or in the Virtual Cockpit view.

Top-Down Orientation

Another view in FSX is a top-down view. This is essentially a view from above the aircraft looking down and can be zoomed in right down to the ground level or zoomed way out looking down at the Earth from outer space.

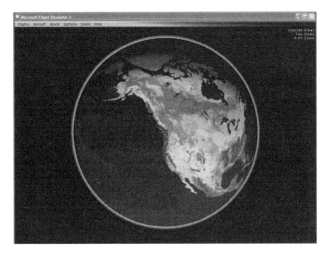

To achieve this view, you can press F12 on your keyboard or select ViewViews | View Mode | Outside View | Top-Down, then press the minus key (-) to zoom out

The orientation of this view by default has the aircraft pointing up on the screen and as you zoom out, it changes to have North be at the top of the screen. You can adjust this orientation to be:

➼ Aircraft Oriented
The front of the aircraft will be at the top of the monitor no matter how far away you zoom out.

➼ North Oriented
The top of the monitor will be showing North no matter how far you zoom out.

➼ North At High Altitudes
The top-down view will start with the front of the aircraft being at the top of the monitor, then at a certain altitude above the aircraft will switch to North being at the top of the monitor.

Help

The Help menu contains a lot of the information found in this book, but not all of it!

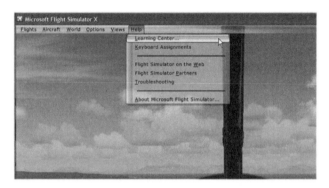

Learning Center

The Learning Center has four tabs:

+ Key Topics
  Selected areas including Getting Started, Step-By-Step Guide, Air Traffic Control, Navigation and more. Click an icon or topic to view more information.

+ Site Map
  This include a series of links to all parts of the FSX help file broken down into common areas; Key Concepts, The World, Aircraft, Post Flight Tools, Options, Multiplayer, Troubleshooting, Important Skills, In the Cockpit, Advanced Flying Skills, Navigation, Air Traffic Control, Flights, Missions, Flight Simulator Extreme, Partners and Reference.

+ Index
  Includes a list of key words and topics sorted alphabetically that can be clicked for more information.

+ Lessons
  Covers all aspects of learning to fly from the basics the forces an aircraft experiences and uses during flight to reading the instruments and of aircraft forces all the way up to and including full ILS approaches for airline pilots.

Keyboard Assignments

The Keyboard Assignments option will open the Kneeboard to the Keys option showing you the main keyboard commands.

Flight Simulator On The Web

Choosing Flight Simulator On The Web from the Help menu will open your default web browser to www.fsinsider.com.

Flight Simulator Partners

This will open the Help menu showing the partners who teamed with Microsoft to develop FSX.

Troubleshooting

The Troubleshooting section of the Help menu provides suggestions to help you track down problems with FSX including Restarting the Flight Sim, video drivers, sound drivers, DirectX issues, graphics issues, Add-on compatibility, memory issues, information on error messages, computer system requirements, reinstalling FSX and online resources.

The ILS System

The ILS (Instrument Landing System) helps guide your aircraft by showing you how to line up with the runway and, in some cases, the proper angle needed to land. To activate the ILS, you'll need to set a runway-specific frequency on your aircraft's NAV (navigation) radio. We'll start with some basics of shooting an ILS approach and then show how to do it easier!

Let's go to the active runway at Chicago O'Hare (KORD) using the Cessna. To get into this situation, select Free Flight from the FSX's opening screen. Click the [Change...] button for the aircraft and set the Aircraft Manufacturer to Cessna. Click on the Cessna 208 and click [OK]. Next, click the [Change] button for the Current Location. Click [Clear Filter] and enter KORD for the Airport ID, then click [OK]. It's easier to do this in the day time so if necessary, change the time of day, however since this is an ILS practice it's not really necessary. Click the [Fly Now] button to place the Cessna 208 on the runway ready to fly at KORD. Once on the runway, we'll switch to the 2D panel view. If your FSX starts in the Virtual Cockpit view, press [Shift] + [A] to switch to the 2D cockpit.

The first thing we'll need is an airport that has an ILS, plus we'll need that ILS frequency in order to shoot the approach. To find a suitable runway, we'll open the Map View. Press the [Alt] key on your keyboard and then select the **World | Map View** command or click the Map View icon on the panel.

The Map View shows you your aircraft's current position and the surrounding area. Your aircraft will be in the center of the map. We'll click on the magnifier on the top of the map view window to zoom in a bit.

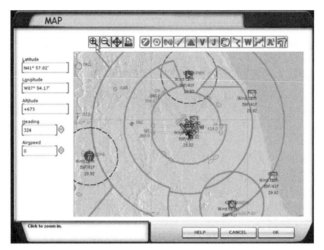

We'll fly down to Chicago Midway since it's pretty close and has an ILS. To move the map down, place the mouse on the bottom of the Map View window. Notice the mouse pointer will change to a large arrow. Clicking in this area will scroll the map in that direction each time the mouse is clicked.

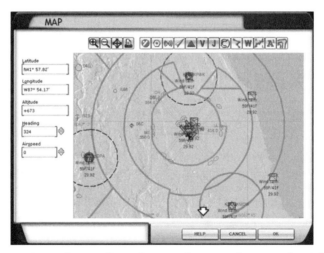

Try to center the Midway airport by scrolling the map down and over to the right a bit, then zooming in on Chicago Midway airport.

You'll notice that if you hover you mouse over the green ILS triangle, you'll see the frequency in the pop-up menu.

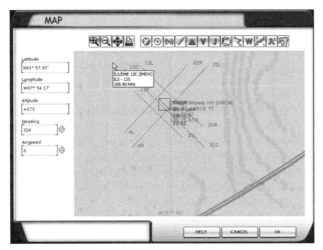

If you want to be sure you have the correct frequency, you can double-click on the center of the airport and get a Facilities window showing you relevant navigation aids and airport information.

We can see from the overview of the airport and the green ILS that runway 13C is easiest to approach from O'Hare. Double-click on the line that reads:

```
ILS                    ILS/DME 13C (IMDW)
```

This will show us the information on 13C on the ILS and has an ILS frequency of 109.90. This is the frequency we'll tune on the NAV1 radio.

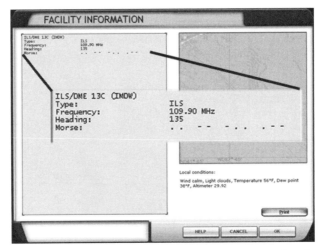

Click OK on the Facilities window and on the map view to return to the Cessna 208 cockpit. Open the Radio Stack by clicking the Radio icon on the tool bar.

The radios on the Cessna 208 require you to change the standby frequency, then swap the active frequency with the standby frequency. On the right side of the top radio, place the mouse over the first digit of the standby frequency as shown in the following image. The mouse will turn to a plus sign (+) or minus sign (-). Click the mouse button when the minus sign is shown until the first part of the frequency reads 109 (see **A** in the following image).

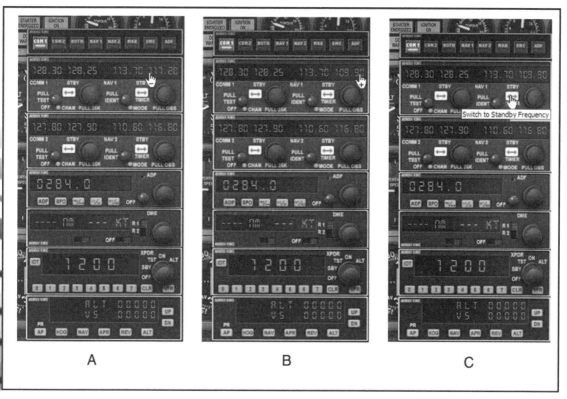

A　　　　　　B　　　　　　C

Once set, move the mouse to the right side of the decimal point and click until the number reads 90 (see **B** in the image above). Once set, click the STBY (standby) button to swap the frequencies and make the 109.90 the active frequency (see image **C** above).

Next, we'll tune in the NAV2 radio right below it in the same manner. Change the Standby frequency on the NAV2 radio to 109.90 and make it active. When set, click the Radio icon again to close the Radio stack.

If you recall from the map view and our compass heading, we are heading northwest and the runway we're heading is southwest of us so we'll need to take off and turn around. We won't worry about ATC in this example so go ahead and take off and as soon as convenient, fly a heading of about 150 degrees.

While in flight, we'll adjust the heading on the VOR2 dial located just right of center on the bottom of the panel. In the lower left of the gauge is the OBS (Omni Bearing Selector).

Placing the mouse on this dial will show a plus or minus sign allowing you to adjust the heading of the dial. Click the plus or minus sign until the top center of the gauge reads about 130 degrees.

Why? Because we are heading to runway 13C and runway "13" means the heading of the runway is 130 degrees. The "C" means that there are 3 runways with the same heading, a left runway which is 13L a right runway which is 13R and a center runway which is 13C.

Once tuned, keep the aircraft heading toward Chicago Midway at about 150 degrees. Keep an eye on the VOR2 dial and you'll see the needles in the center spring to life once the aircraft is in range of ILS from runway 13C at Chicago Midway (see image immediately to the right).

The VOR2 gauge contains 2 needles. The vertical needle is anchored at the top-center of the gauge and the horizontal needle is anchored at the left-center. These needles tell you where you need to fly to follow the Glideslope. What is a Glideslope? A Glideslope is the approach angle needed to land on the runway properly. Keeping the needles centered means that you are on the right track.

The horizontal needle tells you if you are too high or too low of the glideslope. The vertical needle tells you if you are to the left or right of the runway. A common phrase in aviation is "Fly To The Needles." This means that if the horizontal needle is high or starts to drift up, you need to raise the aircraft to get back on track. As the aircraft increases in altitude, the horizontal needle will lower. If the vertical needle is to the right or starts to drifts to the right, you need to fly to the right to get back on track. We can see from the shot here that we are too low and too far to the right. We need to fly up and to the left in order to get back on track.

This covers the basics for flying with the ILS needles. To keep sharp and practice the ILS approaches, you can use the Slew mode as discussed in this book to move the plane as needed to get on course. While doing an approach, you can literally keep your eyes on the panel to maintain the airspeed and watch those needles. If you can keep the centered, you'll land right on the runway (see image immediately to the right).

The Visual Approach Path And Following the Yellow Brick Road

Now that you're familiar with the ILS needles, we'll show another way to practice the approach without staring at the instrument panel. This method doesn't have much use in real navigation, but it will help you to get the feel for landing properly.

For this example, we'll repeat the same procedure of taking off in the Cessna 208 from the active runway at Chicago O'Hare and heading to Chicago Midway again. Before take off, make sure that the NAV1 radio to 109.90 and close the radio stack. Press the W key two (2) times to turn off the instrument panel showing only the mini-panel along the bottom. Go ahead and take off and fly a head of about 215 degrees.

Next we'll turn on the Visual Approach Path. Press the (Alt) key on the keyboard and open the Aircraft menu at the top. Click Visual Flight Path from the menu.

On the Visual Flight Path window:

✈ Click Enable Visual Flight Path check box

✈ Set the Linked Radio to NAV1

✈ Set the Number of Guides to High

✈ Set the Guide Shape to Rectangles

✈ Set the Distance Between Guides to Minimum

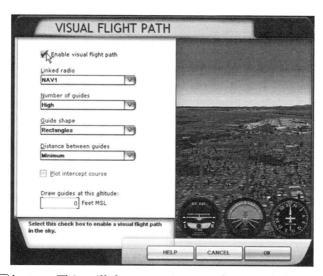

Once set, click the (OK) button. This will draw a series or red rectangle boxes in the air at an angle. These boxes represent the glideslope. As you are flying on the heading of 215 degrees, you should see the red boxes in the air. Fly toward the line of boxes, then turn to fly through the boxes. Keeping the plane within the boxes will take you right down to the runway.

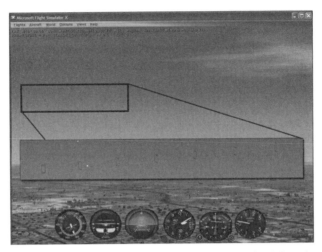

As you get more familiar with the Visual Approach path, you may find that there are too many boxes. You can simply open the Visual Flight Path window again and decrease the number of guides to Medium or Low. You can also increase the distance between the guides to Medium or Maximum. Note that with fewer guides and an increased distance between the guides, it will be more difficult to find the guides. We recommend you keep the number high and the distance between low until you find them and get on track, then you can adjust the quantity.

 Take a look at the ILS Approach Video on the Companion CD-ROM for more information. See the Contents pages for more information about the Companion CD-ROM and all the videos.

Aside from the rectangles, there are also Telephone Poles, a Yellow Brick Road and Hoops. Fly right on top of the telephone poles, on top of the yellow brick road or through the center of the yellow hoops to land on the runway.

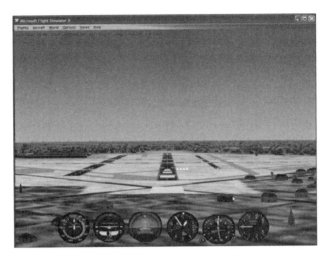

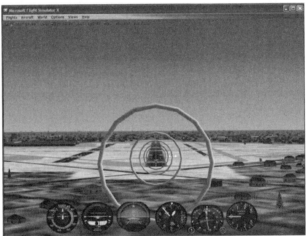

Don't forget to use the Slew mode if you get too far off course. Another thing to do for practicing approaches is to turn down the Simulation Rate of the Flight Sim. Press the Ⓡ key on the keyboard, then the minus (⊟) key to slow down the simulation rate making it easier to fine-tune your approach. Press the Ⓡ key and the plus sign (⊞) to speed it back up. You can also press the Ⓐˡᵗ key and open the Options menu and choose Simulation Rate, then select the desired speed.

Slew Mode And Camera Views

The idea of slewing is simple: Moving your aircraft in FSX without actually flying. If you're practicing an approach and realize you are off course or are about to crash, enter slew mode, raise your aircraft up, and/or move it back to help you get back on course, then turn slew mode off and resume flight.

The slew commands in FSX allow you to:

⤴ Raise or lower the aircraft

⤴ Raise or lower the nose or pitch of the aircraft

⤴ Raise or lower either wing or the bank

⤴ Move the aircraft forward or backward

⤴ Move the aircraft left or right

You enter slew mode pressing the Y key on the keyboard. Once in Slew mode, use the following keys to move your aircraft:

Y	Toggles slew mode on off
Spacebar	Stops all motion, points the aircraft north and levels the aircraft's attitude so it's parallel to the horizon.

Moving (slewing) Slowly

The following keys will slew the aircraft as listed if you press the key once. If you want to increase the slew speed, press the key several times. Make certain that the NumLock is OFF when you use the number keys in the keypad for slewing otherwise the keys on the keypad change the camera view and not the slew mode.

Key	Action
Keypad ⑧	Moves the aircraft forward
Keypad ②	Moves the pane backward
Keypad ④	Moves the aircraft to the left
Keypad ⑥	Moves the aircraft to the right
Keypad ⑤	Stops all motion
Keypad ⑦	Lowers the left wing (banks left)
Keypad ⑨	Lowers the right wing (banks right)
Keypad ①	Rotates the aircraft to the left (counter-clockwise when viewed from above)
Keypad ③	Rotates the aircraft to the right (clockwise when views from above)
ⓠ	Raises the aircraft up
ⓩ	Lowers the aircraft
⑨ (top of keyboard)	Raises the nose of the aircraft (pitch up)
⓪ (top of keyboard)	Lowers the nose of the aircraft (pitch down)

If for example you press the ⑧ key one time to move forward, you can press the ② key to move backward, thus stopping. Press the ② key again to move backward. The same applies with the ④ and ⑥ keys, ① and ③ keys and ⑦ and ⑨ keys.

Moving (slewing) Faster

The next set of commands are for moving the aircraft fast. Pressing the keys below will move the aircraft in the specified direction at the maximum speed.

F1	Decreases the altitude of the aircraft	F5	Raises the nose of the aircraft
F4	Increases the Altitude of the aircraft	F6	Lowers the nose of the airc

The F1 and F4 are common commands. Unlike the slower moving commands, pressing the F1 key to move the aircraft down, then pressing the F4 won't stop the aircraft, instead you will instantly be moving up. To stop, you will need to press the ⑤ key on the keypad, or the Spacebar to stop.

Slewing With Your Joystick

If you have a joystick hooked up to control FSX, you can also use this to slew the aircraft. This method is not recommended for small movements and adjustments because it is rather difficult to control the speed of the slew with the joystick. Moving the stick all the way forward with Slew mode on will move the aircraft forward at it's maximum speed, which is often results in an undesirable sever change in position. The same applies with moving the stick left, right and backward. If you choose to use the joystick to slew, it's helpful to have a joystick with a snap back feature that will automatically return to the center position so in case you do start moving to fast or spinning too fast you can release the stick and stop the planes motion.

One advantage it has is the easy ability to move in two directions at the same time. If you can control the stick and not move it too far, you can move your aircraft backward and to the right at the same time by pulling the stick backward and to the right.

If your joystick has a twist feature normally used for rudder control, this can also rotate the aircraft serving the ⑦ and ⑨ keypad functions.

Slewing With Your Mouse

A new feature to FSX is the ability to use the mouse to control the aircraft. Actually this feature was resurrected from earlier versions of Flight Sim, but now this feature is usable to slew the aircraft as well.

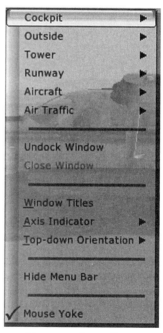

To activate the mouse as the yoke, right-click on the FSX window and choose Mouse Yoke from the pop-up menu (see image on right). This will turn your mouse movements into the aircraft control device. This is limited for slew functions in that the aircraft can only move left, right, forward, backward and every angle in between.

When the mouse yoke is activated, the cursor will change to a large plus sign (+) on the screen. Moving the mouse up or forward will move the aircraft forward and moving it down or backward will move the aircraft backward. Move the mouse left and aircraft will move left, move the mouse to the right and the aircraft will move to the right. Moving the mouse forward and to the right will move the aircraft forward and to the right. The angle direction can be achieved using the keyboard by pressing multiple keys but not at the same time. For example, press the ② key a few times to move forward, then press the ④ key a few times to move the left.

You can also activate the Mouse Yoke feature by pressing the (Shift) + (X) *key combination.*

More Slew and Other Important Controls

A few other key combinations that are worth mentioning and trying to remember.

When you activate the Slew mode by pressing the ⓨ key, notice the red text that appears in the top left of the screen. This text tells you the aircraft's latitude and longitude, altitude above sea level, heading the speed. More information is available by pressing (Shift) + ⓩ. Hold the (Shift) key and tap the ⓩ key. Doing this will change the information display on the top left to show the Frames per Second and the target frame rate. The frame rate is the number of frames the Flight Simulator can draw every second. Pressing (Shift) + ⓩ again will display not only the frame rate, but the latitude, longitude, altitude, heading and airspeed as well.

Other Slew keyboard commands include:

F2	Freeze Altitude	F6	Freeze Pitch
F8	Pitch Down Quickly	F5	Pitch Up Quickly
Ctrl + Spacebar	Slew Reset		

Controlling The Camera Views

One feature of FSX is the enhancement to the camera view controls. Each aircraft in FSX includes a 2D panel, which is a flat image, typically of the left side of the panel, with gauge files placed on top of it. This 2D panel is typically accompanied by pop-up windows including radio stack, GPS, throttles and so on.

Another view common to all aircraft is the Virtual Cockpit view. The virtual cockpit is a 3D model of the cockpit that includes a full panel complete with gauge instruments and animation of the yoke or control stick, throttles, rudder pedals and other movable parts of a cockpit like switches. Other views include an Aircraft view, a Tower view and an Outside view.

In previous versions of FS, you were only able to view the 2D cockpit, one virtual cockpit view, a spot view and a tower view. New to FSX are additional view categories, and within these categories are multiple views. Typical to FSX aircraft are the cockpit views, aircraft views, spot views and tower views. To switch between the different view categories, press the S key or Shift + S. Within the different categories, the different views are cycled using the A and Shift + A keys.

The Aircraft view includes multiple views of the aircraft from various positions including the wing tips pointing back to the fuselage, view of the top of the aircraft above the tail, views of the landing gear and so on. To get to the Aircraft view, press the S key on the keyboard one or more time and read the text in the top right of the screen until it reads Aircraft View. Below the text Aircraft View, is a description of the current view.

Press the A key, or Shift + A to cycle through the various views. The Aircraft view mode camera positions are defined in the aircraft's configuration file, which we'll discuss later in another chapter. Some camera controls in the Aircraft view will have a snap-back feature. This snap-back will allow you to rotate the camera in any direction, but when the key is released, the view will snap-back to the default position.

In the Tower view the camera always points right at the aircraft. The camera position will be shifted to the next closest tower when the A key is pressed.

The cockpit view is cycled between the 2D and 3D cockpit by pressing the A key on the keyboard or Shift + A. By default, the FSX will start an aircraft in the virtual cockpit view. Pressing the A key will cycle through different camera positions within the virtual cockpit.

These views often include the right seat or copilot view, throttle controls, radio stack or special portions of the panel. Once the virtual cockpit views have been cycled the next view will be the 2D cockpit view.

Instead of cycling through the different view modes and views within each mode, you can jump directly to any view from the right-click pop-up menu. Right-click on the FSX window and you'll see the image below:

Under each entry, Cockpit, Outside, Tower, Runway, Aircraft and Air Traffic are the available views for the aircraft.

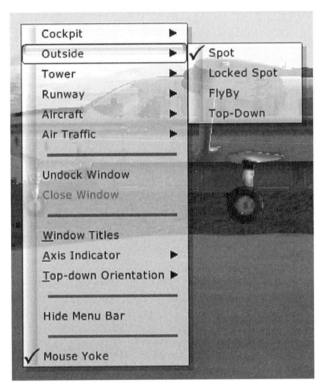

Note the Runway and Air Traffic entries. These are that are not cycled using the Ⓢ and Ⓢhift+Ⓢ keys. The Runway menu will give a list of nearby runways. When clicked, the view will change to the virtual cockpit facing in the direction of the runway. The Air Traffic menu option will provide views of nearby aircraft in the air. These views can also be opened in a new and separate window using the View menu and selecting New View from the menu.

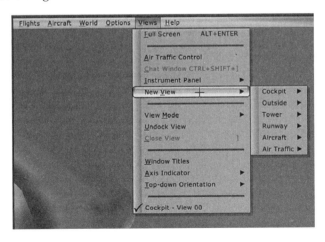

2D Cockpit Views and Windows

There are 3 common ways to open the pop-up windows in the 2D view.

Icons on the 2D Panel

Most aircraft will have special, small icons on the panel that represents the panel it will open. The icons are typically black and white. Click them once to open the panel, click the icon again to close the panel.

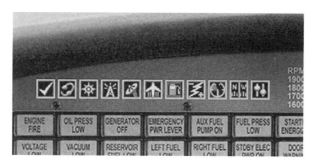

These are the icons as found on the Cessna 208. From left to right, these icons will open the Checklists, ATC window, Map, Radio Stack, GPS, Throttle panel, Fuel Panel, Electronic Panel, Engine Panel, Compass and Other Controls, which in this case is an outside air temperature gauge. Note that the first three icons in this series are not technically 2D panels

Keyboard

The pop-up panels can also be opened with the keyboard by holding the (Shift) key and pressing the numbers across the top of the keyboard. (Shift) + (1) will toggle the main instrument panel on and off. (Shift) + (2), (Shift) + (3) and so on will open up other windows like the GPS, radio stack, throttle and so on. The (Shift) + (#) will open different windows on different planes and the number of windows available will vary between planes as well.

View Menu

At the top of the FSX screen is a menu bar that includes a View menu. Under the View menu you can select Instrument Panel and choose which pop-up window you want to open. Selecting a window will open that window and place a check next to the window in the View | Instrument Panel menu. Repeating the process will remove the check and close the window. If you do not have the menus at the top of the FSX screen, you can press the (Alt) key on your keyboard or right-click the FSX screen and choose Hide Menu bar from the pop-up menu to remove the check mark in front of it revealing the menu bar at the top.

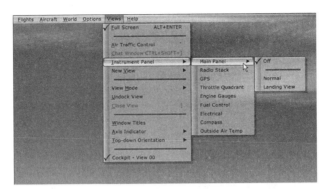

To access the menus at the top of the FSX window, press the [Alt] key on the keyboard.

Click the View menu, then click the Instrument Panel submenu. You can see the different pop-up windows listed. Clicking them will open the window and place a check next to the window title in the menu. To close the window, either right-click on the window and choose Close from the pop-up menu, or click the View | Instrument Panel | <window name> again.

Also notice that the Main Panel in this example has another submenu. The Normal and Landing options are different perspectives of the panel. The "Normal" option provides a nearly full screen view of the panel giving the pilot a full view of the panel. The "Landing" option provides a better view over the panel designed to be used during a landing. The pilot will have fewer instruments in view, but will be able to better see where they are going.

The "Off" entry in the image above simply tells us that the main panel is turned off. Clicking this will change the menu to "On" and will show the main 2D panel. The main panel can also be toggled on and off using the W key on the keyboard. Pressing the W key will turn off the main panel revealing a mini panel in most aircraft. The mini panel contains a series of 4 to 6 primary instruments across the bottom part of the screen. The advantage to this mini panel is to get a full view out the front of the aircraft, but still have the main instruments needed for a safe flight.

The mini panel here shows the airspeed, turn indicator, attitude indicator, altimeter, horizontal situation indicator and vertical speed indicator.

These 2D pop-up windows can be opened in the virtual cockpit as well. If the aircraft you are flying does not have the Garmin 500 as part of it's normal panel or virtual cockpit, you can still open the GPS while flying in the VC.

Aside from the new views, you also have control over the camera. We'll cover some of the ways to move the camera in various views. Note that not all aircraft in FSX will have these abilities but most will. The camera positions are set in a configuration file for each aircraft. Some 3rd party aircraft may not have these views or may not have the same functionality allowed in the camera configuration.

We'll start with the virtual cockpit. We've covered how to cycle through all the views of the virtual cockpit using the Ⓐ and Shift + Ⓐ keys. You can also rotate or turn the camera in most positions as well.

This is done by having the NumLock function ON and pressing the numbers on the keyboard. The number ⑥ on the keypad will rotate the view to the right while the number ④ will rotate the view back to the left. This can be especially handy if you want to look over at a radio stack or center console.

To look up at an overhead panel, press the number ⑧ on the keypad or to look down at the rudder pedals, press the number ② on the keypad.

You can also move the camera at different angle by pressing the other numbers on the keypad. The number ⑨ on the keypad might be better suited to view an overhead panel in the virtual cockpit since it moves the camera both right and up at the same time. The number ⑦ on the keypad will move the view up and to the left. To move down and to the right, press the number ③ on the keypad and to move down to the left, press the number ① on the keypad.

Pressing the number ⑤ on the keypad will point the view straight down into the seat. I'm sorry but I can't come up with a good reason for that one!

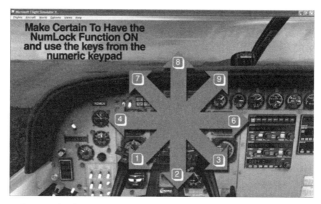

The same camera controls apply for most other views. The Tower views however are different. A tower view, which can be found by pressing the Ⓢ key one or more times is a locked view with the camera positioned at the control tower and cannot be rotated.

The keypad keys only move the cameras direction or angle; left, right, up down and so on. To actually move the camera, you can use the following key combinations to actually move the camera's location:

Shift + Enter	Move the camera Up	Ctrl + Backspace	Move the camera Forward
Shift + Backspace	Move the camera Down	Ctrl + Shift + Enter	Move the camera Right
Ctrl + Enter	Move the camera Backward	Ctrl + Shift + Backspace	Move the camera Left

Once you have adjusted the cameras position, you can use the keypad with the NumLock on to rotate the camera angle. Combining the cameras angle commands with the commands to move the camera allow you to place the camera anywhere within the aircraft cockpit. If you happen to have an aircraft with a virtual cabin, you can use these commands to move the camera into the virtual cabin area and take a seat (after setting the autopilot first of course!).

In the cockpit's 2D panel view, the keypad keys also will control the view, but in the same way they do in the virtual cockpit. Instead of a panning or rotating view, you'll get a view of the virtual cockpit. For example, pressing the ④ key on the keypad will give you a view looking straight to the right with a rendering of the cockpit as seen in the virtual cockpit. The number ⑨ on the keypad will look up at an angle to the right showing part of the panel and part of the door.

Now that we know how to use the views, you're ready to learn how to create new views.

Floatplanes & Feeling The Salt In Your Hair

Are you looking for a refreshing change in your flying? If so, you should consider flying a floatplane or seaplane because doing so will add new experiences of flying in FSX. Flying a floatplane or seaplane opens up new opportunities to explore areas such as the Bahamas, the Azores and remote lakes and rivers.

Before continuing, we need to explain seaplanes, floatplanes and amphibians. A floatplane is just one type of seaplane (a flying boat is another type). A floatplane is a fixed wing aircraft that is designed to take off and land (or "alight") on water. You might consider any type of aircraft that lands on water as a seaplane. But that is not necessarily true because helicopters may also be fitted with floats to facilitate their usage on water, however they're not referred to as "seaplanes" so we won't be talking about those in this chapter.

Also, don't confuse floatplanes with another type of seaplane called *amphibians*. These seaplanes have retractable wheels and can land on a conventional runway or on water; a true floatplane can only take off and land on water.

As you may have seen already in FSX, a floatplane has slender pontoons mounted under its fuselage. Although two floats are common today, some floatplanes, especially those from the World War II era, had a single float under the main fuselage and two small floats under the wings. Only the "floats" of a floatplane normally touch the water so the fuselage remains above water.

This is different than the other type of seaplane, the flying boat, in which the fuselage provides the main source of buoyancy. The fuselage functions similar to the hull of a ship in the water. Most flying boats have small floats mounted on their wings to keep them stable in the water.

Floatplanes can only land or take off on water with little or no wave action and, like any aircraft, have trouble in difficult weather conditions. The size of waves a seaplane can withstand depends on many things, including the aircraft's size, hull or float design and its weight.

Search and rescue units are among the largest operators of seaplanes today due to their efficiency and their ability to both spot and rescue survivors. Land-based airplanes can only locate survivors and perhaps drop supplies but cannot pick up the survivors and the limited range and size of many helicopters may prevent them from large scale or distant rescue operations.

Seaplanes are also often used in remote areas such as Alaska, Canada and areas with a large number of lakes convenient for takeoff and landing. These aircraft may operate on a charter basis, provide scheduled service or be operated by residents of the area for private and personal use. Greece uses seaplanes to connect its many islands to the mainland and seaplanes are also used throughout the Caribbean for similar reasons. You'll be able to fly a route over the Florida Keys that we describe later in this chapter.

Seaplane History

You may be surprised to learn that the seaplane is almost 100 years old. French engineer Henri Fabre flew the first seaplane, called Le Canard ("The Duck"), in March 1910. The aircraft took off from the water and flew 800 meters.

His designs and experiments were soon followed by other aircraft pioneers, including the Voisin brothers Gabriel and Charles, who purchased several of the Fabre floats and fitted them to their Canard Voisin airplane. The Canard Voisin became the first seaplane to fly over the River Seine in October 1910. The aircraft was also the first seaplane to be used militarily in March 1912 when it flew from the French seaplane carrier, La Foudre.

Early seaplane development in the United States began at Hammondsport, New York by American aviation pioneer Glenn Curtis. The first American seaplane flight occurred in January 1911. The United States used the Curtiss N-9 seaplanes during World War I as primary trainers, and over 2,500 Navy pilots learned to fly in them. A few N-9s were even used to develop an "aerial torpedo," which was an unmanned seaplane that would hit a distant target.

The Curtiss seaplane was developed in the UK as the Felixstowe series of flying boats whose design was then taken back to the US for production. The Felixstowes were used in the World War I to patrol for German submarines.

The first transatlantic flight of a seaplane occurred on March 27, 1919, when a US Navy seaplane made the flight.

In 1936 a group of wealthy US industrialists, including Henry Morgan, Marshall Field and E.R. Harriman, wanted an faster way of commuting from their homes on Long Island to the financial district of Wall Street. They commissioned Roy Grumman to build ten airplanes that could take off from their private airstrips and land on the water near the financial district. The result was the ten-seat Grumman G-21 Goose aircraft. The aircraft was quite successful and was soon adopted by the US Navy and US Coast Guard. Both the US and UK used the Goose during World War II in the roles of transport, reconnaissance, rescue and training. It was while it was in service with the RAF that it received its nickname "Goose." The Goose was used after the war in areas from the Alaskan wilderness to the sunny Pacific. Several Gooses (two or more of the aircraft have never been called geese) are still flown today in many areas, including modified forms, such as the Turbo-Goose.

Extensive seaplane research and development for military uses slowed after World War II due to the development of the helicopter and the modern aircraft carriers. The U.S. Navy, however, continued to operate seaplanes and seaplane tenders, especially in the Far East until the mid-1970s.

Flying A Floatplane In FSX

By this time you should have realized that your seaplane has some distinctive characteristics, most noticeably in appearance, over a conventional aircraft. Therefore, you probably also now realize that flying it means you need to learn certain procedures and techniques. Some of these may apply more to real world situations but you should also learn them for flying in FSX.

So, let's enjoy flying a seaplane in FSX. We'll use the FSX default deHavilland Beaver throughout this chapter for our aircraft but you can use any seaplane you wish.

Taxiing

To get started with some practice taxiing and takeoffs, lets's select a real seaplane base in FSX and a flight scenario. The airport we'll use is called Flying Bonefish and it's located in the Florida Keys near Marathon.

- ✈ Select the **World | Time and Season...** command and set clock to 12:00 and Season to Summer.

- ✈ Select the **World | Weather...** command and set the weather to Fair Skies.

- ✈ Select the **World | Go To Airport...** command and make certain United States is selected for the Country/Region and Any for the State/Province. Type in FA75 for the Airport and select N for the Runway.

By this time you should have realized that your seaplane has some distinctive characteristics, most importantly appearance and utility, over a conventional aircraft. Therefore, you probably also now realize that flying it means you need to learn certain procedures and techniques. Some of these may apply more to real world situations but you should also learn them for flying in FSX. One example of how flying a seaplane is different than flying a conventional aircraft is when taxiing. The procedure for a seaplane obviously has to be much different than taxiing on a nice long level taxiway at your favorite airport. As a seaplane pilot, you'll either taxi with a lot of power or taxi at low idle, but never in between, especially for long distances.

The reason for this all or nothing attitude is due to your aircraft's propeller(s). Water can wear down the prop blades over time just like sand, gravel and other debris. In case you haven't priced real world propellers lately, they aren't cheap. Fortunately we don't need to worry about that in FSX but we should still follow the real world example and avoid RPM settings between 1,000 and that required to keep your aircraft taxiing briskly. The basic idea to remember is to keep the RPM either low enough so little water is sucked through the prop or high enough so any water is sprayed back behind the prop.

Idle taxi and fast taxi

Also, you probably won't be surprised to know that you have a few options on the type of taxi technique you can use. The simplest technique is the *idle taxi*, which, as its name suggests, you keep the power at idle while maneuvering. This procedure typically gives you a few knots of forward speed although this may also depend on the wind and other factors. This disadvantage of this technique is that your flight controls are virtually ineffective at such a slow speed. Therefore, another way to control your aircraft is necessary.

Fortunately, the Beaver (and most seaplanes) have a control called water rudders for this purpose. These are retractable keels at the trailing edge of floats. You can set the water rudder control up or down by adjusting the lever located on the lower left of the instrument panel (see image below). Click the handle to toggle between up and down.

You should set the water rudders in the water while you're taxiing to provide better handling of your seaplane. This is especially true in tight spots. Keep in mind, however, that you'll still need to provide some forward speed for the water rudders to work; if your aircraft isn't moving, the water rudders won't do much good.

Note the water rudders at the back of the two floats. You should set the water rudders in the water while you're taxiing to provide better handling of your seaplane.

The situation when it's best for you to apply a *fast taxi* speed (also called *step taxi*) is when you need a longer taxi distance such as when you need to taxi to the far end of a lake to turn around for takeoff. Remember, do not go at a medium speed but transition to a taxi fast enough to bring the hull or floats "on step" or "on plane."

NOTE

The term "on step" is more often used as a nautical term, but the part or parts of a seaplane that are in the water are designed using the same principles as boats. You want to get the hull or floats up and out of the water as much as practicable. This reduces drag considerably, which also plays a big hand in your seaplane being able to accelerate enough to take off.

Full elevator back pressure is required for a fast taxi to prevent the floats from digging in to waves. It also helps your seaplane get up on plane faster. Always remember the power level…simply go full power until up on step. As your seaplane begins to accelerate, it starts to plow. This is a decision point for you. You can either keep the back pressure on the stick/yoke or release it slightly. If you keep holding the nose up high, you'll likely remain in a plow taxi. It's usually recommended relaxing the elevator a little bit so your seaplane continues its acceleration to get up on plane

You don't want to takeoff when you're on plane so reduce power slightly to maintain the taxi. You can tell if you're on step in FSX by noticing a nice wake trail behind your aircraft. When you're on plane, you should be able to keep the longitudinal axis (nose) of your seaplane relatively level with the surface while maintaining the wake, but without taking off. This may require experience and trial/error to determine the right settings for the particular seaplane you're flying.

One important note on step taxis. You'll be moving fast enough for the water rudder to have some affect on aircraft control so you should consider retracting the water rudder for fast taxis.

Beginning Your Takeoff

When you've taxied to where you want to begin your takeoff, position your seaplane towards deep water. Make certain you're clear of objects and into the wind as much as possible. Regardless of your location, you should always have a plan in mind as you're preparing to begin the takeoff roll on how you're going to climb out and begin your flight. Some remote areas are surrounded by fairly significant terrain and you may need to turn immediately after takeoff and follow a stream through a valley or maybe even circle your way up to a safe altitude directly overhead the body of water from which you just departed.

Be certain the water rudders are in the up position for your takeoff. This may be more of a real world procedure because the tail rudder and water rudders aren't usually in perfect alignment so the water rudders could have the nose of the seaplane turn while you try to counter with the aerodynamic rudder. The result is that the two devices may end up fighting each other or, worse, if the two aren't rigged right and you touchdown on landing thinking the rudder pedals are neutral. A slightly bent water rudder can make things rather disturbing (and scary) as soon as it digs into the water.

Although the water reflections, waves and general appearance of water in FSX is quite impressive, the water conditions still aren't much of an issue even for seaplane pilots so we'll only talk about normal takeoff and landing techniques.

Takeoffs, characteristically, are executed with partial flaps, for example, usually one or two notches. This helps your seaplane lift out of the water and up onto plane faster. Start all takeoff runs with the elevator pulled aft and full power applied. As the aircraft gets up on step, relax the back pressure slightly to allow your seaplane to accelerate without the excess drag of digging in the rear end of the floats or aircraft tail.

Text continues on page 160------------->

Other Neat Things To Try, er, Fly

Catalina Island

Another great area to take your seaplane in FSX is southern California, especially Catalina Island. Select the **World | Go To Airport...** command and type in L11 for the Airport and select N for the Runway.

This will put you in the waters just off shore of Avalon and you'll be in an impressive area for flying your seaplane. Takeoff and explore the various coves and inlets of Catalina Island.

Although you might first think of Alaska or other remote areas for flying your seaplane, consider warmer climates, too. The islands of the Carribean, for example, offer great areas to explore, as does Hawaii and Greece.

Sailing

If you're ready to try something different in your seaplane that is also done in the real world, try to sail. This isn't an FSX Easter egg but instead you can use the flight controls in a specific way to use the wind to steer your seaplane in the desired direction.

Although we're mentioning sailing as a fun thing to try, it also has its practical side as well. For example, if you want to get to a tight spot, such as a beach in a cove, sailing in is much smarter and safer than trying to idle taxi in with a wind to your back and then trying to turn around.

To try this, set the wind speed at about 20-25 knots into custom weather. Your seaplane should bob around to face directly into the current of air. Once facing into the wind you will be pushed slowly backwards.

To float towards the left simply turn the ailerons to the left and step on right rudder or do the opposite to float to the right. This technque involves dropping the aileron on the right side of the wing that ends up creating more drag, pulling this wing aft. The rudder input pulls the tail out into the direction you want to go. Both of these items work together so the wind gently pushes the seaplane to the left.

Remember your goal in this case is to take off and not taxi so keep the power at the maximum permissible setting. Use the rudder pedals if any directional control is required. If one of the wings begins to rise up due to the turn, or because of wind, apply aileron gently to counter the rise.

Landings

One thing about landing your seaplane on water is that you won't have a lighted, paved, smooth, radio controlled 10,000-foot runway in front of you. So, one problem to overcome involves depth perception because it may be more difficult than you expect to determine your altitude above water surfaces. Fortunately, we know of several ways of dealing with the depth perception problem:.

1. Land so that your shadow of your seaplane is easily visible as it would be from the chase plane view.

2. Watch the altimeter. This is especially true if you're landing in an ocean because if the altimeter is set correctly, it should read zero when you touchdown, thus you can plan your descent accordingly. However, this method won't always work if you're landing in a lake because you must consider the local terrain elevation.

3. Use the terrain ahead of you to judge altitude. By observing how a jetty or outcropping of land appears in relation to the land behind it, you can have a good idea of when you're about to touch down. If the pier, jetty, dock, etc., look as if it is below or forward of the background, you still have a bit to descend, but if they appear at the same level, you're almost on the water.

Set your flaps to either partial to full flaps and water rudders in the up position. (Setting partial flaps ensures a higher nose attitude and so reduces float dig-in risks.)

The best way I have found to land a seaplane in FSX is to get within about 50 to 100 feet of the water and then pitch up and set power to establish a very slight descent, for example, 50-100 feet per minute. The downside with this idea is that it requires a lot of water space and you may have to maneuver around terrain to get to a good landing spot. Therefore, if you're concerned about space, fly along a shoreline or make your approach to cross a shoreline immediately before touchdown to help with reference, thus reducing water run distance. This idea also has some problems because water near the shore in FSX may not be "deep enough" for you to use.

When you touch the water, bring the power to idle and gently pull back on the elevator. This will slow you down until you come off of step. Then you should be ready to taxi to parking or the dock.

A Florida Keys Floatplane Adventure For You To Fly

The chain of islands called the Florida Keys are well-known as a beautiful and relaxing place to spend a vacation. Because the "keys" are isolated from the Florida mainland, aircraft and boats are used to bring in many people and most of the supplies.

The Florida Keys start at the southeastern tip of the Florida peninsula and extend in a gentle arc south-to-southwest and before turning west to Key West, the westernmost of the inhabited islands, before ending at the uninhabited Dry Tortugas (about 113km from Key West).

They lie along the Florida Straits and provide a land barrier for the Atlantic Ocean on the east from the Gulf of Mexico on the west. The population of the Florida Keys is just under 80,000 people according to the 2000 census but because the population is concentrated in a few areas, such as Key West, you're likely to fly over many uninhabited islands.

Microsoft Flight Simulator Flight Plan
Holiday Isle -> Chalk's Key West
Distance: 71.4 nm
Estimated fuel burn: 17.9 gal / 107.7 lb
Estimated time en route: 0:40

Waypoints	Route	Alt (ft)	Hdg	Distance	GS (kts)	Fuel (gal/lb)	Time off
				Leg		95.0	0:00
FA05				Rem	Est	Est	ETE
				71.4	Act	Act	ATE
EYW (113.50) (VOR)	-D->	1138	258	68.5	103	17.2 / 103.2	0:39
				2.9		/	
61FD (airport)	-D->	0	202	2.9	103	0.7 / 4.2	0:01
				0.0		/	

Not For Operational Use

There are about 1700 islands in the Florida Keys although I cannot guarantee that you'll find them all in FSX but nevertheless, they're there for you to explore. Select your favorite floatplane and enjoy the area!

We're flying the route mainly by a combination of GPS and VOR navigation so you'll need to refer to your GPS gauge occasionally. This will especially be true on the approach to Chalks. To set up the flight, make the following settings in FSX:

✦ Select your favorite floatplane that you want to fly on this flight. The distance is slightly over 70nm so it's not far.

✦ Select the **World | Go To Airport...** command and make certain United States is selected for the Country/Region and Any for the State/Province. Type in FA05 for the Airport and select N for the Runway.

✦ Set the time for 12:00 and the Season for summer by selecting the **World | Time & Season...** command.

✦ Set the weather for "Fair Weather" by selecting the **World | Weather...** command.

✦ Dial in the EYW VOR (113.50) if you want to use VOR navigation instead of the Flight Planner.

✦ Takeoff from FA05 and make a left climbing turn to 2,500 feet. Make certain to follow the tips on page 155 for takeoffs.

✦ You can either follow US Highway 1 south if you want to fly over land or follow the flight plan on a heading of 258-degrees and fly mostly over the water with Highway 1 to the left. If you do follow the highway, make certain to keep the EYW VOR in range.

✦ Continue tracking the EYW VOR to on top.

✦ 15nm out from EYW, descend to 1000 feet. You should be near 7fA1 airport at this point.

✦ Maintain your heading to EYW (should be approximately 258 degrees).

Enroute over the Keys

✦ You should soon see KNCX out the left window. It's probably a good idea to stay to the right (west) of the airport to avoid traffic problems.

✦ On top EYW, turn heading 202 degrees and follow the track line to the airport.

✦ Check your airspeed and flap setting at this point. Also make certain to look for watercraft in the area. See page 158 for more information.

✦ Land 61FD and taxi to the beach, island or wherever you would like to go.

Coming to a stop at Chalk's

Man On A Mission

Do you enjoy flying missions? Most FSX users do because missions add a new element to flight simulation. By combining the realism of flight simulation and a sense of game play, missions have broadened the appeal of flight simulation to a whole new generation

What Is A Mission

A mission is basically a flight situation in FSX where the user has to perform certain tasks. These tasks can be anything from flying an aircraft through hoops, to landing an aircraft on a certain runway or they can be much more involved like landing a helicopter on an oil platform or flying an aerobatics aircraft through pylons. The difference between a mission and a simply saved flight is that a mission provides real-time instruction and feedback as you are flying. If you succeed at a certain task, you are given a new task. If you fail, the mission has ended and when you successfully complete a mission, you are rewarded.

Creating missions involves using tools that come with the Flight Simulator X Deluxe Edition. These tools are referred to as Software Development Kits or SDKs. We are not going to dig into all the aspects of creating a mission in this chapter, but we are going to have a look at using the tool that can be used to create missions. Why look at the tool if we're not going to create a mission? Because the tool can do more than create missions. It can also be used to customize scenery.

Software Development Kits And Missions

The Software Development Kits or SDKs are essentially documentation and a collection of specific tools. The SDKs contain technical information that breaks down the structure of the files used by the simulator and provides guidance to those who wish to design new things for use in the Flight Simulator. The information in the SDKs is specific in that it covers all the aspects of, for example, the panel configuration file (Panel.cfg), but they doesn't really show you how to create a panel or apply the information in all cases.

The SDKs on missions are a bit different. There is a lot of information that will walk you through creating a basic mission.

As mentioned before, we're going to use the same tool that can be used to create missions to create custom scenery areas. As with most things, saying it is easier than doing it but we'll get you from here to there as smoothly as possible.

Here's what we have to do in order to customize our scenery:

→ Install the Software Development Kit files to you computer

→ Set up the FSX to recognize and load the proper tools.

→ Learn about the Object Placement Tool

Installing The Software Development Kits

To install the SDKs, you must have the FSX Deluxe Edition because the SDKs aren't available with the Standard Edition of FSX. The SDKs are included on the FSX Deluxe Edition DVD. To install the SDKs, insert FSX DVD #1 into your computer's DVD drive. If the disc starts to run FSX or install it, cancel the installation. Double-click the "My Computer" icon on your desktop.

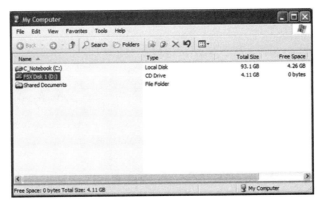

Now RIGHT click the DVD-ROM drive that contains the FSX DVD #1 labeled "FSX Disk1" and select **Explore** from the pop-up menu.

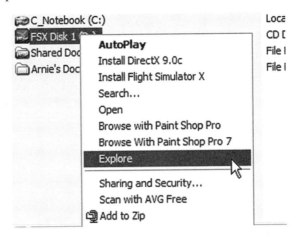

Here you'll see the contents of the FSX DVD.

One of the folders on the DVD is called SDK. Double-click this folder and then double-click the Setup or SETUP.EXE file within that folder to begin install of the SDK.

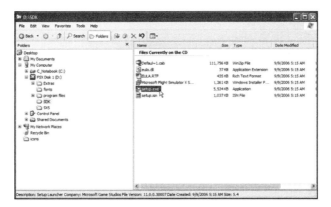

By default the SDKs will install into the folder:

C:\Program Files\Microsoft Games\ Microsoft Flight Simulator X SKD

but you'll have the option to change this folder. The decision to change the path is important. The next section will set up part of the SDK called the Object Placement Tool. Setting up the Object Placement Tool requires the Object Placement tool be installed to a certain location in direct relation to the FSX.

If you have FSX installed the default drive and location (C:\Program Files\Microsoft Games\Microsoft Flight Simulator X), then proceed with the installation of the SDK to the default location.

If you have installed FSX to another drive, or another folder then you will want to install the SDK to the same drive. For example, if you have installed FSX to "D:\FSX", we recommend you install the SDK to D:\Microsoft Flight Simulator X SDK. It's best not to change the folder name of the SDKs installation folder. We'll cover the reason soon.

Implementing the Object Placement Tool

Unfortunately installing the SDKs does not make them ready to use. The next step is to tell FSX that there is a new file to load and where that file is located. This is done by modifying the file called DLL.XML. This file in most cases is located in the following location:

```
C:\Documents and Settings\<your User Name>\Application Data\Microsoft\FSX
```

To get to this folder, double-click the "My Computer" icon on your Desktop, then double-click the folder as listed above. <Your User Name> will be different for every computer. If your name is Jim and you set up the computer under your name, the folder may be c alled "Jim". Some systems may have the folder called "Compaq Administrator". Explore the folder until you find the file DLL.XML file.

Once you locate the file, right-click it and choose **Open With**, then slide over and choose **Notepad** from the pop-up window. If you don't have the **Open With** entry, you can choose **Choose Program...** and select the program from the list and select **Notepad** from the list.

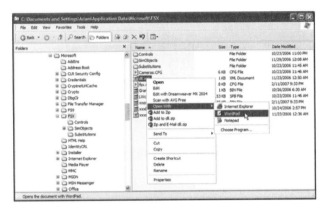

The DLL.XML file contains multiple entries that are "almost" set up. We're not going to go into all the details of the entries in this file, but we are going to take a look at part of it. Notice a section in the file that looks like this:

```
<Launch.Addon>
   <Name>Object Placement Tool</Name>
   <Disabled>False</Disabled>
   <ManualLoad>False</ManualLoad>
   <Path>..\Microsoft Flight Simulator X SDK\SDK\Mission Creation
Kit\object_placement.dll</Path>
   </Launch.Addon>
```

The line "<LaunchAddon>" tells FSX that there is a new file for it to load.

The next line, "<Name>Object Placement Tool</Name>" sets the name of the addon. The text <Name> starts the name and the </Name> ends the name. The text in the middle is the name of the new file.

The next line is tricky:

```
<Disabled>True</Disabled>
```

This line tells FSX if the new addon is disabled or not. An entry of "true" means that the addon is disabled. In order for FSX to load this addon, we need to change this to False. After editing, the line should look like this:

```
<Disabled>False</Disabled>
```

The next line does not need to be altered since the addon will not be manually loaded, instead it will be automatically loaded with FSX starts. Do not change the line:

```
<ManualLoad>False</ManualLoad>
```

The following line sets the path to the addon. In this case, the addon is the file "object_placement.dll". FSX already knows where it is being run from. The path needs to tell FSX where the addon is located starting from the main FSX folder. The text:

```
..\
```

at the start of the file tells FSX to move up one folder. If for example FSX is installed to:

```
C:\Program Files\Microsoft Games\Microsoft Flight Simulator X
```

Then entering the text ..\ will change the folder to:

```
C:\Program Files\Microsoft Games
```

From there, the path then moves into a new folder called "Microsoft Flight Simulator X SDK", then into the "SDK" folder and then into the "Mission Creation Kit" folder. Lastly, the file name of the addon is entered, "object_placement.dll".

This is why the installation of the SDKs is so vital. In order for FSX to be able to load the Object Placement Tool, the path to the Object_Placement.dll file must be correct.

If you are in a situation where you cannot set the proper path, you can do a search for the file "object_placement.dll", then copy the file into the FSX's main folder. Once the file is in place, you can then set the <Path> line to:

```
<Path>object_placement.dll</Path>
```

To recap, in most cases you will only need to change the line "<Disabled>True</Disabled>" to "<Disabled>False</Disabled>". Once that is done, save the file.

If you cannot see the object placement tool in FSX as discussed in the next section, then try locating and copying the file "object_placement.dll" to the FSX's main folder and then change the line "<Path>..\Microsoft Flight Simulator X SDK\SDK\Mission Creation Kit\object_placement.dll</Path>" to "<Path>object_placement.dll</Path>" and save the file.

Customizing Your Scenery

Now that we have the SDKs installed, we're ready to go into FSX and load the Object Placement Tool. To do this, open the FSX and use Free Flight to position your aircraft at Friday Harbor (KFHR) airport on the default runway. As you can see this is a pretty empty airport with not much around. We're going to open the Object Placement Tool and spruce it up a bit.

To open the Object Placement Tool, press the Alt key on your keyboard and click the **Tools** menu at the top of the FSX screen and choose **Object Placement Tool** from the menu.

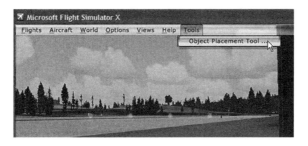

This will open the Object Placement Tool:

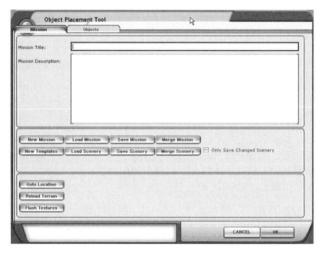

This is the main screen of the Object Placement Tool. Most of these options are used to create missions. We're only concentrating right now on the two tabs at the top, Mission and Object, as well as the (Load Scenery) and (Save Scenery) buttons.

To start, click the Object tab at the top.

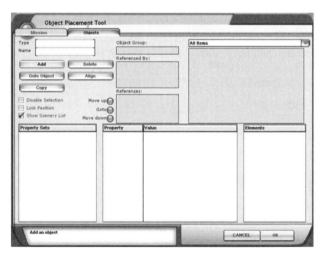

Again, most features are designed for creating missions, which we won't talk about here. Let's start by selecting an object and positioning it on the screen and you'll see how easy it is creating your own scenery. Click the (Add) button and the screen will change a bit giving you two drop down boxes. These drop down boxes allow you to select the object category in the top drop-down list, then the specific object from that category in the second drop down list.

From the top drop-down list, select **Scenery**.

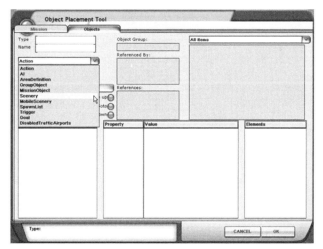

From the second drop-down list, select the object you want to insert. The list is quite extensive including items such as vehicles, buildings, animals, plants and much more. Since we're at an airport, we'll add a hanger so we'll select "gen_hanger07".

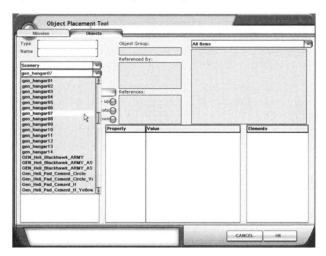

Once selected, the object will appear behind the Object Placement Tool. If the Object Placement Tool is taking up too much room on the screen, you can simply drag it out of the way. Click on the top of the Object Placement Tool (actually right on the text that treads Object Placement Tool at the top of the window will do) and drag it out of the way. We recommend moving it to the bottom of the screen or off the screen so you can still see the top of the window.

Notice that after we have selected the object, in this case gen_hanger07, that the object will appear on the screen, actually in the same spot that the aircraft is sitting. This probably isn't the best place to place the hanger, so we'll work on moving it.

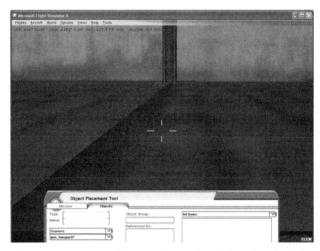

To move the hanger on the screen, we need to see the entire object. To do this, we'll move the aircraft first. Notice in the bottom right corner of the screen that the Slew mode is now active so we can use the keyboard to move the aircraft. Also notice that FSX is paused. Press the P key to unpause FSX so you can move the aircraft. (See the "Slew Mode And Camera Views" chapter for more information.) Make certain NUM LOCK is off and then press 2 on your keyboard keypad to move the aircraft backward. As long as the Object Placement Tool is open, the aircraft will move up at the same time it's moving backward. This will show the entire object sitting right on the runway. When the aircraft gets back far enough to see the entire hanger and the airport, press 5 on the keypad to stop the planes motion.

To make the object officially part of our new scenery project and make it so we can edit it's position, click the Add button on the Object Placement Tool located just below the drop down boxes. If necessary, drag the Object Placement Tool up in order to see the Add button.

This will officially add the object to our project.

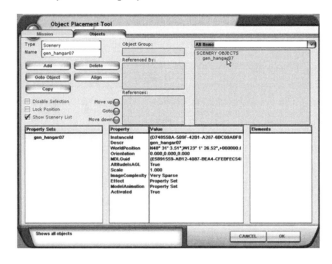

After you click the [Add] button and the object is part of the project, we see that is has been added to the list in the top right and that we have a series of Properties with editable values. We'll go over the object's Properties in order here and how to edit them.

InstanceId

This is the Instance Identification. Every object whether it is a scenery object or an event trigger for a mission – every thing added to a project will have a unique InstanceId.

Descr

This is the description of the object. You can change this if you want. If you have 5 hangers that are all the same, you may want to alter the Descr so you can tell them apart.

WorldPosition

This is the Latitude and Longitude and Altitude of the object. If you want to adjust the object position to match an exact location, you can enter the coordinated here. The Altitude by default is above ground level (See AltitudeIsAGL property)

Orientation

The Orientation property sets the Pitch, Bank and Heading of the object in that order. Pitch will tip the object forward and backward. Bank will tip the object left and right. Heading will rotate the object.

MDLGuid

This is a specific 32-digit number that is unique to each object. This is different from the InstanceId. The InstanceId will be different for every object in every mission/project. The MDLGuid is always the same for a specific object. This ID is how FSX knows which object to load.

AltitudeIsAGL

This is the 'Altitude Is Above Ground Level' property The acceptable entries for this field are either True or False. True means that the altitude set in the WorldPosition property is above ground level. When set to false, then the altitude in the WorldPosition property is NOT above ground level, which means it can only be Above Sea Level.

Scale

This is the scale of the object. A setting of 1 draws the object a full or normal size. A setting of 2 would be twice it's original size and a settings of 0.5 will draw the object at half of it's original size.

ImageComplexity

FSX has an image complexity setting on all of its scenery objects. This settings can be Very Sparse, Sparse, Normal, Dense, Very Dense or Extremely Dense. Users can choose which level of complexity FSX will display from the Options | Settings | Display menu.

Effect

This property is used in mission creation if the object will have an effect attached to it such as a light, smoke or fire.

ModelAnimation

This property is used in mission creation if the object is to have animation.

Activated

This property determines if the object is active or inactive. If active, the object will appear, if inactive, the object will not appear.

Let's slide the Object Placement Tool out of the way and take a look at the object in front of us and see what we can do to move it.

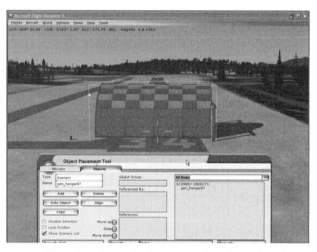

Notice the green box surrounding the object. This means the object is selected or current and ready for editing either by editing the Properties in the Object Placement Tool, or by adjusting the object visually on the screen. I think we'll do a little of each.

Click on the hanger and drag it on the screen to reposition it. We'll move it over to the right just off the runway.

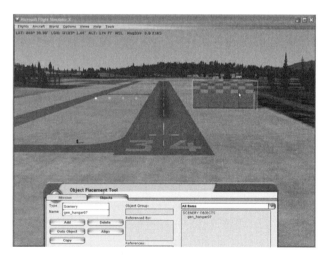

Next, let's rotate the hanger 90 degrees. To do this, drag the Object Placement tool back up and we'll adjust the three set of numbers on the Orientation property by changing it to 90.000. Now that we've moved the hanger, we can see both the hanger and most of the Object Placement Tool.

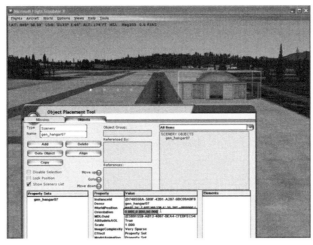

We'll make a few more adjustment on the Object Placement Tool including decreasing the scale a bit, moving the hanger over a bit and and resetting the ImageComplexity setting.

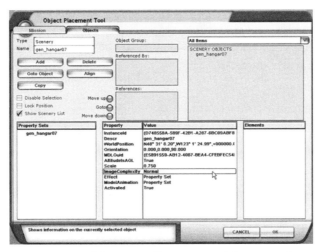

Using the information we've covered here, see if you can add a control tower up to the left of the runway.

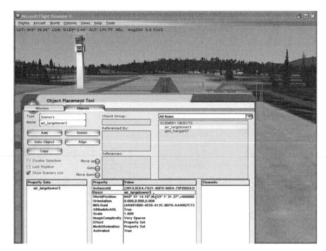

Next we have to save our file and then convert it to permanent scenery.

To save the file, click the Mission tab at the top of the Object Placement Tool and click the Save Scenery button. This will open a Save As window that will save your project as a text file written in XML format. The details of the contents of the XML file are not important, but suffice it to say it contains all the information needed to place the scenery objects in FSX. We'll save our file as "SceneryTest1".

By default the Save As window will try to save the file in the "Flight Simulator X Files" folder, which is in the My Documents folder. The location of the file does not matter as long as you can find it again.

The next step is to close the Object Placement Tool and FSX and then convert the file from the new XML file into a scenery *.BGL file. Close the Object Placement Tool by clicking Cancel, then No to saving the changes. The Object Placement Tool assumes that you are creating a mission and asks you if you want to save the mission. Since we've saved the Scenery file and are not creating a mission, we don't need to save the mission file.

Also note that when closing the Mission builder, the objects we placed will no longer be visible. This is normal. They will only be visible in the Object Placement Tool until we convert it to a real scenery file.

Converting the XML file

To convert our new XML file into a permanent BGL file we can either compile the object using the BGLComp.EXE file that was installed with the FSX SDKs, or we can do it using another much simpler method.

BGLComp.EXE

BGLCOMP.exe is what is referred to as a command-line compiler. Even though it is a program, it does not have an interface. Double-clicking on the file will do basically nothing. It will flash a black screen quickly.

Using BGLComp requires using a DOS prompt and browsing in DOS to the folder where BGLComp exists. This would require clicking on Start and choosing Run and entering COMMAND and clicking [OK]. Now change the path to the BGLComp.EXE's folder. Type the following:

```
CD..
```

And press the [Enter] key. Then type again:

```
CD..
```

Now we need to enter the path to the BGLComp folder. This gets tricky because DOS only accepts eight (8) characters per folder name. So to get to the SDK folders, we need to enter:

```
CD Progra~1
```

And press press the [Enter] key. This will move us into the Program Files folder. Since DOS only accepts 8 characters, you have to abbreviate. You take the first 6 letters of the folder name, then add ~1 to it. If you have multiple folder that start the same, you can use ~2, ~3 and so on. So progra~1 is 8 characters and DOS will recognize this.

Repeat this process to get into the Microsoft Games folder. You may need to use micros~2, micros~3 or micros~4 or even higher to get into that folder. If you go into the wrong one, you can use cd.. to go back one level and try another.

Repeat the process again to go into the "Microsoft Flight Simulator X SDK" folder, which is probably another micros~2 or micros~3 entry.

Repeat the process again and go into the "SDK" folder, then again into the Environment Kit folder (enviro~1), then into the "BGL Compiler SDK" folder... and all of this is just to get to the BGLComp.exe. We still have to then enter the path to the SceneryTest1.BGL file!

An avid computer user can avoid all of this by doing a few things:

1. Saving the XML file into a simpler folder path like the root of your C: drive

2. Copying the BGLComp.exe file to a simpler folder path

This would make entering the paths to the compiler and then the file name much easier.

Now if you are sitting there reading this with your head in your hands thinking, "I'll never be able to create scenery this way — it's too confusing!" you can relax. You're not alone and we are here to show you an easier way to do it!

We've included a program on the Companion CD-ROM called the "Scenery Shortcut." It's a basic program that allows you to simply browse to your XML file and then set the folder you want the new scenery BGL file to be created in.

To install the program, insert the Companion CD-ROM into your CD-ROM drive. Choose the "Scenery Shortcut and flights" option. Then follow the prompts on the screen to install the scenery shortcut and saved flights referenced in other chapters in *Tips, Tricks & Trips*. Once installed, open the program by double-clicking the Scenery Shortcut icon on the Desktop.

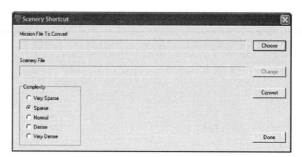

To use Scenery Shortcut, simply click the Choose button on the top right of the window to select the XML file to convert. This will default to the My Documents folder. Double-click the Flight Simulator X Files folder and click the SceneryTest1.XML file. Click [Open] to load the file into Scenery Shortcut.

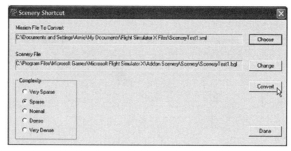

If we take a close look at the Scenery Shortcut after loading the XML file, we'll see that not only the top line is filled in, but it also has the location and file name for the Scenery File line as well. This path is the default location of FSX with the "Addon Scenery\Scenery" folder added onto the path.. The end is capped with the BGL file name with the same name as the original XML file.

If needed, you can change the location of the BGL file by clicking the second [Change] button.

The last thing to set is the Complexity. If you recall we also set the Scenery Complexity in the Object Placement Tool – so why do we need to set it again? Why not? Think of it as a second chance! Actually, the Scenery Shortcut can convert the Scenery XML as well as regular Mission XML files, each of which can be saved from the Object Placement Tool. Mission XML files do not have a Scenery Complexity setting so you can set one with the Scenery Shortcut.

The Object Placement Tool allows you to set the Scenery Complexity for each object. When these files are compiled with BGLComp, each scenery object will retain its individual complexity setting. When compiled with the Scenery Shortcut, all objects in the file will assume the new Scenery Complexity setting defined in the Scenery Shortcut program.

Click the Compile the button to create the scenery file. Notice the text "Scenery File Created!" next to the Convert button.

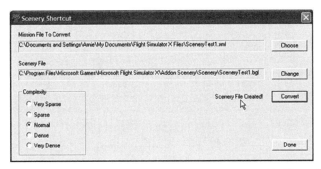

The next step here is to load FSX again and see the new scenery. We'll make a quick stop in the Scenery Library to be sure that the Addon Scenery folder is added and active in the Scenery Library to assure that FSX will load the new scenery.

Let's open FSX and click the Settings tab on the opening screen. On the Settings screen, click the Scenery Library button.

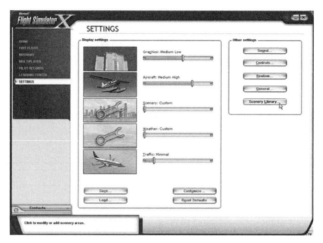

In the Scenery Library we see a list of the scenery areas FSX is loading. Since we saved the new scenery file into the Addon Scenery folder, we need to be sure that the Addon Scenery folder is being loaded by FSX.

Looking through the list you should see "Addon Scenery" in the list. It does not have to be on the top of the list, but it does have to be on the list and have a check in front of it.

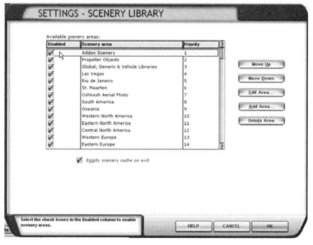

If you do not have a check in front of Addon Scenery, go ahead and place one there and click OK.

If you do not have Addon Scenery in the list you will need to add it. Click the Add button the right side. This will open the Microsoft Flight Simulator X's main folder. Double-click the Addon Scenery folder and click OK.

This will add it to the top of the list. Click [OK] again to accept the new addition. FSX will rebuild the database for the scenery files. This tells us that FSX has recognized new scenery files and is incorporating them into the FSX world.

Now that we have made sure that the new scenery files are being loaded by FSX, let's return to the Free Flight Option and change the airport to Friday Harbor runway 34.

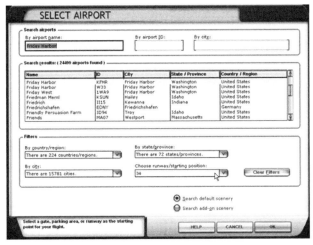

Once we get there we'll see the new scenery file, let's slew up and zoom out a bit so we can see both of the buildings.

Editing New Scenery

Now that we've proved that we can add scenery, let's say you want to make a change or add some more objects.

The first step to edit the scenery we just made is to disable it in the Scenery Library. How can we edit it if we disable it? We know that FSX reads the BGL file to know where to draw the scenery objects, but what we need to realize is that the Object Placement Tool does NOT use the BGL file, it uses the XML file. If we were to load the Object Placement Tool, then load the XML file, we would have 2 copies of the objects visible in FSX – the BGL file being read by FSX and XML file being loaded by the Object Placement Tool. It will be much easier to edit the scenery if there is only one version visible.

Lets go back into the Scenery Library and remove the check from the Addon Scenery. Press the [Alt] key and open the World menu and enter Scenery Library. Click the check mark in front of Addon Scenery to remove the check and click [OK].

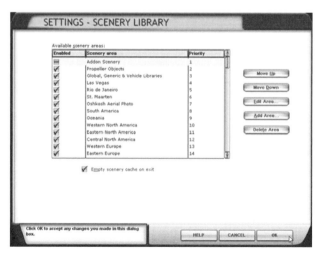

FSX rebuilds the scenery database again; when that is complete, the objects at Friday Harbor are gone.

OK, we we're ready to do some editing and we'll add an object here as well. Go ahead and press the Alt key and click the Tools menu and click the Object Placement Tool.

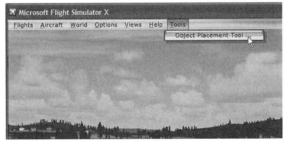

Click the Load Scenery file, then we'll select the ScenertTest1.XML file we saved earlier.

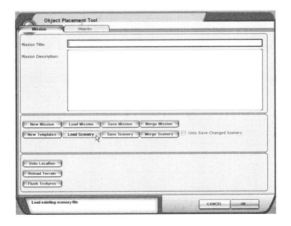

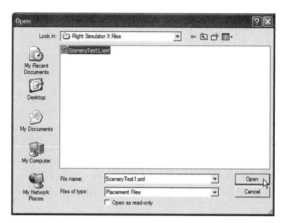

Click the Objects tab at the top. Now let's go ahead and move the Control tower back toward the center of the airport. To do this, click on the "air_largetower_3" from the list in the top right. This will select the tower. You'll notice that it will have a green box around it.

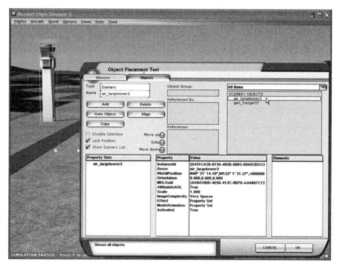

In order to move the selected object, you will need to remove the Lock Position button.

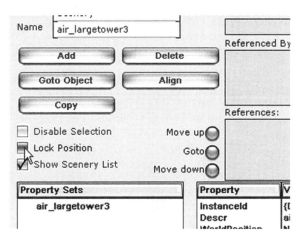

Once unchecked, you can click and hold the mouse button down on the object, in this case the control tower and drag the mouse to reposition it.

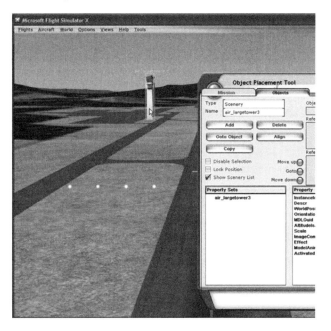

NOTE

Be very careful with your mouse here. If you happen to jerk the mouse and release the button, the object can disappear. What happens is the object goes off the screen and it can be very difficult to locate and correct the position In fact, it's often easier to cancel your changes and reload the project. For this reason, we recommend clicking on the Mission tab at the top and clicking the Save Scenery button after every change. This way you can go back if a major mistake is made.

Once in position, we'll go ahead and add a few vehicles. We'll start with "VEH_Land_AmbulanceUS" Click the Add button and select Scenery from the first drop-down list. Use the second drop-down list to select VEH_Land_AmbulanceUS.

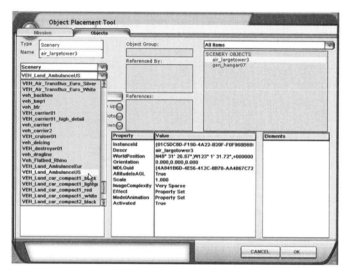

Click the [add] button to add it to the project. Move the Object Placement Tool out of the way so we can see the object. Click and drag the ambulance to the new location.

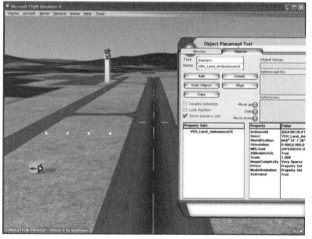

We'll rotate the object 90 degrees also.

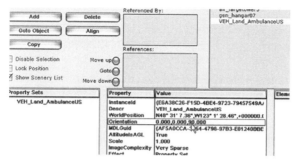

We've also added the following objects and positioned them next to our ambulance:

```
Veh_air_FireTruck_US_Red
Veh_air_fueltruck
Veh_deicing
```

Once positioned, we'll click back on the Mission tab and click (Save Scenery) and overwrite the ScenertTest1.XML file.

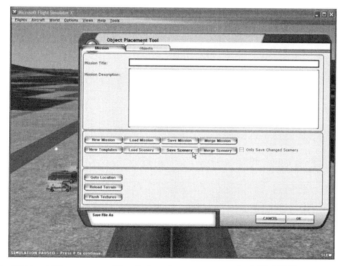

Now we can close the Object Placement Tool. Again, you can click (Cancel) and you <u>do not</u> need to save the mission file.

Now we can minimize or close FSX and convert the new XML file with Scenery Shortcut. Open Scenery Shortcut and select the SceneryTest1.BGLfile and verify the Scenery File path and name as before and click Convert. The old file will be overwritten.

Once converted, we'll go back into FSX and make a stop in the Scenery Library again. We need to click the box in front of Addon Scenery to tell FSX to load the scenery from this folder.

Pimp My Panel

R eady to get you hands dirty? We'll look at the structure of your aircraft's instrument panel in this chapter we'll so we can better understand how these panels work in your aircraft. We'll start by defining what we mean by a panel.

Let's Define Panels & Gauges

Each aircraft that you can fly in FSX has a panel. The panel typically contains two versions — a 2-D and a 3-D panel. The 2-D panel is a flat bitmap image that has individual gauges mapped on it and a series of pop-up panels like the GPS, radio stack and throttle quadrant. The 3-D panel is the virtual cockpit. The shape and layout of the virtual cockpit is stored in the aircraft's model file (*.MDL file) found in the aircraft's Model folder. The panel.cfg file also tells FSX what gauges to load on the virtual cockpit, where to draw them and how big they are to be drawn.

Gauges

What are gauges exactly you ask? A gauge is a collection of individual pieces of code that FSX reads to know what information to display on the screen. Gauges access information about the plane like airspeed, altitude and so on. They take this information and draw it in a way that makes sense to us. Other gauges allow you to set or change information in the Flight Sim, like changing the radio frequencies or setting the barometer by clicking in a certain plane on the gauge.

Gauges can be either XML files, GAU files or DLL files. XML gauges are text files that contain code to draw the gauge. There are rules that must be followed to create a new XML gauge, most of which are covered in the FSX Software Development Kits. The XML files reference bitmap images. An airspeed indicator for example, may use multiple images including a background image of the dial, then another image of just the needle. When the gauge is loaded by FSX, it draws the background image on the panel and the needle on top of it pointing to zero. The gauge reads the airspeed of the aircraft as determined by FSX then uses this information to rotate the needle on the gauge. It's the programmer's job to make sure that the needle on the gauge points to the actual aircraft speed.

The XML files and associated bitmap images are commonly compressed into a single file that FSX can read. The compressed file is not an ordinary zip file, it's a specially compressed file called a CAB file. The Cessna 208B references a file called Cessna208B_XML.cab, which we will investigate a bit more later.

The GAU files are similar to the CAB files in that they contain multiple gauges, but they are not standard text files. They are compiled files created by writing code in the language "C" or "C+". The GAU files are more like mini-programs or DLL files than they are gauges and because of this they can do things that XML gauges cannot like read registry entries, load database files and so on. In earlier versions of Flight Simulator, planes would have a separate GAU file for each gauge used on a panel. This was quite inefficient because it was similar to running a separate program for each instrument drawn on the panel. By combining the gauges into a single file, designers were able to save system resources allowing them to be used by the Flight Simulator for better performance. These GAU files that contain multiple sub gauges are commonly referred to as clustered gauges. Many of the older GAU gauge files are not compatible with FSX.

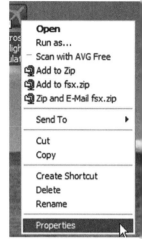

The new preferred format for the GAU gauge files are the DLL Files. These are virtually identical to the clustered gauges, except they are only recognized by FSX and possibly by future versions of Flight Simulator.

To get started, we'll open the panel.cfg file and take a look at the different sections. To do this, we'll browse into the aircraft folder. Since many users will have their FSX installed into a variety of locations and drives, we'll use a foolproof method to get to it. Locate the icon you use to open the FSX. Place the mouse over this icon and press the right mouse button. This will open a pop-up window. Left click on Properties on this pop-up menu (see image on right).

This will open the Properties of the icon. On the General tab, click the Find Target button.

This will open a window showing you the contents for the FSX's main folder. Use the scroll bar as needed to locate the Sim Object folder and double-click it. Now you should see the folder Airplanes, Animals, Boats, GroundVehicles, Misc, Rotocraft. Double-click the Airplanes folder. With the Airplanes folder open, we'll click the View menu and choose Details. This will put all of the folders alphabetically in a single column.

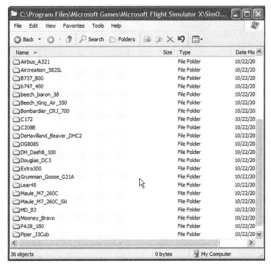

Opening the C208B folder will show us the folders that make up a complete aircraft. For now, all we're concerned with is the Panel folder so let's go ahead and open it.

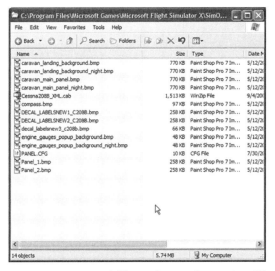

Here we see a series of images, a compressed file and a configuration file called Panel or Panel.cfg. we'll come back to the compressed file a little later on. For now, double-click the file called Panel or Panel.cfg. Windows may ask you how you want to open the file.

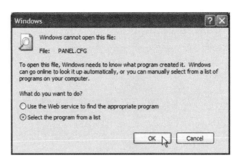

On this window above, click "Select the program from a list". Since the panel.cfg file is a text file, scroll down the list of programs and choose Notepad or WordPad from the list. Make sure the box that is labeled "Always use the selected program to open this kind of file" is checked and click the OK button. This will open the panel.cfg file.

The panel.cfg file starts off with the information used to draw the aircraft 2-D panel. The top of the file starts with the Window Titles. In the example of the Cessna 208B, the top of the file looks like this:

```
[Window Titles]
Window00=Main Panel
Window01=Radio Stack
Window02=GPS
Window03=Throttle Quadrant
Window04=Engine Gauges
Window05=Fuel Control
Window06=Electrical
Window07=Compass
Window08=Landing View
Window09=Outside Air Temp
Window10=Mini Panel
```

The parts of the panel.cfg file that are in brackets ([ ]) are called sections. The first section, the [Window Titles] section defines the aircraft's panel windows. The windows are in order:

```
Window00=
Window01=
```

And so on. After the definition comes the name of the window:

```
Main Panel
Radio Stack
GPS
```

And so on in this case. These names will appear in FSX under the Views | Instrument panel window.

Below these window titles is a separator line that looks something like this:

```
//————————————————————————
```

The forward slashes (//)at the beginning of the line is called a "comment". Comments are instructions not read by a program and are used for information only. For example a programmer might add comments to a programs code that can be used to remind them what a certain section of the code does. In this case it is used as a separator. FSX will not read lines that have forward slashes in front of it.

Following the separator is the information that FSX reads to render the window. Section [Window00] typically defines the main 2-D panel and this case is no exception. The following statements draw the main window:

```
file_1024=caravan_main_panel.bmp
file_1024_night=caravan_main_panel_night.bmp
size_mm=1024
position=7
visible=1
ident=MAIN_PANEL
```

The line "file_1024=" tells FSX which image to load. In this case, it's loading the files caravan_main_panel.bmp. Notice the "1024" before the equal sign (=). This is in reference to the screen resolution. In previous versions of FSX, there could be multiple entries telling FS which image to load for different screen resolutions, like file_640= and file_1024=. This would load one image if the screen resolution was set to 640x480 and another image if the screen resolution as 1024x768 or higher. With FSX, it requires a screen resolution of at least 1024x768.

The line "file_1024_night=" tells FSX which image to load at night. In this case, the file name is caravan_main_panel_night.bmp.

The next line, "size_mm=1024". This line defines the size of the main window. In this example, there is only one entry, 1024. This means that the size of the window will be 1024 pixels by 768 pixels. If an odd sized image is used, the numbers in this line can be used. We'll see this in the next window...

The line "position=7" tells FSX where to drawn the window on the screen. Each area on the screen has a number assigned to it from 0 through 8.

```
Position=0 is the top left
Position=1 is the top center
Position=2 is the top right
```

```
Position=3 is the left center
Position=4 is the exact center of the screen
Position=5 is the right center
Position=6 is the bottom left corner
Position=7 is the bottom center of the screen
Position=8 is the bottom right corner of the screen
```

The next line, "visible=1" is pretty straight forward. This is set to either 1 or 0. When set to 1, this window will be drawn when the cockpit view is loaded by FSX. A setting of 0 will not be visible when the cockpit view is loaded by FSX.

The line "Ident=MAIN_PANEL" is a bit more tricky. 'Ident' stands for Identifier. Other windows will be referred to as "RADIO_STACK_PANEL", "GPS_PANEL" and so on. This is an internal name that FSX uses. These names are tied internally to a number. The icon gauges/instruments that you click to open the GPS instrument radio stack and so on have a number in the gauge. When the icon is clicked, it tells FSX to open the window that has the 'Ident' within the gauge file. This is a bit confusing so we'll clarify in a bit. Let's move one to the next part in the panel.cfg file to see how the gauges are placed on a panel, then we'll take a look at the gauge files themselves to see how they work.

Following the part of section [window00] that draws the window is the gauge definitions. This part tells FSX which gauges to load and where to draw them on the screen. Here is a sample from the sent part:

```
gauge00=Cessna208B_XML!airspeed, 419,331
gauge01=Cessna208B_XML!altimeter, 710,331
gauge02=Cessna208B_XML!annunciator_panel_1, 485,244
gauge03=Cessna208B_XML!annunciator_panel_2, 849,322

. . .
gauge25=SimIcons1024!Kneeboard Icon,  510, 212
gauge26=SimIcons1024!ATC Icon, 532, 212
gauge27=SimIcons1024!Map Icon, 554, 212
gauge28=SimIcons1024!Avionics Icon, 576, 212
gauge29=SimIcons1024!GPS Icon, 598, 212
gauge30=SimIcons1024!ECU Icon, 620, 212
gauge31=SimIcons1024!Fuel Panel Icon, 642, 212
gauge32=SimIcons1024!Electrical Panel Icon, 664, 212
gauge33=SimIcons1024!Engine Instruments Icon,  686, 212
gauge34=SimIcons1024!Compass Icon, 708, 212
gauge35=SimIcons1024!Other Controls Icon, 730, 212
. . .
```

In looking at the gauge definitions, we see this format:

```
Gauge##=<gauge name>!<sub gauge name>, X position, Y position
```

The gauge## is simply a sequence of numbers going in order from gauge00, to gauge 01 and so on until all the required gauges for that window are placed.

The <gauge name> is the name of the gauge file. In this case we see the Cessna208B_XML gauge and the SimIcons1024 gauges. These are main gauges that can contain multiple sub gauges. Think of it as a folder name with files within the folder. The Gauge is like a folder and the sub gauges are like files within that folder.

The <sub gauge name> is a specific piece of code designed to do a certain task within a main gauge. In this example, we have the Cessna208B_XML file as the main gauge. This holds all the gauges that are specific to the Cessna 208B. Within that file are individual XML files that perform certain tasks.

The numbers following the gauge definition tells FSX where to draw the gauge on the panel. Lets take a look back at the line:

```
size_mm=1024
```

This tells us that the main window is 1204 pixels wide and will be the standard 768 pixels high. Lets look at the first gauge definition:

```
gauge00=Cessna208B_XML!airspeed, 419,331
```

Again, the numbers at the end of the line tell us where to draw the gauge on the panel. This definition always starts in the top left corner of the screen. The top left is referred to as 0,0. This means that it is 0 pixels over from the left and 0 pixels down from the top. Our first line will start drawing the top left corner of the gauge 419 pixels from the left edge of the screen and 331 pixels down from the top.

Most gauge definitions like this will have two additional numbers that will represent the size of the gauge. We'll come back to these in a bit.

Lets move on to the next section in the panel.cfg file...

The next section, [window01], is a bit different from the first section:

```
[Window01]
Background_color=2,2,2
size_mm=250,504
position=8
visible=0
ident=RADIO_STACK_PANEL
gauge01=Bendix_King_Radio!Bendix-King Radio Audio,    0,  0,250, 44
gauge02=Bendix_King_Radio!Bendix-King Radio Nav-Comm 1,  0, 45,250, 92
gauge03=Bendix_King_Radio!Bendix-King Radio Nav-Comm 2,  0,136,250, 92
gauge04=Bendix_King_Radio!Bendix-King Radio ADF,        0,227,250, 65
gauge05=Bendix_King_Radio!Bendix-King Radio DME,        0,290,250, 65
gauge06=Bendix_King_Radio!Bendix-King Radio Xpndr,   0,353,250, 78
gauge07=Bendix_King_Radio!Bendix-King Radio AP,         0,430,250, 74
```

As expected, the new section has a '01' at the end instead of a 00 like the first one. But the first line reads:

```
Background_color=2,2,2
```

Instead of loading a bitmap image like in the first section, this line defines a background color. The color is set in RGB, which stands for Red, Blue and Green. The numbers range from 0 to 255. 0,0,0 would be pure black, so 2,2,2 is pretty close to pure black. On a side note, 0,0,0 is pure black, but in FSX, pure black and only pure black is rendered as transparent or invisible.

Why would you want an invisible background? Some gauges, like certain GPS gauges are not perfectly square and have rounded edges. If you define a window section, it has to be a square or rectangle shape. If the background color is black and the gauge has a rounded edge, you will still see the black behind it. If you have a transparent background, then you still have the window definition that you can map a gauge to, but the rounded edges on the gauges will be visible with the background panel or scenery visible on the edges of the gauge.

The next line, "size_mm=250,504" defines the size of the window to be drawn. This size is 250 pixels wide and 504 pixels tall.

The next line, "position=8" tells us that the window will be drawn in the bottom right corner of the screen.

The next line, "Visible=0" tells us that when we load the 2-D cockpit view that this window will NOT be visible.

The ident for this window is set to RADIO_STACK_PANEL. As mentioned earlier, this is tied to a number that is referenced in the gauge file. A panel designer can use either these standard names, or the associated number from the gauge. We'll show you how to access this number in a bit.

Next we get into the gauge definitions for this window:

```
gauge01=Bendix_King_Radio!Bendix-King Radio Audio,    0,   0,250,  44
gauge02=Bendix_King_Radio!Bendix-King Radio Nav-Comm 1,  0,  45,250,  92
gauge03=Bendix_King_Radio!Bendix-King Radio Nav-Comm 2,  0,136,250,  92
gauge04=Bendix_King_Radio!Bendix-King Radio ADF,             0,227,250, 65
gauge05=Bendix_King_Radio!Bendix-King Radio DME,             0,290,250, 65
gauge06=Bendix_King_Radio!Bendix-King Radio Xpndr,      0,353,250,  78
gauge07=Bendix_King_Radio!Bendix-King Radio AP,              0,430,250, 74
```

As discussed before, the gauges are listed in order. This is the radio stack panel so all gauges used are in the Bendix_King_Radio gauge file. Notice the numbers at the end of the line. There are 4 numbers listed here instead of only 2 like in the first section.

When only two numbers are used as in the first section, the gauge is drawn at 100% of the size of the image as it was programmed. When four numbers are used, they tell FSX how large the gauge is to be drawn. Take the first line as an example:

```
gauge01=Bendix_King_Radio!Bendix-King Radio Audio,    0,   0,250,  44
```

Remember, the size of this entire panel as defined by the line "size_mm=250,504" is only 250 pixels wide and is 504 pixels tall, not 1024 x 768 like the main panel. The gauge definition for the Audio panel here starts: 0, 0. This means that the top left corner of the Audio gauge is dawn in the very top left corner of the new window. The next numbers, 250, 44 tells FSX that the gauge is to be drawn 250 pixels wide and 44 pixels tall. Notice that the size of the window was only 250 pixels wide so this gauge will cover the new window from left to right but will only cover the top 44 pixels of the panel.

The next line, "gauge02=Bendix_King_Radio!Bendix-King Radio Nav-Comm 1, 0, 45, 250, 92". This tells us that the Nav-Comm gauge will be loaded starting zero (0) pixels over to the left or in other words right on the left edge of the panel, and 45 pixels down from the top. Recall that the first gauge was drawn down only 44 pixels and this one starts at 45 pixels down. This will leave a 1-pixel gap between the top gauge and the second gauge. The last 2 numbers tell us that the gauge is drawn 250 pixels wide, again covering the entire width of the panel and 92 pixels high.

The remaining sections are all similar and there is no need to cover what each section does specifically. You can read them if desired to see how they are drawn.

If you wanted to add a new pop-up window to the panel, you could do so by adding a new entry into the [Window Titles] section at the top that might look something like this:

```
Window11=My Custom Gauge
```

Then scrolling down through the panel, add a new section after the [Window10] section that defines your new gauge.

The text "My Custom Gauge" would appear in the Views | Instrument Panel menu in FSX and clicking it would open your new window.

At the end of the panel.cfg file are the Virtual Cockpit sections. These are labeled [vcockpit01], [vcockpit02] and so on. These are a bit more difficult to describe and understand since they are specific to the aircraft you are working with. Here's the first part of the [vcockpit01] section:

```
[Vcockpit01]
file=panel_1.bmp
Background_color=0,0,0
size_mm=512,512
visible=1
pixel_size=512,512s
texture=$C208_1
```

The first line specifies a bitmap image that is to be loaded over top of the virtual cockpit model. IN this case the file is called panel_1.bmp and it located in the panel folder along with the panel.cfg file.

The second line specifies a background color or 0,0,0, which as we know is invisible.

The next line set the size of the panel, here it's set to 512,512 or 512 pixels wide and 512 pixels tall.

The next line tells is that this window will be visible when the virtual cockpit view is active in FSX. This entry should be on for each virtual cockpit gauge window.

The "pixel_size=512,512s" is actually not defined in the Software Development Kit but we believe it refers to the size of the image that is loaded. Having the size of the pixels set to the same as the panel (size_mm entry) sets a one-to-one ratio.

The last line "texture=$c2008_1" is an internal reference to the model (*.mdl) file. The model is designed with a certain 'tag' on the virtual cockpit parts that will have gauges on them. This is how FSX knows where on the model to draw the gauges that are defined in this section in the panel.cfg file.

The rest of the section is the same as the other sections. The gauge is defined followed by the number of pixels from the left, the number down from the top, then the number of pixels wide the gauge will be drawn and then the number of pixels high the gauge will be drawn.

New sections cannot be added to the virtual cockpit since they have to be designed into the model of the aircraft. You can however add a new gauge if there is room on virtual cockpit panel.

Gauge files can be found in 2 main locations within the Flight Simulator. One location is the Panel folder of the aircraft. Most of the aircraft that come with FSX have their main gauges in the Panel folder. The other location is the Gauges folder found in the FSX's main folder. To find them quickly, we can go back to the Panel folder where we opened the panel.cfg file.

The file we are looking for is called Cessna208B_XML.cab. Cab files, as mentioned earlier are compressed files. Windows may be able to open the compressed file to see what's in it. But it won't easily be able to view the files within the file. We recommend you install WinZip for this (available for download at www.winzip.com. After you install WinZip, double-click on the cab file and it will open in WInZip showing you the contents of the file.

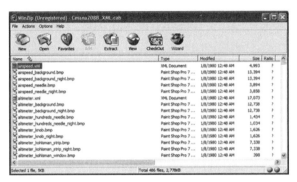

In this file we can see the XML files like airspeed.xml and altimeter.xml and the bitmap images like airspeed_background.bmp and altimeter_background.bmp. Scrolling down through the rest of the file will reveal more XML and BMP files. The XML files in this file are the sub gauge names. If we look back at the panel.cfg file, we see the line:

```
gauge00=Cessna208B_XML!airspeed, 419,331
```

This tells FSX to load the file "Cessna208B_XML.cab", then read the sub gauge "airspeed.xml".

For now we can close WinZip. Let's take a look at the Gauges folder. You can either click the Back button the window showing the contents of the Panel folder, or go through the Right-Click Properties on the FSX icon again and click the Find Target button. To reveal the main FSX folder again, Double-click the Gauges folder.

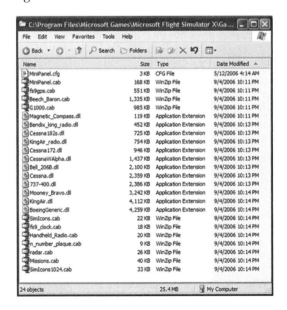

We already mentioned the "ident" and how text used for the "ident" is internally referenced to a number. Let's take a look in the SimIcons1024.cab file and then open some of the XML files to determine what these numbers are.

Double-click the SimIncos1024.cab file to view it in WinZip. We'll also click the Type column two times to sort the column by type so we can see all of the XML files grouped together.

Let's right-click on the "Radio Icon.xml" file and choose "View With NOTEPAD.EXE". This will open the file in Notepad and show us the following:

```
<?xml version="1.0" encoding="utf-8"?>
<Gauge Name="Radio Icon" Version="1.0">
    <Image Name="radio_icon.bmp"/>
    <Mouse>
        <Help ID="HELPID_GAUGE_TOGGLE_RADIO_WINDOW"/>
        <Cursor Type="Hand"/>
        <Click>50 (&gt;K:PANEL_ID_TOGGLE)</Click>
    </Mouse>
</Gauge>
```

The part of the line that we're interested here is:

```
<Click>50 (&gt;K:PANEL_ID_TOGGLE)</Click>
```

This says that when the icon is clicked, it references the number 50. If you wanted to, you can replace the line in the panel.cfg file that reads:

```
ident=RADIO_STACK_PANEL
```

with the line:

```
ident=50
```

Both these examples above will produce the same results when the Radio Stack icon is clicked. Here is a cross-reference list of some of the main Ident names versus their number counter parts:

```
THROTTLE_PANEL          10
RADIO_STACK_PANEL  50
COMPASS_PANEL           75
```

```
IFR_MAIN_PANEL            1
COLLECTIVE_PANEL          200
GPS_PANEL                 225
OVERHEAD_PANEL            250
FLAPS_TRIM_PANEL          252
FUEL_PANEL                253
ELECTRICAL_PANEL          125
```

Other features of the panel.cfg file

There are a few other things that can be found in a panel.cfg. The most common one found in 3rd party panels, but freeware and commercial are size and position controls added to the pop-up windows. These controls allow you to specify the exact width of the pop-up panel and its position on the screen regardless of the position= and size_mm settings.

Let's look back at the Radio Stack pop-up section [window01] of the Cessna208B:

```
[Window01]
Background_color=2,2,2
size_mm=250,504
position=8
visible=0
ident=RADIO_STACK_PANEL
```

When you click the Radio Stack icon on the panel, it will open the radio stack in position 8, which is the lower left corner.

If you want to make the radio stack bigger and have it appear in a specific area on the screen, you can add 2 lines the [Window01] section in the panel.cfg file like this:

The numbers after the equal sign (=) must be between 0.00 and 1.00 for the "Window_pos=" line. The first number will be the X position setting the distance from the left edge of the FSX screen and the second number will be the Y position setting distance down from the top edge of the screen. One the position is defined, FSX will draw the top left corner of the pop-up panel starting in that location.

On the "Window_size=" line, FSX will render the size of the panel with a number of 1.00 being full size as defined by the size_mm= entry. If you enter numbers larger than 1.00, the window size will be drawn larger.

Here's what the radio stack will look like with the settings:

Aliasing Panels and gauges

As we discussed earlier, there are only 2 places a gauge can be stored in FSX – the aircraft's panel folder and the main Gauges folder. When trying to load a gauge, FSX looks in the aircraft's \Panel folder first and if it's not there, it looks in the \Gauges folder. But what happens if the perfect gauge you want for your panel is on the Lear45 panel? There are 3 possible solutions:

1. Copy the Lear45's gauge from the Lear's \Panel folder to the main Gauges folder.
2. Copy the Lear45's gauge from the Lear's \Panel folder to your aircraft's \Panel folder.

Both of these options require another copy of the gauge thus using more drive space. Why use up the space when the gauge is already on the hard drive? Why not just use it from the folder it's already in? Good question... and the answer is options 3:

3. Reference the Lear 45's gauge from the Lear 45's \Panel folder.

This is called Aliasing the gauge. To use an alias, you enter a path to the gauge's location. You need to know a few things before you can alias a gauge:

1. The name of the gauge file name or cab file name
2. The sub-gauge name within the cab file
3. The exact folder and path the cab file is in.

Let's use the Cessna 208's panel as our example. Let's replace the airspeed indicator as noted in this line:

```
gauge00=Cessna208B_XML!airspeed, 419,331
```

with the airspeed indicator of the Lear 45. Granted, there is no logical reason to do this, but it will show us how to alias a gauge from an existing plane.

Let's gather our information:

1. gauge file name: Lear_45_XML.cab
2. sub gauge name: asi.xml
3. path to file: Lear45\Panel

In order to get FSX to locate the correct folder, we have to know that FSX is already looking in the panel folder of the Cessna 208B. This is true if we are working with the Cessna 208, the Extra 300 or the any other plane either a default FSX plane or a 3rd party aircraft. We have to enter a path that will direct FSX to a different folder. This path has to tells FSX to:

- Back up one folder to the aircraft's main folder, in this case that's the C208B folder
- Back up another folder to the main Airplanes folder.
- Move down one folder into the Lear45 folder
- Move down one folder into the Lear 45's Panel folder
- Enter the name of the new gauge file

To move up one folder, we enter this information:

```
../
```

To move up 2 folders, we enter this:

```
../../
```

This takes care of steps one and two. The next step is to simply enter the path to the new folder, which is:

```
Lear45\Panel
```

Next is the name of the new gauge file:

```
Lear_45_XML
```

Last is the exclamation point to define the sub gauge, then the sub gauge name.

```
!asi
```

Put it all together and our alias entry will look like this:

```
Gauge00=../../Lear45/Panel/Lear_45_XML!asi, 419,331
```

Here's what it looks like in FSX:

But now notice the gauge is too small! The reason is due to the extra two numbers. Recall that when only two numbers are used, in this case 419, 331, the gauge is rendered at 100%. The gauge was obviously custom-made to match the Cessna 208's panel. The Lear45's airspeed gauge is obviously the same – custom made for the Lear 45 panel. So how do we make it fit? We have to add the extra two numbers at the end to make the gauge a littler larger than it was designed.

Notice in the image above that the top left corner of the gauge is not quite in the right position either. This is because the Lear 45's airspeed gauge is more squared with a gauge frame with the corners cut off and Cessna's gauge was just the circle in the center of the frame as drawn on the panel. To adjust this, we'll need to modify the number 419 and 331 a bit to move it over and up a bit. Let's try these numbers:

```
gauge00=../../Lear45/Panel/Lear_45_XML!asi, 405,320,135,135
```

Here's what we get:

Now you have all the information you need to place just about any gauge onto any panel or to resize and replace gauges on existing panels.

Flying Using Your Keyboard

espite the impressive joysticks, yokes and other controllers now available, many of us still feel more comfortable using our keyboards to handle certain aircraft controls and to select commands and options. Although using the keyboard is no longer practical as the primary flight control, many simmers prefer using the keyboard in certain circumstances (for example, controlling the ailerons, elevator and rudder).

Although dozens of keyboard commands are available, but since you'll probably never use most of them, you won't need to learn all of them. However, by remembering the most important keys, you'll become a more expert simmer.

Before using the keyboard in FSX, please read and make certain you understand the following:

When you see a single key listed in the following keyboard command descriptions, all you need to do is press that key. For example:

P

means to simply press the P key. If you see a key combination, such as:

Ctrl + T

press and hold down the first key (Ctrl in this example) and then press the second key simultaneously (T in this example).

Before beginning

Before talking about default keyboard assignments, you should know that you can customize keyboard controls in FSX. For example, if pressing the S key seems more natural for a view out the side window, you can customize FSX so that whenever you press the S key, you're looking out the left window.

To change the keyboard assignments, select the **Options | Settings | Controls...** command. Then select the BUTTONS/KEYS tab to bring it to the front. Select either the "Normal" or "Slew" option. The key controls you can change will depend on which option you select. Select each option and notice how the Assignment list changes depending on which option you select.

Find the [Reset Defaults] button before you begin making changes. It's near the bottom of the Controls Assignments dialog box. If you want to cancel any changes you've made to your key assignments, click the [Reset Defaults] button. This will return the Flight Simulator default settings to the keyboard assignments.

The "Event category" lists the buttons, settings or controls that you can change. Click the drop down menu to change a specific control. For example, if you want to change Control Surfaces, then select "Control surface commands" to customize the keyboard assignments for the commands that apply only to the Control Surfaces.

You'll change the keyboard assignments in the "Event category" list. Select an event in the "Event category" list (the options that appear under "Event" depend on what you selected in the "Event category" list). Click the [Change Assignment...] button to change the keyboard assignment for the selected command. Then press the key(s) in the Select Assignment dialog box that you want to assign to the command.

Click the [Delete Key Assignment] button to remove the current keyboard assignment from the command you've selected in the Event table. Be careful using this button because you won't be prompted first to confirm the action.

Adjusting keyboard sensitivity

You can experiment with the keyboard sensitivity settings so the controls are either more sensitive or less sensitive to your key presses. These affect only the primary flight surfaces (ailerons, elevators and rudders).

Select the **Options | Settings | Controls...** command. Then select the CALIBRATION tab to bring it to the front. Drag the slider controls under Keyboard sensitivity (left to decrease or right to increase sensitivity) to the desired settings.

Autopilot commands

One area where you'll find an advantage of using the keyboard is operating the autopilot. Use the following key combinations:

Airspeed hold on/off	Ctrl + R
Altitude hold on/off	Ctrl + Z
Approach mode on/off	Ctrl + A
Attitude hold on/off	Ctrl + T
Autopilot master switch on/off	Z
Back course mode on/off	Ctrl + B
Heading hold on/off	Ctrl + H
Localizer hold on/off	Ctrl + O
Mach hold on/off	Ctrl + M
NAV1 hold on/off	Ctrl + N
Wing leveler on/off	Ctrl + V
Yaw damper on/off	Ctrl + D

Control Surface commands

You probably will use your joystick or yoke for controlling your aircraft but you can also use the keyboard to manage your aircraft's control surfaces.

Aileron trim left	Ctrl + Num Pad 4
Aileron trim right	Ctrl + Num Pad 6
Arm autospoilers	Shift + /
Bank left (ailerons)	Num Pad 4
Bank right (ailerons)	Num Pad 6
Center ailerons and rudder	Num Pad 5
Elevator trim up	Num Pad 1
Elevator trim down	Num Pad 7
Extend flaps (in increments)	F7
Extend flaps fully	F8
Extend/Retract spoilers/airbrakes	/
Pitch down (elevator)	Num Pad 8
Pitch up (elevator)	Num Pad 2
Retract flaps (in increments)	F6
Retract flaps fully	F5
Yaw left (rudder)	Num Pad 0
Yaw right (rudder)	Num Pad Enter

Engine commands

You'll use your joystick or yoke to control your aircraft's engine in most cases but you'll also need to use the keyboard in certain situations.

Arm auto-throttle .... [Shift] + [R]
Carb heat/ De-ice on/off .... [H]
Cut throttle .... [F1]
Decrease prop RPM .... [Ctrl] + [F2]
Decrease throttle .... [F2]
Engage auto-throttle takeoff/
   go-around mode .... [Ctrl] + [Shift] + [R]
Engine auto start .... [Ctrl] + [E]
Enrich mixture .... [Ctrl] + [Shift] + [F3]
Full throttle .... [F4]
Increase prop RPM .... [Ctrl] + [F3]
Increase throttle .... [F3]
Lean mixture .... [Ctrl] + [Shift] + [F2]
Reheat/Afterburner on/off .... [Shift] + [F4]
Select engine .... [E]
Select jet starter .... [J]
Select magnetos .... [M]
Set mixture to idle cutoff .... [Ctrl] + [Shift] + [F1]
Set mixture to rich .... [Ctrl] + [Shift] + [F4]
Set prop RPM to high .... [Ctrl] + [F4]
Set prop RPM to low .... [Ctrl] + [F1]

General aircraft commands

Use these commands to control general aircraft situations.

Apply left brakes .... (num) [*]
Apply right brakes .... (num) [-]
Apply/Release brakes .... [.]
Landing gear up/down .... [G]
Manually pump landing gear .... [Ctrl] + [G]
Master   battery/alternator   switches   on/off
 .... [Shift] + [M]
Set parking brake .... [Ctrl] + [.]
Smoke system on/off .... [I]

Instrument commands

Use the following key combinations to control the instrument commands.

Decrease selection slightly .... [Shift] + [-]
Decrease selection .... [-]
Increase selection slightly .... [Shift] + [=]
Increase selection .... [=]
Pitot heat on/off .... [Shift] + [H]
Reset altimeter .... [B]
Reset directional gyro .... [D]

Light commands

Use the following key combinations to control the interior and exterior lights.

All lights on/off .... [L]
Strobe lights on/off .... [O]
Landing lights on/off .... [Ctrl] + [L]
Panel lights on/off .... [Shift] + [L]

Multiplayer commands

Use these key combinations when you're flying with other pilots on the Internet, LAN, modem or a direct connection.

Chat window on/off .... [Ctrl] + [Shift] + [J]
Cycle through other players .... [Ctrl] + [Shift] + [O]
Follow other player .... [Ctrl] + [Shift] + [F]
Switch focus to chat window .... [Enter]
Pause Full Session .... [Ctrl] + [P]
Transfer/Accept control .... [Shift] + [T]

Radio commands

Use the following key combinations to control the navigation and other radios.

ADF ident on/off .... [Ctrl] + [5]
Select ADF .... [Ctrl] + [Shift] + [A]
Select COM radio .... [C]
Select DME .... [F]
Select NAV radio .... [N]
Select OBS .... [Shift] + [V]
Select transponder .... [T]
VOR1 ident on/off .... [Ctrl] + [1]
VOR2 ident on/off .... [Ctrl] + [2]

Simulator commands

Use these commands to control FSX general functions.

ATC window on/off .... [`]
Autorudder on/off .... [Ctrl] + [Shift] + [U]
Exit Flight Simulator immediately .... [Ctrl] + [Pause]
Exit Flight Simulator .... [Ctrl] + [C]
Joystick on/off .... [K]
Mission compass objective (next) .... [K]
Mission compass objective (previous) .... [Shift] + [K]
Mission compass pointer on/off .... [U]
Pause FSX .... [P]
Reset current flight .... [Ctrl] + [;]
Save current flight .... [;]
Simulation rate .... [R]
Slew mode on/off .... [Y]
Sound on/off .... [Q]

Slew commands

Use these commands to slew your aircraft. Slewing is a special non[-]flight mode that lets you move quickly in FSX. This mode is very useful for repositioning your aircraft anywhere in FSX. The slew commands will only work when you enter slew mode (pressing [Y] enters and exits slew mode).

 NOTE

For more information on Slew commands in FSX, read the "Slew Mode And Camera Views" beginning on page 143.

Slew mode on/off .... [Y]
Reset aircraft orientation so it's level ...... [Ctrl] + [Spacebar]
Toggle coordinates/frame rate .... [Shift] + [Z]

Altitude Up/down

Move down quickly .... [F1]
Move down slowly .... [Z]
Move up quickly .... [F4]
Move up slowly .... [Q]

Move Forward/backward

Move backward .... Num Pad [2]
Move forward .... Num Pad [8]
Freeze vertical movement (altitude) .... [F2]
Freeze all movement .... Num Pad [5]

Move sideways

Move left .... Num Pad [4]
Move right .... Num Pad [6]

Pitch

Nose down quickly .... [F8]
Nose down .... [F7]
Nose up quickly .... [F5]
Nose up .... [9]
Freeze pitch .... [F6]

Bank (roll)

Bank left .... Num Pad [7]
Bank right .... Num Pad [9]
Freeze banking .... Num Pad [5]

Heading (yaw)

Rotate left .... Num Pad [1]
Rotate right .... Num Pad [3]
Freeze rotation .... Num Pad [5]

Views

Pan view down .... [Shift] + [Enter]
Pan view left .... [Ctrl] + [Shift] + [Backspace]
Pan view right .... [Ctrl] + [Shift] + [Enter]
Pan view up .... [Shift] + [Backspace]

View commands

Use the following key combinations to control direction and other information on views.

2-D Cockpit view .... [F10]
Aircraft labels (on/off) .... [Ctrl] + [Shift] + [L]
Coordinates/frame rate .... [Shift] + [Z]
Create new view window .... [[]
Cycle coordinates/frame rate .... [Shift] + [Z]
Eyepoint (move back) .... [Ctrl] + [Enter]
Eyepoint (move down) .... [Shift] + [Backspace]
Eyepoint (move forward) .... [Ctrl] + [Backspace]
Eyepoint (move left) .... [Ctrl] + [Shift] + [Backspace]
Eyepoint (move right) .... [Ctrl] + [Shift] + [Enter]
Eyepoint (move up) .... [Shift] + [Enter]
Eyepoint (reset) .... [Ctrl] + [Spacebar]
Kneeboard (on/off) .... [Shift] + [F10]
Open new window .... [[]
Panel (view next) .... [W]
Panel (view previous) .... [Shift] + [W]
Panel transparency .... [Ctrl] + [Shift] + [T]
Set zoom to 1X .... [Backspace]
Switch to previous view .... [Ctrl] + [Shift] + [Tab]
View next category .... [S]
View next in current category .... [A]
View previous .... [Ctrl] + [S]
View next window .... [Ctrl] + [Tab]
Virtual cockpit (shortcut) .... [F9]
Switch to top-down view .... [F12]

Don't Be Afraid Of The Blades

Flying a helicopter is quite different than flying a fixed-wing aircraft both in real life and in flight simulation. We assume that you already know the basics of flying a fixed-wing aircraft and so to help you make the transition to helicopters, we'll give you a few hints and tips to get you up and flying quickly and safely.

For an aircraft to fly, it must be moving forward. To get the aircraft to move forward, you simply increase the throttle. The increased engine power turns the propeller faster. The blades of the propeller are twisted slightly to "bite the air" and this thrust pulls the aircraft forward. The wind rushing over wings lifts the aircraft off of the ground.

On a helicopter, the blades of the rotor are on top. Similarly, when you increase the throttle, the rotor spins faster and the helicopter lifts off of the ground.

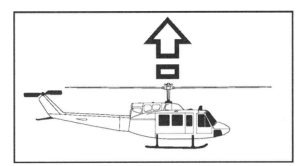

For a helicopter to move forward, you tip the axis of the rotor forward so instead of pulling it straight up, the blades pull it both upward and forward as shown here:

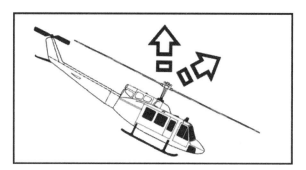

To do this, you'll have to push your control stick forward. In a aircraft, pushing the stick forward causes the nose to drop and the aircraft descends. In a helicopter, pushing the stick forward also lowers the nose, but also tips the blades forward. The result is that the helicopter is pulled upward and forward at the same time. Be careful though! If you push the stick too far forward, the helicopter will descend just like an aircraft.

The rotor is acting against the pull gravity. Gravity pulls the helicopter down and the rotor pulls it up. When you tip the nose forward, you are changing this relationship. The trick is to tip the nose forward enough to move forward while at the same time maintaining enough upward lift to keep the gravity from pulling the helicopter towards the ground. Again, if you tip it too far forward, gravity wins and the helicopter descends.

What does the tail rotor do?

Helicopters have two rotors — one is on top and the other is on the tail. As we've just seen, the top rotor provides upward and forward thrust. The tail rotor keeps the body of the helicopter from spinning. Suppose the top rotor of a helicopter is spinning clockwise as shown in the following image:

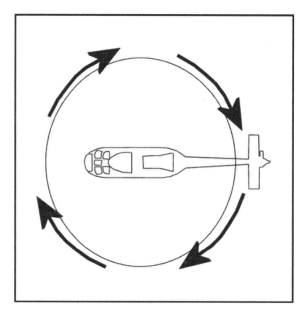

The engine that is turning the rotor is mounted to the body of the helicopter. It basically needs something to push against to turn the blades. This "something" is the body of the helicopter. This might be OK when the helicopter is sitting on the ground. You can turn the rotor with the engine while sitting on the ground because the body is held to the ground by gravity and friction of the wheels or skids on the helicopter. When the helicopter lifts off the ground, you've counteracted the gravity with the lift of the blades but removed the friction that is holding the body while the engine continues to turn. What happens here is that the body of the helicopter starts to turn in the opposite direction of the blades.

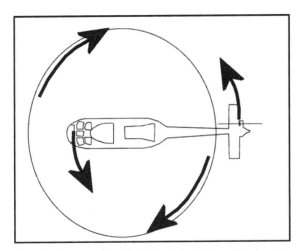

But obviously no one can fly a helicopter like this. The job of the tail rotor is to counteract the spinning of the body of the helicopter. Using our example, the tail rotor spins, similar to an aircraft propeller, to push the body of the helicopter clockwise (when viewed from above), just like the top rotor. As you increase the throttle, the top rotor spins faster to lift off and the tail rotor also turns faster to keep the helicopter body from spinning.

How does a helicopter hover?

A helicopter is hovering when it appears to be floating in one place above the ground and is not gaining or loosing altitude nor moving forward or backward. When you first lift off, the helicopter is close to a hover. If you slowly increase the throttle when you are on the ground, the helicopter will start to lift. The more you increase the throttle, the higher and faster it will climb. Once airborne, if you decrease the throttle slightly, just enough to arrest the lift, you will be in a hover. In FSX, the helicopter may start to drift forward or backward a bit after a few seconds though.

But the trickiest part is transitioning from forward motion into a hover. We've learned how to gain forward motion, but we didn't cover slowing down. The same concept we have for moving forward applies to slowing down or flying backward (Note that FSX does not like helicopters to fly backward for very long. FSX shows zero airspeed when you are moving backward in a helicopter and eventually it will spin out of control).

The next image shows how you achieve a hover. Notice that it goes from nose-down to get forward motion, then levels off to maintain a cruise speed, and then goes nose up to slow down. Once the forward motion has stopped, then helicopter is again leveled off and the altitude is controlled with the throttle. One important note to remember when flying a helicopter is not to use the control stick to gain or lower altitude as you would flying a fixed wing aircraft. The speed of the rotors controls the altitude and the speed of the rotors are controlled by the throttle.

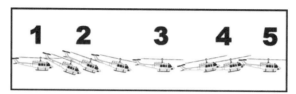

1 – Hovering after lift-off

2 – Gaining airspeed/accelerating

3 – Cruising

4 – Lowering airspeed/decelerating

5 – Hovering

How do you land a helicopter?

If you learn to hover, you'll be able to land a helicopter. To land, you basically achieve a hover and then decrease the throttle to lower the helicopter. If you start to descend too quickly, increase the throttle to break the descent.

But you may also be in situations when you need to spin your helicopter around ninety degrees and land on a dime, just like they do in the Hollywood movies. This is done using the "collective." The job of the tail rotor is to counteract the top rotor to keep the body of the helicopter from spinning. When you adjust the collective, you're changing the speed of the tail rotor. The rudder control is used in FSX to adjust the collective. Using a joystick with twisting action for the rudder control is highly recommended for flying helicopters in FSX.

When the collective is increased (joystick twisted one way or one pedal pushed down), the tail rotor spins faster thus pushing the tail of the aircraft around – not too fast usually, but it does push the body of the helicopter. Using our example, it would turn the body of the helicopter counterclockwise.

Decreasing the collective (rudder twisted the opposite way or the other pedal pushed down) decreases the speed of the tail rotor causing the overhead rotor to overpower the tail rotor and causing the body of the helicopter to turn it in the opposite direction or clockwise using our example.

If the helicopter is moving in level flight and you change the collective, you'll slow down due to the wind resistance on the side of the helicopter body as it pivots, but overall speed isn't decreased significantly – you'll just be flying backward, which is not recommended, especially in FSX.

If the nose is tipped forward, you can adjust the collective to spin the helicopter around. This may also make the helicopter go backward for a bit, but not for long. When the rotor is tipped forward you are gaining speed, when you turn around 180 degrees, you still have much of the speed, but you are still tipped forward. This causes the helicopter to slow down quickly. Now the rotor is pulling the helicopter forward while it's momentum is going backward.

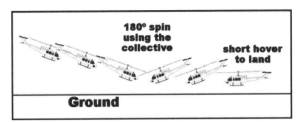

It doesn't take long for the rotor to overpower the momentum and stop the helicopter's motion. When this happens, it's time to level off, hover, then land. In the movies and I'm sure obviously in real life, experience expert pilots can do a spin landing without too much extra thought. For the novice, it is not recommended, but fun to try in Flight Sim!

Why does the control stick move left and right if adjusting the collective and moving the stick forward and backward controls all the helicopters motion?

The movement of the stick left and right actually tips the individual blades of the rotor, but only on one side of the helicopter. This will create more 'bite' on one side of the helicopter causing it to lift more on one side than on the other. The result is the helicopter will bank to the right or left a bit and start to move in that direction. The effect is very similar to how the ailerons work on an aircraft.

To turn right in an aircraft, you lower the left aileron to increase the lift on the bottom of left wing and raise the aileron on the right wing to increase the drag on the top of the right wing. The result is a lifting of the left wing and a lowering of the right wing causing the aircraft to bank or turn.

The effect is similar when you want to move your helicopter left and right. Push the control stick to the right (but not too much!) to move right. When the blade spins around overhead, your helicopter tips. When the blade rotates to the left side of the helicopter, it tips more to "bite" more to get more lift. When it spins back around to the right, it levels off or tips in the opposite direction to cause even lift or less lift than when on the left side. This obviously happens very fast. The result is a slight tip in the helicopter causing the direction of the lift to change. Instead of straight up or forward and up like during acceleration, it is now more up, forward and to the right. When you want to stop, counteract the direction by moving the stick to the left until sideways motion is stopped.

The following describes the basic maneuvers you should try with your helicopter in FSX:

Hovering

Lifting straight up with your hand only on the throttle, then adjusting the throttle to obtain a hover. Once you hover for a bit, decrease the throttle to decrease altitude and land. Practice this until you can land softly. If you are hitting the ground too hard, remember to adjust the throttle up and down very slightly to control your descent.

Rotating

Lift off from the ground and use the Collective (Rudder Control) to pivot the aircraft 180°, then set it back down.

Forward motion

Lift off from a runway or helipad straight up and hover. Pick a spot right in front of you not too far away to land. Move the stick forward watching your airspeed. Level off, and then pull back to slow down as you approach the spot. Achieve a hover and lower the throttle to land. Practice this until you can land where you want.

Sideways motion

Lift off from a runway or helipad straight up and hover. Look to the left or right to find a place to land using the hat switch. Move the control stick in that direction. Move the stick in the opposite direction to stop motion and hover, then land. Practice this until you land where you want to, then repeat it for moving in the opposite direction.

Forward motion to a hover

Lift off from a runway or helipad and hover. Find a target to hover over like a boat on the water or a building. Use the collective (rudder) to line up with the object and push the control stick forward to fly to it. Pull back on the stick as you approach the object and level off when your speed is almost zero and achieve a hover. Practice this until you can hover where you want.

After completing these few exercises, you'll be able to fly a helicopter in FSX!

Take a look at the Flying A Helicopter Video on the Companion CD-ROM for more information. See the Contents pages for more information about the Companion CD-ROM and all the videos.

FSX Files & Folders

To get a better understanding of FSX, we're going to take a look at the files and folders used by FSX on your system. We're not going to get into elaborate detail on every file, just some of the important files that can be easily edited. You should know now that there are approximately 42,000 files in the FSX folder and we obviously can't cover the exact purpose of every file, but we can cover a lot of them!

To get started, we'll show you the easiest way to get to your FSX's main folder. Right-click on the icon you use to open FSX and choose Properties from the pop-up menu (see image on the right). This will show you the properties of the icon (see image below).

What do the Properties of the FSX icon have to do with the files and folder? The key here is the Find Target button. Clicking the Find Target button will open a window showing you the contents of the FSX folder. From here we can start covering what each folder does and what types of files are in each folder. So click the Find Target button.

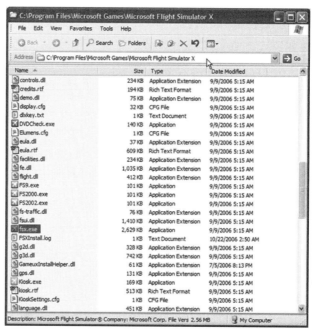

The FSX.EXE file will be highlighted when the window opens. In order to get a better perspective, Click the Folders button at the top. This will show us a list of the folder on the left side and the contents of the selected folder on the right.

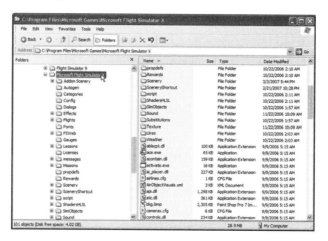

The Microsoft Flight Simulator X folder is selected in the above image. This is know as the main or root folder of FSX. The right side is showing the subfolder and files of the FSX's main folder. The folders will be at the top of the list and files will be below that.

We'll start with some of the files in the root folder so scroll down past the list of folders. You will see a list DLL files and EXE files as well as a few images and configuration files. It's helpful if you have the file extensions visible. To do this, click the **Tools** menu at the top of the window and select **Folder Options**.

Click the View tab at the top and remove the check from the "Hide extensions for known file types" box. Then click the [Show hidden files and folders] button.

This will assure that we will see all of the files and file extensions. Click [OK] to close the window.

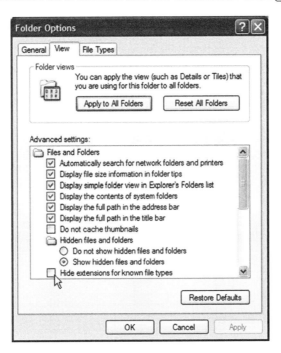

As noted before, most of the files in this folder are not editable, but we'll give a quick rundown of some of files and what they do and point out a few that are editable. We're not going to get into the structure of any these files, but some are worth opening to take a peek at just how FSX knows how to do certain things!

Some files are pretty self-explanatory like these:

```
Atd.dll
Flight.dll
Fs-traffic.dll
FSX.exe
Gps.dll
Multiplayer.dll
Panels.dll
Sound.dll
Terrain.dll
Visualfx.dll
Whether .dll
Window.dll
Some files of interest that can be opened are:
Airlines.cfg
Cameras.cfg
Display.cfg
Stars.dat
Suneffect.cfg
Terrain.cfg
```

A *.cfg or configuration file is a text file that FSX reads. These files typically hold information that FSX reads to know how to display things or settings FSX uses to perform certain actions. The easiest way to open a file that Windows does not recognize is to right-click the file and choose "Open With" from the pop-up window. This will open a window asking you if you want to search the web for a program to open it or if you want to choose the program for a list. We'll choose the program for a list. From this list, you can choose Notepad or WordPad. We recommend Notepad and in order to make Windows recognize the configuration files so we don't have to do this every time, we'll click the "Always use the selected program to open this kind of file" box and click [OK].

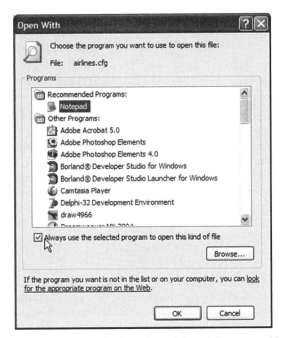

We can see when this file is open that it includes a list of the airlines used by FSX. You can edit these names or add new ones to the list.

The Cameras.cfg defines the default camera positions for an aircraft. All of the FSX aircraft have camera positions defines in the aircraft.cfg file, which we'll ge to later on. If you install a 3rd party aircraft that does not have these new positions defined, FSX will use these default locations.

The Display.cfg file is used by FSX to set certain display parameters that are required for different video cards. Unless you are certain of what you are doing, we recommend not adjusting this file.

The Stars.dat file is similar to a configuration file and can be opened in a similar manner to the configuration files. We'd recommend choosing WordPad instead of Notepad though becasue WordPad maintains more formatting options that may be used in DAT files. This particular file includes the configuration of the stars and constellations as seen in the night sky in FSX. This is an interesting file to see which constellations are included and how they are configured!

The Suneffect.cfg file tells FSX how to draw the effects of the sun and moon.

The Terrain.cfg file is very extensive and defines the types of textures FSX uses in certain areas on the ground. The exact details of this file could fill a book by itself so we'll not get into its details.

Addon Scenery

Let's move into the first folder. Locate the Addon Scenery folder on the left side of the window and click it one time. This will show you the contents on the right side. The contents include 2 folders, Scenery and Texture. On a clean install of FSX, clean meaning that no new files or third party software has been installed to it, the Scenery and Texture folders will be empty. Why are they here if that are empty? Because it's the easiest way to add new scenery files to FSX. You simply place the new scenery files (*.BGL files) into the Addon Scenery's Scenery subfolder and the new texture files, typically bitmap or *.bmp files, into the Texture folder. FSX will automatically load these files.

As a rule of Flight Sim, all scenery files must be in a folder called "Scenery". Scenery files (*.bgl files) will not be loaded by FSX unless they are in a folder called Scenery.

Autogen folder

The next folder, Autogen, includes a configuration file and then a series of *.SPB files. The SPB files are not editable. The configuration file is however and it appears to set up the objects that appear in certain areas in FSX.

Make sense? Let me explain it another way... I'm sure you recall that when flying in FSX in the city, you see city-style buildings, when flying over farm land you see farms, when in the mountains you see trees and in the desert you see brush and so on. Suffice to say that you see the objects you expect to see in the different areas. FSX breaks down the different areas, desert, mountains, city, farmland and so on. The terrain in these areas is known as 'landclass'. FSX uses the file DEFAUL.XML in the Autogen folder to know which objects to drawn in these areas. XML files, like the default.xml can also be opened like the configuration files. Either Notepad or WordPad can be used to open these files. If you double-click on the file, they will probably open in Internet Explorer.

Categories

Moving on to the next folder called "Categories", we see a series of bitmap images (*.BMP files) and an XML file. The bitmap images can be opened by double-clicking them. They will open with your default paint program and you can again open the XML file with WordPad or Notepad. What do these files do? They set up the mission categories (fitting name for the folder!) as seen in FSX by clicking the Mission tab. Let's take a look at the Mission tab in FSX:

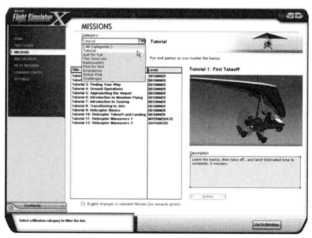

Now let's look at part of the FSCategories.xml file:

```
<Descr>Fun and games as you master the basics.</Descr>
<Title>Tutorial</Title>

<PreviewImage>banner_tutorials.bmp</PreviewImage>
```

The Title section is what appears in the Category drop-down list on the Mission Tab. When the category is selected, the "Descr" or Description appears to the right. The "PreviewImage" line tells FSX which bitmap images from the "Categories" folder to load. This image will be displayed to the right of the list of missions within the selected category.

If you are a mission designer and wanted to create a new category of mission, you would simply need to create a bitmap image that 335 by 75 pixels and save it in the categories folder, open the FSCategories.XML file in Notepad and add the following:

```
<SimMissionUI.ScenarioCategory id="{*NEW GUID*}">
    <Descr>*NEW DESCRIPTION*</Descr>
    <Title>*NEW TITLE*</Title>
    <PreviewImage>*NEW BITMAP IMAGE NAME*.bmp</PreviewImage>
</SimMissionUI.ScenarioCategory>
```

Obviously you will need to substitute your information. Getting your new missions into the new category is another matter which we will cover when we get to the Mission folder.

 A GUID is a 32-digit identification code containing letters and numbers. You will need to generate a new GUID. The best thing to do is check on-line for a GUID Generator program.

Config folder

The Config folder contains *.HTM files that will open in Internet Explorer or your default web browser. These contain information on adjusting the video settings on your computer.

Dialogs folder

The Dialogs folder contains 118 *.spb files which are not editable. Since the name of the folder is Dialogs, we can assume that the content affects the dialog windows visible in FSX. The names of the *.spb files in the folder tend to support this. For example:

dlganalysis.spb – Flight Analysis dialog window

dlgCertPrivate.spb – Certification of Private Pilot

dlgdisplayaircraft.spb – Options | Settings | Display menu Aircraft tab

dlgtimeseason.spb – World | Time and Season menu

Effects folder

The Effects folder holds *.FX files. Effect files contain code that FSX reads to know how to draw effects like flashing lights, smoke, sparks, fireworks and so on. Often effects will use textures (bitmaps images), which are located in the Texture folder under the Effects folder.

*.FX files are text and can be opened with Notepad or WordPad.

Flights folder

The Flights folder in previous versions of Flight Simulator held the users saved flights. When you saved a flight using the Flights | Save Flight menu, the files would be saved in this folder. In FS2004, the saved flights were saved in the My Documents\Flight Simulator Files folder. FSX saves its flight files in the My Documents\Flight Simulator X Files folder. Try as I may, I cannot seem to find the purpose of the files in the Kiosk folder under the Flights folder. The "Other" folder under the Flights folder contains the default flights used by FSX in other countries.

If desired, the *.FLT files are text files and can be opened with Notepad or WordPad. It contains all the information requires by FSX to put the plane back in the exact same position it was in when the flight was saved including the location, altitude, heading, speed, view (panel, virtual cockpit, spot, etc.) and so on. The *.WX files are not text can cannot be edited with a text editor, but they do contain the information used to restore the weather conditions. They are loaded at the same time the flight is loaded.

Fonts folder

The Fonts folder holds the fonts that FSX uses on the different menus and on certain instruments/ gauges.

FSWeb folder

The FSWeb folder contains lot of *.htm files which when double-clicked will open in your default web browser, like Internet Explorer for example. These are the pages that will appear in FSX on the Learning Center option in FSX.

Gauges folder

The Gauges folder contains common gauges or instruments that appear on the aircraft's instrument panel and in the virtual cockpit. Typically only common gauges go in this folder. Most downloaded or 3rd party aircraft will place the gauges in this folder. Other 3rd party aircraft including most of the aircraft that come with FSX will be found in the individual aircraft's \Panel folder. We'll get to that a little later on.

Lessons folder

The Lessons folder holds the saved flight and real-time instruction files used in the Learning Center. If you click the Learning Center option on FSX's opening screen, select a lesson and scroll down to the bottom, there will be a spot to click on that reads "Fly The Lesson Now". Clicking this link will launch the appropriate flight lesson from this folder. Under the Lessons folder are additional folders that hold the different flight lessons for the different levels of instruction including "Priv" for private pilot training, "Inst" for instrument ratings, "Solo" for solo flights and so on.

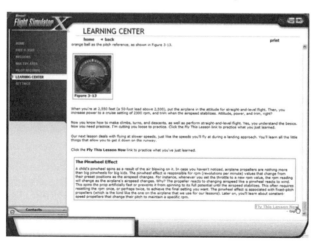

Licenses folder

The Licenses folder contains "*.xrm-ms" files which can be opened in WordPad. We do not recommend editing these files. They appear to be files used to register FSX with Microsoft on-line.

Messages folder

The Messages folder contains folder similar to those found in the Lessons folder. The *.msg files in this folder are text files that can be opened in WordPad. They contain the text messages that will appear when flying the lessons. You can edit these if you want, but then you will have difficulty completing the lessons properly!

Missions folder

The Missions folder contains 9 folder. These folders break down the Missions that come with FSX into different categories like Challenges, Just For Fun, Airline Pilot and so on. Under each of these 9 folders are separate folders for each mission that is in FSX.

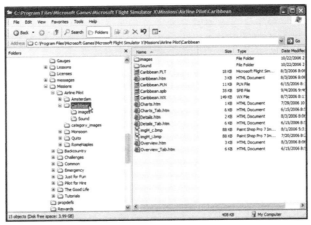

Using the example above, we've browsed into the Airline Pilot folder, then into the Caribbean folder. Here we can see the HTM files that will open in your default web browser like Internet Explorer if double-clicked. These will be visible in FSX when you select a mission in FSX. The .FLT file is the saved flight that FSX loads that will place the aircraft at the airport or in flight depending on the mission and the flights associated weather file (.wx file). The *.SPB file are the mission files that contain the mission programming itself so FSX knows when to play an audio file, which objects to draw, where and how to draw them and so on. The Images folder holds the images that are loaded by the *.HTM files and the Sound folder holds the audio files or *.wav files that are played during the mission. For fun, you can open the Sound folder and double-click on the *.wav files to hear the audio.

Propdefs folder

The Propdefs folder contains a series of *.XML files that are template files. We recommend that you do not modify these files.

The Rewards folder contains *.RWD files which are not editable. These set up the rewards that are given when missions are passed.

Scenery folder

The Scenery folder holds numerous subfolders.

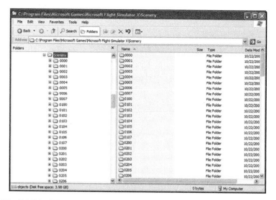

The folders numbered 0000, 0001, 0002 and so on represent a portion of the world. Look at a flat map of the world with the International time/date line on the far left and break it up into 11 even section from left to right and 7 sections from top to bottom. The first 2 digits of the folder number represents the section from left to right across the map. Section 00 would be starting at the International Time/Date line, then section 01 would be to the right of that and so on. The second two digits represent the sections from top to bottom. Section 00 would be at the top of the map, section 01 would be below that and so on.

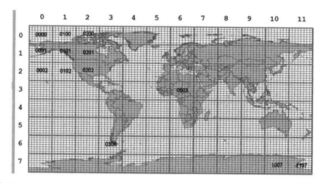

After the numbered folder are other scenery folders used by FSX including scenery for certain areas.

AFRI
  Africa

ASIA
  Asia

AUST
  Australia

BASE
  Global base scenery including seasonal information, time zones and the likes.

CITIES
   Specific scenery areas for major cities, like Las Vegas, OshKosh, Wisconsin, Rio de Janeiro, and St. Maarten

EUREE
   Eastern Europe

EURW
   Western Europe

GLOBAL
   scenery files for the entire globe including Mission Objects, vegetation, vehicles, bridges, airport objects and more.

NAMC
   Central North America

NAME
   Eastern North America

NAMW
   Western North America

OCEN
   Oceania – Australia and New Guinea areas

PROPS
   Unknown for certain.

SAME
   South America

WORLD
   General world scenery

Script folder

The Script folder contains a LIB folder, which has a series of *.ABL file. ABL files are Adventure Basic Language. Some long time users of Flight Simulator may recall the Adventures. There were written in the Adventure Basic Language. These files can be opened with WordPad if needed, but we recommend not editing them.

ShadersHLSL folder

The ShadersHLSL folder contains 5 folders: Common, FixedFunction, General, Misc and Terrain. These folders hold effect files used by FSX to control the water effects and reflections, terrain display effects, shadows and so on.

Sim Objects folder

The Sim Objects folder folds all the dynamic objects used in FSX.

Airplanes
   Contains the aircraft you can fly, as well as the AI aircraft models

Animals
   Includes the wild animals you see in FSX

Boats
>   Includes all the boats seen in FSX

GoundVehicles
>   Holds all of the cars and trucks you see driving on the roads and around airports.

Misc
>   Contains miscellaneous objects typically ones used in mission like the flourbombs, bucket, water drop and so on.

Rotorcraft
>   Contains the helicopters you can fly in FSX.

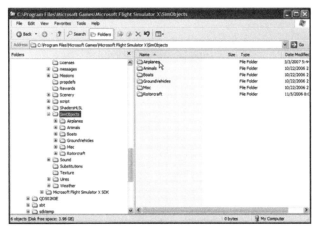

Each of these folders contains a separate folder, one for each object. How does FSX know which of these objects are to be flyable planes and which ones are used as trucks and which ones are animals and so on? It's not so much the name of the folder they are in as it is in the files that are within the folder. Let's take a closer look at the Airplanes folder. In here we see a separate folder for each aircraft.

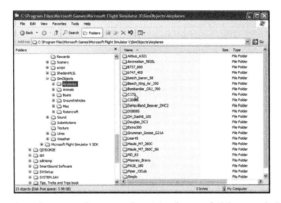

We're going to take some time here and cover the Airplanes folder and the structure of an aircraft folder and we'll be able to see just how FSX knows to load an aircraft. We'll use the C172 folder as an example has a few tricks in it. If we can understand this, we can understand any aircraft folder. Let's go ahead and open the C172 folder.

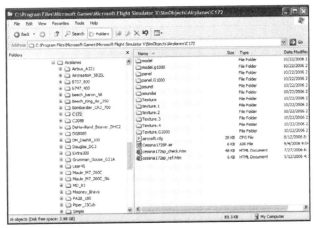

Every aircraft in FSX will have at least 4 folders to it: Model, Panel, Sound and Texture. As you can see here, we have 2 Model folders, 2 Panel folders, 2 sound folders and 6 texture folders! We'll show in a short bit just how FSX knows which folders to use. First, we'll define what each folder contains.

The Model folder holds the models or *.MDL files. The MDL files contain the drawing code FSX uses to display the aircraft. This code is not editable and cannot be opened. The MDL file not only holds the drawing information of the 3D model but it also tells FSX which images, called textures, to project on the model. This definition tells FSX which texture to draw and which part of the texture to draw on each part. Notice there are 2 MDL files in the Model folder:

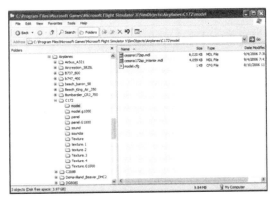

One folder is the main or exterior model and the other is the interior or Virtual Cockpit. So how does FSX know which model to draw and when? This is where the Model.cfg file comes in. This is a simple file that contains the following information.

```
[models]
normal=Cessna172SP
interior=cessna172sp_interior
```

The Normal line defines the external model and the interior line defines the model to draw in the virtual cockpit.

The Panel folder is covered in another chapter in this book. It contains the panel.cfg file which tells FSX which background images to draw for the instrument panel and which gauges to draw on that image. It also defines which gauges to draw in the virtual cockpit and where to place them. Many aircraft will also include the gauge file, or *.cab file in the panel folder as well.

The Sound folder contains the sounds that FSX will play when flying the plane. There are different sounds heard when the view is in the cockpit and when the view is outside the aircraft. How does FSX know which sound to play when? Again we turn to the configuration sound, in this case the Sound.cfg file.

The Texture folder holds the images that are applied to the Model (*.mdl file). Each texture folder has the same texture file names. Again you ask, how does FSX know which texture folder to load? The answer lies in the Aircraft.cfg file found in the aircraft's main folder. We'll get to this file in a second. Let's take a quick peak in the texture folder...

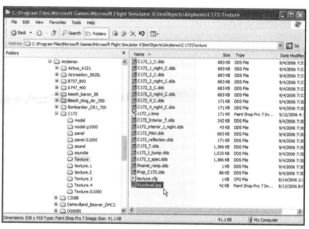

Here we see a collection of *.DDS files as well as a configuration file and a file called Thumbnail.jpg. The thumbnail.jpg is a standard JPG image that can be opened. This file loaded by FSX on the aircraft selection window. This is the preview of the aircraft.

NOTE

DDS files are specially compressed images that cannot be opened with a standard painting program. You will need a special program to convert these images to an editable format like "DDS Converter 2" or "DXTBMP", both are freeware program and can be found on-line with a simple search. Another program that can handle these files is the FS Repaint Program from Abacus Software found at www.abacuspub.com. FS Repaint actually loads the MDL files of the aircraft and reads the texture application and displays the aircraft model with textures as they appear in FSX. This allows you to create new liveries for your aircraft by replacing existing ones, or create new texture folders. It also includes a tool that lets you repaint the textures and see what it will look like without saving and loading FSX after each texture change. The textures can be repainted either in FS Repaint with a built-in editor or by sending them to another paint program like Paint Shop Pro or PhotoShop.

We've talked a lot about the aircraft.cfg file so lets go ahead and go back to the C172 folder and talk about the files in there, including the aircraft.cfg file. The files in the main C172 folder are:

```
Aircraft.cfg
Cessna172SP.air
Cessna172sp_check.htm
Cessna172sp_ref.htm
```

We'll start at the bottom of the list and work our way up. The last two files, the cessna172sp_check and cessna172sp_ref files are *.HTM files and can be opened by double-clicking them.

The "_check" in the file name lets us know that file is the checklist. This is essentially a series of instructions used by the pilot to make sure the aircraft is operating normally and provides information specific to the aircraft that the pilot uses to fly the aircraft.

The "_ref" in the file name lets us know that the file contains reference information such as the maneuvering speeds, cruise speeds, never exceed speed, stalling speed and so on otherwise know as "vspeeds".

Both the 'check' and 'ref' files are available on the kneeboard when the aircraft is loaded in FSX.

The Cessna172sp.air file is a file used by FSX to lay a foundation of how the aircraft will perform or handle in FSX. The specifics of how the aircraft performs are set in the aircraft.cft file.

Ok are you ready? We're going to get into the aircraft.cfg file. This file is one of the most commonly edited file in FSX.

Let's go ahead and open up the aircraft.cfg file with Notepad. The different parts of the file, or sections are defined within brackets [ ]. The first sections of the file define the different liveries.

```
[fltsim.0]
title=Cessna Skyhawk 172SP Paint1
sim=Cessna172SP
model=
panel=
sound=
texture=1
kb_checklists=Cessna172SP_check
kb_reference=Cessna172SP_ref
atc_id=G-BAFM
ui_manufacturer="Cessna"
ui_type="C172SP Skyhawk"
ui_variation=" Blue, Gold"
ui_typerole="Single Engine Prop"
ui_createdby="Microsoft Corporation"
```

description="A stable and trustworthy plane, most pilots have logged at least a few hours in a Cessna 172, since it's the most widely available aircraft in the rental fleet, and is used by most flight schools. Since the first prototype was completed in 1955, more than 35,000 C172s have been produced, making it the world's most popular single-engine plane. One of Cessna's first tricycle-gear airplanes, the 172 quickly became the favorite of a growing class of business pilots. Its reliability and easy handling (along with thoughtful engineering and structural updates) have ensured its continued popularity for decades."

The start of the file, "[fltsim.0] tells FSX that this is the first livery. All liveries should be defined in numerical order starting with 0, then 1 and so on. From here, we'll cover the section line by line:

"Title="

The Title line has to be unique for each version/livery of the aircraft. Avoid changing the title line of existing aircraft in FSX. This title is used in the *.FLT files, the saved flights in FSX. This is how FSX knows exactly which version of which aircraft to load when starting a flight.

"Sim="

The Sim line defines the air file that FSX will use. Notice that the text after the equal sign (=) is the same as the */air file name in the C172 folder. The aircraft will not appear in FSX is the sim= line is not the same as the air file name.

"Model="

This line tells FSX which Model folder to load the aircraft's model file (*.mdl file). If you recall there were 2 Model files – once called "Model" and one called "Model.G1000". FSX knows to look in the folder called Model for the aircraft's *.MDL file. Scroll down the aircraft.cfg file and tale a look at the [fltsim.4] section. In this section, the "model=" line reads:

model=G1000

After reading this file, FSX knows to look in the Model folder, then it looks for a folder called "model.G1000". Basically the text after the period on the model folder name is what would go in the "model=" line.

"Panel="

This is very similar to the model= line. Again take a look at the [fltsim.4] section of the file and we'll see this line:

panel=G1000

Just like with the "Model=" line, the text after the period, in this case 'G1000", gets entered after the equal sign to tell FSX to load the panel from the "Panel.G1000" folder.

"Sound="

Just like the Panel and Model lines, the Sound is the same way. You can set FSX to use different sounds for different versions of an aircraft.

"Texture="

And again, the Texture folder tells FSX which texture folder to load the textures from.

Why would you need the ability to use different folders? Let's say for example that you have two versions of an aircraft – a regular and turbo charged version. These would have different models for the different engines and obviously different sounds as well as different paint schemes all for basically the same model of aircraft. The different planes would probably have different panels as well so you can set both planes up in the same folder.

"Kb_checklists="

In this line, the "KB" stands for Kneeboard, then the text after the equal sign tells FSX the name of the file to load on the Checklist tab on the kneeboard. In the C172, the checklist is a *.htm file, but can also be a text file with a *.txt extension.

"Kb_reference="

Similar to the "kb_checklists" line, the "kb_reference" line tells FSX which file to load on the Reference tab on the Kneeboard. In the C172 folder, this file is also a *.htm file, but can also be a text file.

"atc_id="

This line sets the Air Traffic Control Identification. This the tail number of the aircraft as defined on the textures in most cases, but the planes that come with FSX and some 3rd party planes have the ability to have changeable tail numbers.

"ui_manufacturer="

This line sets the User Interface Manufacturer. When viewing the aircraft available in FSX, you'll notice they are broken down by manufacturer, publisher and the style of aircraft. The text after the equal sign here tells FSX which category to display the aircraft. If the manufacturer set here does not already exist, FSX will create it.

"ui_type="

This line sets the User Interface Type. The text after the equal sign is what will appear under the thumbnail preview of the aircraft when the manufacturer is selected along with the variation.

"ui_variation="

This line sets the User Interface Variation. The text after the equal sign is what will appear under the thumbnail preview of the aircraft when the manufacturer is selected along with the variations.

"ui_typerole="

This line sets the User Type/Role. This is another category similar to the Manufacturer. The text entered here will appear under the Aircraft Type drop-down list. The text here describes the type of aircraft, such as, Single Engine Prop, Commercial Airliner, Glider, Rotorcraft, Twin Engine Turboprop and so on.

"ui_createdby="

This line sets the User Interface Publisher. This is another category similar to the Manufacturer and Type/Role. The text entered here will appear under the Publisher drop-down list. Many 3rd party developers will enter their company name in here allowing you to sort the list of planes showing only those made by that publisher.

The quotation marks are optional in all of these sections.

"ui_description="

This line is the User Interface Description. The text after the equal sign is a basic description of the aircraft which will appear when the aircraft is selected on the Details button when selected aircraft.

If we scroll down through the file we see quite a few more sections. We'll cover a few more them.

[General]

The General section sets up some of the Air Traffic Control information including the ATC_TYPE and ATC_MODEL. These will be used by ATC when contacting the plane along with the ATC_ID in the [FLYSIM.#] section.

The EDITABLE line is a leftover from FS2000. Flight Simulator 2000 included an editor program that would provide a user interface to edit the aircraft.cfg file. A setting of 1 (editable=1) meant that you could edit the parameters in the aircraft.cfg file in the editor and a setting of 0 (editable=0) meant that you could not edit it in the editor.

The PERFORMANCE line is simply text that typically contains information about the plane that appears below the description on the Details in Aircraft.. Any text can be added here.

The CATEGORY line sets, what else, the category of the object. I say object because these are used not only in the Airplanes configuration file but in all folders under SimObjects. Some common categories include Airplane, Helicopter, GroundVehicle, ControlTower, SimpleObject and so on.

The CAMERADEFINITION.# sections define the camera positions available to the aircraft. There are typically 2 different types of Camera Definitions. One set has a single number in the section name and the other has three digits. The sections with one digit are typically views of the aircraft from the outside like views of the Right Wing, Left Wing, Tail and so on. The three digit sections hold views of the interior or virtual cockpit of the aircraft including The Right Seat, Radio Stack and Light Switches in the case of the C172.

The TITLE line under the camera definition section is simply a title that appears in the top right corner of FSX when pressing the S and/or A keys on the keyboard.

The GUID line is again a 32-digit code that is unique to each camera position.

The ORIGIN defines the object or point on which the camera is oriented and can be set to the following:

Cockpit
    The camera is locked at a fixed position in the 2D cockpit.

Virtual Cockpit
> Camera is set at the eye point, which is farther down in the aircraft.cfg file, which we will get to later.

Center
> This is used in an aircraft's external view or spot plane that has the camera point at the center of the aircraft's visual model.

Pilot
> This is used in an aircraft's external view or spot view that has the camera positioned at the pilot inside the aircraft's visual model.

Tower
> This is an external camera located at a control tower that is nearby the aircraft's current location.

Fixed
> This is an external camera set in a fixed position

The line SNAPPBHADJUST stands for "Snap-Pitch-Bank-Heading-Adjust". This setting can equal one of the following:

NONE
> The Camera position will be fixed and will not move when the joysticks 'hat' switch is moved, or the numbers on the keyboard's keypad is pressed.

ORDINAL
> The camera will move in 90-degree increments instead of a panning effect.

SWIVEL
> The camera will pan around in a circle in any direction.

ORTHOGONAL
> This is used for top-down views and will essentially rotate the camera clockwise or counter-clockwise.

The line SNAPPBHRETURN stands for Snap-Pitch-Bank-Heading-Return. This is either True or False. If set to True, the camera will snap back to the default position (set below). The hat-switch on the joystick will adjust the camera's position, but when the hat-switch is released, the camera will snap back. If set to False, the camera will stay in the position it is when the hat-switch is released.

The PANPHBADJUST is the same as the SnapPbhAdjust and the PANPHBRETRUN is the same as the SnapPhbReturn.

The Track line is only used on an external camera position and sets whether the camera will move along with an object (track it) or not.. It can be set to one of the following:

NONE
> This setting has no tracking. Movement is left up to the user.

FLYBY
> Moves the camera along with the aircraft using the positions using positions set later on in the section. After the flyby, FSX will recalculate the cameras position.

TRACK
> This setting has the camera track the object/aircraft and maintains its position, like in the tower view. The camera is set on the aircraft and turns keeping the aircraft in the center of the screen.

TRACKBANK
    Same as the Track

FLATCHASE
    The Camera will move with the object and maintain a fixed distance.

FLATCHASELOCKED
    The Camera will move with the object and maintain a fixed distance and the camera movements will be rigid.

The SHOWAXIS line sets whether the axis indicator will be visible in that view or not.

The ALLOWZOOM line is either True or False and sets whether the plus (+) and minus (-) keys will zoom the camera in and out when this view is active.

INITIALZOOM sets the default zoom setting. A setting of 1.0 is normal zoom. A higher number will have the view zoomed in when the view is active and when the setting is lower than 1, like 0.5, the view will be zoomed out.

The SHOWWEATHER sets if the weather visualizations will be visible in this view.

The INITIALXYZ has 3 numbers that set the X, Y and Z coordinates. To explain how the X, Y and Z coordinates are set, we'll sit in the cockpit looking straight ahead. The X coordinate would be left to right. The Y coordinate would be up and down and the Z coordinate would be forward and backward. The trick is determining where the origin or 0,0,0 point is!

These coordinates set the actual location of the camera in relation to the origin (0,0,0) position on the plane. The first number sets the X coordinate, the second number sets the Y coordinate and the last number sets the Z coordinate.

The line INITIALPBH sets the initial pitch, bank and heading of the view. This can also be difficult to determine how to set these. The numbers for the pitch ranger from –90 to 90 and the bank and heading range from –180 to 180. The first number sets the pitch, the second number sets the bank and the last number sets the heading.

The XYZADJUST line sets whether the camera will respond to position changes like with the joystick's hat-switch.

The CATEGORY line tells FSX in which view this camera position will come into play. When cycling to the virtual cockpit in FSX using the S key, the main camera position will appear first. This is set in a different section of the aircraft.cfg file, which we'll come to shortly. When pressing the A key in the virtual cockpit, you will begin to cycle through the views who's origin is set to Virtual Cockpit.

MOMENTUMEFECT sets whether or not the cameras will move with the momentum of the aircraft. For example, if you are in the cockpit sitting on the runway and you hit the gas you will be pulled back into the seat. Setting the MomentumEffect to True will move the camera back when you accelerate or pull the camera to the left or right when turning, or move it up and down when climbing or diving. The effect is not much, but enough to notice.

The CLIPMODE entry is a bit extensive to cover here, or in the SDKs. According to the SDKs:

"A discussion of clip plane management is beyond the scope of this document. However, the concept is relevant to the camera system because it determines whether the camera favors near or far objects in the view"

Some of the sections and parameters in the aircraft.cfg file are pretty obvious. We're not going to cover every entry as that would take a book in itself, but we'll cover some of the entries here:

[WEIGHT_AND_BALANCE]

Sets the Max Gross Weight and Empty Weight in pounds and the station loads. The station loads can be things like passengers, pilots, baggage and so on. The STATION_LOAD.# lines define the weight in pounds and the position of the different loads. The position is again in X, Y and Z coordinates based on the center of the model.

The STATION_NAME.# lines define the name of the station loads. These names will appear in FSX under the Aircraft | Fuel and Payload menu. In this menu you can adjust the weights of the station loads. By default the Cessna 172 here has no weight set for the 2 rear passengers and the baggage.

[FLIGHT_TUNING]

This section of the aircraft.cfg file allows you to adjust some of the most noticeable aspects of how the aircraft will perform in FSX. By default all settings are set to 1.0. In creasing the number will increase the effect and decreasng the number will decrease the effect.

cruise_lift_scalar – the amount of lift on the aircraft when cruising.

parasite_drag_scalar – the amount of drag on the aircraft.

elevator_effectiveness – the effect of the elevator. If you want the aircraft to respond quicker and when you pull back or push forward on the stick, increase this setting.

aileron_effectiveness – Similar to the elevator, increasing the Aileron_effectivenenss will make the plane bank faster.

rudder_effectiveness – Increasing this setting makes the rudder effect on the aircraft much more pronounced. With the Auto-Rudder turned off in FSX's Realism Settings can make the aircraft do a power slide in the air if set higher enough!

In the Cessna 172, we can see that some of the parameters are defined for us. Notice that they are preceded by two forward slashes. As noted in the panel.cfg file, the slashes tell FSX to ignore text to follow until the carriage return (the next line starts).

Most of the sections in here are noted for us so we won't cover them. I'll take this time to note that changing these settings will affect the way the aircraft performs – and not always in the exact way you expect it to. For example, increasing the POWER_SCALAR and adding 2 more pistons to the engine parameters won't necessarily make the aircraft fly faster. Sections and parameters in this file are linked with each other and changing one value may throw off another setting. This is why editing flight dynamics is so difficult and very few simmers are able to do it effectively. Let's go through a few more sections...

[CONTACT_POINTS]

This section controls how the aircraft will sit on the ground and how it will handle on the ground. This section proceeded by this information:

```
//0   Class
//1   Longitudinal Position        (feet)
//2   Lateral Position             (feet)
//3   Vertical Position            (feet)
//4   Impact Damage Threshold      (Feet Per Minute)
//5   Brake Map                    (0=None, 1=Left, 2=Right)
//6   Wheel Radius                 (feet)
//7   Steer Angle                            (degrees)
//8   Static Compression           (feet)   (0 if rigid)
//9   Max/Static Compression Ratio
//10  Damping Ratio                (0=Undamped, 1=Critically Damped)
//11  Extension Time               (seconds)
//12  Retraction Time              (seconds)
//13  Sound Type
```

It's great to have this information handy right here, but it's incomplete. It does not define what a 'class' is! A class in this case is the type of contact point – tire, float, scrape, ski and so on. Here are the basic numbers supported by FSX:

0 = None

1 = Wheel

2 = Scrape

3 = Skid

4 = Float

5 = Water Rudder

A Scrape point is used on the wing tips to detect when (if) the wings hit the ground and on the nose and tail of the plane.

[VIEWS]

The EYEPOINT line under the views section is the default virtual cockpit position. When you enter the virtual cockpit, this is where the camera will be positioned looking straight ahead.. These numbers are again X, Y and Z coordinates.

[RADIOS]

The Radios section defines how the radios operate on the aircraft. Isn't this defined by the radio gauge you ask? Well, it used to be. Now there are different types of radios, some that you simply tune the frequency and others where you tune the standby frequency, then swap the active and standby frequency. Also, some aircraft may not have a COMM2 radio or a ADF radio and these can be disabled here by changing the first one (1) after the equal sign to a 0. If the radio simply has you change the frequency, then you would set a 0 for the second number. If you change the standby, then swap it with the active, you set the second number to one (1).

[LIGHTS]

The Lights section defines what type of lights are on the aircraft, where they are positioned and the effect file used to draw the light. The types of lights are defined in the file:

1=beacon

2=strobe

3=navigation

4=cockpit

The first number here defines how the light is treated by FSX. For example if you click the Strobe switch on the instrument panel, each light entry here with number 2 will toggle on and off with the switch. The following numbers are the X, Y and Z coordinates on the aircraft where the light is positioned. The last entry is the name of the effect file as found in the Effects folder under FSX, without the extension of ".fx".

[EFFECTS]

This section defines which effect file from the Effects folder under FSX will be shown.

WAKE
  This sets the effect file that will be displayed when you are taxiing on the water or are in the water.

WATER
  This is the effect that will play when the aircraft is in the water. In this case a splash effect of water spraying around the plane.

DIRT
  The effect played when taxiing in the dirt.

CONCRETE
  The effect that is applied when contacting the concrete surfaces in FSX.

TOUCHDOWN
  This is typically the black runways marks left when landing on a runway.

[REFERENCE SPEEDS]

This section lets you set the true airspeed in knots when the stall and over-speed warnings will appear.

OK enough about the aircraft.cfg file. Even though you probably won't have enough information from this book on how to edit the plane to your liking 100%, you might have enough information to no longer fear the file and to experiment with the settings. A word of caution though, please make a back-up of the aircraft.cfg file. Open the aircraft.cfg file, choose File | Save As and enter a new name, make the changes, then use the Save As again and save over the aircraft.cfg file. This way you will have an original back up of the aircraft.cfg file.

This also brings us to the end of the Airplanes folder. The next folders, Animals, Boats, GroundVehicles and Misc are similar to the "Airplanes" folder, but they contain only a file called SIM.CFG instead of an aircraft.cfg file and there is also no *.air file. The folders within these next four folders typically contain a Model, Texture and occasionally a Sound folder.

The Rotorcraft folder is identical to the Airplanes folder except that it holds the helicopters in FSX. You can also place helicopters in the Airplanes folder if desired. The files and folder are identical, except you may find entries in the helicopter/rotorcraft aircraft.cfg file that are not found in the Airplanes aircraft.cfg file.

Sound folder

Moving on down we find the Sound folder. This folder contains *.wav files. These wav files are sounds that are told to play from effect files and other environment-type sounds like wind, thunder, rain and the ground proximity warning files. Feel free to double-click on a few files and have a listen!

Substitutions folder

The Substitutions folder is empty in most cases. This may be a temporary or back-up storage folder for FSX.

Texture folder

The Texture folder holds the textures or images for the scenery files used in FSX. New scenery that is added to FSX can have the texture files placed in this main Texture folder, or in the Texture folder that sits in the same folder as Scenery folder. For example, you can put the scenery *.BGL files in the Addon Scenery\Scenery folder, then you can place the texture files in either the Addon Scenery\Texture folder or here in the main Texture folder. It is recommend you NOT place them in the main texture folder as you will loose track of them in case you want to remove them later.

*.BMPp files
    Bitmap images, usually compressed using a DirectX compatible format for faster loading and processing by the video card called DXT compression. These file can be opened with a freeware program called DXTBMP.

*.DDS file
    These are also DirectX files but in a newer format. These can be opened with freeware programs like DXTBMP and DDSConverter2 as well as some specific pay-ware conversion programs. When these textures are opened, they will be upside-down or inverted.

*.R8 files
    These are also texture files used by earlier version of FS like FS98 and earlier. These images are very unique in that they are 256 color images, but in the earlier versions of FS where they were used, the Flight Simulator had a certain number of colors reserved in each texture's palette so there are less than 256 colors used on any *.r8 texture file. You would have to find an older

program that could open or convert these images. Obviously FSX still recognizes these files though.

Other files in this folder like*.0 and *.1 are the same format as the *.r8 textures.

Uires folder

The Uires folder holds images used by FSX. When you open FSX and see the opening screen, all of the elements on those screens are in the folder as separate images. Feel free to double-click a few bitmap images and have a peek. I recommend NOT saving or altering them.

Weather folder

The Weather folder holds what else but the weather files used by FSX. The Clouds subfolder contains about 350 different cloud configuration files. The Themes subfolder holds the default weather settings that the user can select from the World | Weather menu:

Bldstorm
    Building Storms

Cfronts
    Cold Fronts

Fair
    Fair Weather

Foggedin
    Fogged In

Grayrain
    Gray and Rainy

Stormy
    Stormy Weather

Tstorm
    Thunderstorms

Whiteout
    White Out

Wwonder
    Winter Wonderland

This completes the discussion on the files and folders that are installed with FSX in the main FSX folder. Hopefully with this new information, you will have increased your understanding of how FSX works and what you can do to change the FSX environment a bit more to your liking.

Managing New Scenery In FSX

Besides adding new aircraft to Flight Simulator X, adding new scenery is the most frequent activity for users. You have more than one way to add new scenery files to FSX and how you add the scenery depends on the type of scenery that you're adding. The largest number of new scenery files by far are "enhanced" airports. While there are more than 24,000 airports in FSX, only a few are fully detailed. This leaves a very large number of airports that scenery designers are able to improve.

We'll leave the subject of scenery design to future articles and limit our discussion here to configuring Flight Simulator X to use new scenery. When you initially install FSX on your computer, a folder called Addon Scenery is created within the main FSX folder.

The quickest way to add new scenery is to copy the new scenery files to the FSX Addon Scenery\Scenery folder.

How does FSX know how to use the scenery in this folder? The answer is the Scenery Library Manager.

 NOTE All scenery files used by FSX have the file extension *.BGL* and are commonly referred to as *.BGL files. These *.BGL files MUST be in a folder called Scenery. So that FSX knows to how to handle the scenery files, the **parent folder** must identified to the Scenery Library Manager. For example, suppose that you add new scenery files to the Addon Scenery\Scenery folder. In this case, the parent folder Addon Scenery must be made known to the Scenery Library Manager.

The Scenery Library Manager

To examine the contents of the Scenery Library, open FSX and click the Settings option, then click the [Scenery Library] button.

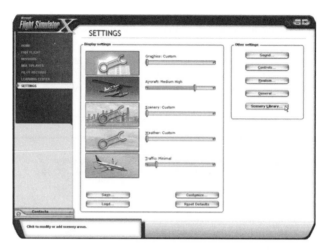

Here is a list of scenery areas that FSX and the order in which they are to be loaded. The order in which they are loaded is called the *priority*. FSX begins to load scenery from the bottom of the list and working towards the top of the list. At the bottom of the list is the world base-scenery followed by more detailed areas. The higher the priority, the earlier FSX loads it. A scenery area with a lower priority is loaded after a scenery area with a higher priority. This is counter-intuitive from the usual sense of the word priority. A lower priority scenery area appears on top of the other higher priority scenery.

The Active column tells FSX whether to load the scenery. When making changes to scenery areas, as discussed in the chapter on using the Object Placement tool (see the "Man On A Mission" chapter for more information). Making an area inactive will keep it in the Scenery Library but tells FSX not to load scenery in that area.

Notice that the Addon Scenery folder is at the top of the list. Click Addon Scenery in the list and click the Edit Area button to get a closer look at what information FSX is using on a scenery area.

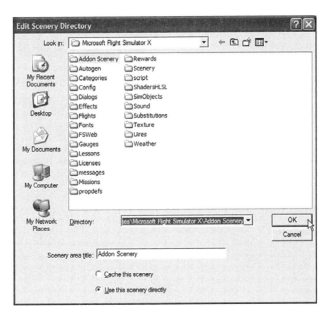

We can see here that it's not very much information. The listing shows is the main folder, a title that appears in the Scenery Library list and options to cache the scenery or use it directly.

OK, now we know that FSX has a list of scenery and this list tells FSX which scenery files to load and in which order to load them, but where does it save this information? The answer is the Scenery.CFG file. Let's look at the contents of the scenery.cfg file to better understand how it works. We may even learn a few things that you can do in the scenery.cfg file that you can't do in the Scenery Library from inside FSX.

The Scenery.cfg file

From the Desktop, double-click the My Computer icon. Now double-click the C: drive. This will show you a list of folders on your hard drive. The folder we are looking for is called "Documents and Settings". Locate and double-click this folder.

In here, double-click the All Users folder. From here, we need to open the Application Data folder.

 If you do not see the Application Data folder, it may be hidden by Windows. Click the Tools menu and choose Folder Options. In here, click the View tab at the top. Select the "Show Hidden Files and Folders" option. You might also want to turn OFF the "Hide File Extensions for Known File Types". This will show you the file extensions so you can be sure you are working with the correct file.

In the Application Data folder, open the Microsoft folder and lastly the FSX folder. To quickly recap, we need to double-click on the following:

```
My Computer
C:
Documents and Settings
All Users
Application Data
Microsoft
FSX
```

In the FSX folder, we see a few folders including Facilities, SceneryCache and SceneryIndexes. These folders are not related to what we are doing, but to cover the bases, they hold the cached scenery information and a list or index of the scenery files being loaded. The Facilities folder holds DAT or data files that appear to contain a list of all the navigation information like airport names and locations, IDs, Intersections, NDBs and VORs.

All we're concerned with in here is the Scenery.cfg file. This is a text file which can be opened with Notepad or WordPad. Let's go a head and open it. Here's what the start of the file looks like.

```
[General]
Title=FS9 World Scenery
Description=FS9 Scenery Data
Clean_on_Exit=TRUE
[Area.001]
Title=Default Terrain
Texture_ID=1
Local=Scenery\World
Layer=1
Active=TRUE
Required=TRUE
Remote=
[Area.002]
Title=Default Scenery
Local=Scenery\BASE
Layer=2
Active=TRUE
Required=TRUE
Remote=
```

The GENERAL section defines some basic properties about the file including the title, which simply says "FS9 World Scenery". This is obviously a left over from the older version of Flight Simulator, otherwise known as FS2004 or FS9, a brief description and whether or not FSX will clean the scenery cache on exit or not. When set to True, FSX will have to reload all the scenery every time it's opened. When set to False, FSX may load a bit faster as it will keep the scenery cached making it faster to load.

Following the GENERAL section are the individual sections for each scenery area FSX will load. Lets look at the first section to understand how it works.

```
[Area.001]
Title=Default Terrain
Texture_ID=1
Local=Scenery\World
Layer=1
Active=TRUE
```

```
Required=TRUE
Remote=
```

The TITLE line is the text that appears in the Scenery Library. This is also what is entered when adding a scenery area in the Title area.

The TEXTURE_ID line can be set to either 1 or 0. These are special settings that should not be changed. According to the FSX SDKs, "Texture_ID=0 sets the global default texture directory to be searched if the requested texture cannot be found from the given path. This is also the location of global textures that have no other directory to reside in. Texture_ID=1 is the default terrain texture directory." The only time this is used in the first section.

The LOCAL line sets the path to the scenery folder that holds the BGL files. FSX already knows where it's main folder is so all this path has to do it tell FSX where to go from the main folder. In this case it goes into the Scenery folder, then into the World folder. As noted before, FSX knows that all BGL files must be in a folder called scenery so we can expect to find the *.BGL files loaded by this are in FS's main folder under the folders: Scenery\World\Scenery.

The LAYER line sets the priority. As you can see this is set to layer one, which means FSX will load it first. The following layers will then be loaded over top of this area. It's a little confusing because the layer is set to one, but the priority in the Scenery Library will have a much higher priority number.

The ACTIVE line simply tells FSX if it is to load the scenery in this section or not. This can be changed in the Scenery Library by checking or unchecking the Active box.

The REQUIRED line sets if the area is required for FSX to operate or not. Most areas are not required and are set to False. The first section is set to True because without the foundation of the world, FSX cannot load the scenery on top.

The REMOTE line is not used in any examples in the default scenery.cfg file. According to the SDKs: "When using a remote path the scenery is copied from the path shown to a uniquely named folder created by Flight Simulator. The scenery files are then read from the new folder, a sub-folder of the Cache folder. Remote paths are very useful when reading scenery files from a location that cannot be accessed as quickly as the local hard drive, for example, from CD drives or a remote server. The format of the path can be one of the three defined for local paths. Only one of REMOTE or LOCAL should be used."

Excluding Scenery

One feature that FSX supports in the scenery.cfg that is not used in the default set up is an Exclude Area definition. Basically what the Exclude Area does is it tells FSX to exclude or not to draw certain thing. The area is defined by adding a line to a section in the Scenery.cfg file, then defining Latitude and Longitude coordinates. We'll give a quick example here...

An excludes are is defined in the scenery.cfg file be entering the following information:

```
Exclude=<Northern Latitude>,<Western Longitude>,<Southern Latitude>,<Eastern
Longitude>,<type>
```

The locations can be determined by positioning your aircraft in the top left corner of the airport and gathering the coordinates and then gathering the coordinates from the bottom right corner of the airport:

To position the aircraft in these locations, use Slew mode to move the aircraft. When in Slew mode, the coordinates will appear in the top left corner of the FSX screen. Here are the coordinates we got from the top left position:

```
LAT: N47º 28.12' LON: W122º 19.44
```

We'll round these off a little and use:

```
N47 28 and W122 19
```

These coordinates will work as the first two positions in the exclude area we're adding. For the bottom right coordinates we've gathered:

```
LAT: N47º 25.65' LON: W122º 17.23
```

We'll round these off a bit also and use:

```
N47 25 and W122 17
```

These will round off the third and fourth parts of the exclude area. The maximum size of an exclude area is 90 degrees of longitude and 45 degrees of latitude.

The last part of the exclude area tells FSX exactly what you are excluding. This can be Objects, VORs, NDBs or all of the above. This is entered as text as shown:

```
objects
vors
ndbs
all
```

So if we put it all together, we get this:

```
Exclude=N47 28,W122 19,N47 25,W122 17,all
```

This text can be added into the Scenery.cfg file into an existing section, preferably the Addon Scenery section. Here's what we come up after modifying that section:

```
[Area.124]
Title=Addon Scenery
Local=Addon Scenery
Remote=
Active=TRUE
Required=FALSE
Layer=124
Exclude=N47 28,W122 19,N47 25,W122 17,all
```

Note that the numbers for the [area.###] title and the layer=### may be different in your scenery.cfg file. This is normal.

Once the change is made, you can save and close the Scenery.cfg file and go back to FSX. When you open FSX, it will build a new database for the scenery.

If you already has FSX running when you modified the file, you can simply open the Scenery Library and click the OK button. This will force FSX to reload the scenery.cfg file and build a new database. You can either press the Q key on your keyboard and End Flight and then enter the Settings and choose Scenery Library, or press the Alt key and open the **World | Scenery Library** menu.

Let's go back to KSEA airport (yes it'll still show up in the list) and see what it looks like:

Surprise, there's no airport! That's right – we excluded all VORs, NDBs and 3D objects, which include airports, from FSX. This is like a clean slate! You can now use scenery design tools like FS Design Studio v3.5 or higher or the Object Placement Tool from the FSX SDKs and Scenery Shortcut to renovate this area as you see fit.

We've included a program called "Scenery Shortcut" on the the Companion CD-ROM for you to learn more about FSX scenery. For more information on this program and the Companion CD-ROM, see page viii (in the Contents section).

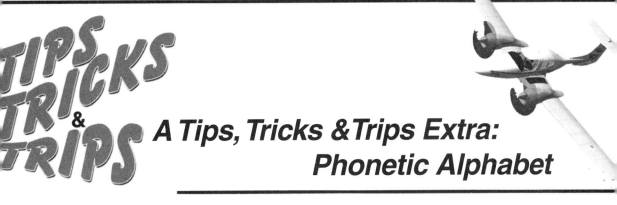

Pilots and ATC use a phonetic alphabet known as the International Radiotelephony Spelling Alphabet to spell letters instead of saying the letters themselves. Although this may seem unnecessary, pilots and ATC use this alphabet to avoid confusion. For example, some letters may sound the same over radio, such as "b" and "e." The phonetic alphabet is used in radio communications around the world by maritime units, aircraft, amateur radio operators and the military.

Although we often call it a "phonetic alphabet," that is a bit of a misnomer because it has no connection to phonetic transcription systems like the International Phonetic Alphabet. Instead, the International Radiotelephony Spelling Alphabet assigns code words to the letters of the English alphabet acrophonically so that critical combinations of letters (and numbers) can be pronounced and understood by those who transmit and receive voice messages by radio or telephone regardless of their native language, especially when the safety of navigation or persons is essential.

Besides pilots (and the FAA), the alphabet is also used by the International Telecommunication Union (ITU), the International Maritime Organization (IMO), the North Atlantic Treaty Organization (NATO) and the American National Standards Institute (ANSI).

The Alphabet

You're probably aware of many of the words already. The words are English because communication between pilots and control towers must be in English whenever two nations are involved, regardless of their native languages. Keep in mind this only refers to international flights so another phonetic alphabet may be used on a domestic flight inside say Italy.

Although the words are pronounced the same, you may see the words spelled slightly different, depending on your location. For example, you may see the non-English spellings Alfa (instead of Alpha) and Juliett (instead of Juliette) used because Alfa is spelled with an *f* in most European languages. Furthermore, the English and French spelling "alpha" would not be properly pronounced by speakers of other languages who may pronounce the "ph" as if it were a "p". Juliett is spelled with

247

a "tt" for native French speakers who treat a single "t" as silent; the English word Juliet is Juliette in French, but the ICAO did not adopt the final "e" because it might be misunderstood by native Spanish speakers as the final syllable "teh".

A	Alpha	(AL fah)
B	Bravo	(BRAH VOH)
C	Charlie	(CHAR lee)
D	Delta	(DELL tah)
E	Echo	(ECK oh)
F	Foxtrot	(FOKS trot)
G	Golf	(GOLF)
H	Hotel	(hoh TELL)
I	India	(IN dee ah)
J	Juliett	(JEW lee ETT)
K	Kilo	(KEY loh)
L	Lima	(LEE mah)
M	Mike	(MIKE)
N	November	(no VEM ber)
O	Oscar	(OSS cah)
P	Papa	(pah PAH)
Q	Quebec	(keh BECK)
R	Romeo	(ROW me oh)
S	Sierra	(see AIR rah)
T	Tango	(TANG go)
U	Uniform	(YOU nee form)
V	Victor	(VIK tah)
W	Whiskey	(WISS key)
X	X Ray	(ECKS RAY)
Y	Yankee	(YANG key)
Z	Zulu	(ZOO loo)

Deviations/changes

Although the words above are standard, some regional deviations do occur. You aren't likely to encounter these changes in FSX but they're still interesting to know. For example, using "Delta" for the letter D is avoided at several United States airports because it's also the callsign for Delta Air

Lines. In these cases, "Dixie" is usually used instead of Delta. Also, "Foxtrot" is commonly shortened to "Fox" at some airports in the US and Canada.

The word "Baker" is often used in Japan for "Bravo" because that word is difficult for Japanese to pronounce. The word "Hawk" is sometimes used in the Philippines instead of "Hotel."

The word "Lima" is seldom used in Indonesia because it means number five (5); instead, "London" is most often used for letter L.

Usage

Pilots use the alphabet to spell out parts of a message or <u>call sign</u> that are critical or otherwise hard to recognize during voice communication. For example, the message

```
proceed to map grid DH98
```

could be transmitted as

```
proceed to map grid Delta-Hotel-Niner-Eight
```

Also, several letter codes and abbreviations using the phonetic alphabet have become popular with pilots and military personnel, such as:

Bravo Zulu
> Referring to the letter code BZ, which means "well done"

Checkpoint Charlie
> Refers to the famous gate-border position in Berlin during the Cold War more formerly called Checkpoint C.

Zulu
> Refers to Greenwich Mean Time or Coordinated Universal Time.

A Tips, Tricks & Trips Extra: Glossary

Accident
An event in which any person suffers serious injury or death or in which the aircraft receives substantial damage.

ADF (Automatic Direction Finder)
An instrument in an aircraft that displays the relative bearing to an NDB.

ADIZ (Air Defense Identification Zone)
The airspace over land or water within which the ready identification, the location, and the control of aircraft are required in the interest of national security.

AH (Artificial Horizon)
An instrument that displays pitch and roll information.

AI (Attitude Indicator)
See AH (Artificial Horizon).

Air carrier
A person or company that whose business involves air transportation whether cargo or passengers.

Air taxi
An aircraft operator whose business involves operations for hire or compensation. The aircraft used must have 30 or less passenger seats and a payload capacity no larger than 7,500 pounds.

Airport
An area on land or water where aircraft can takeoff or land. It also includes any buildings and other facilities.

ALS (Approach Light Systems)
Approach light systems provide a visual means of determining the landing threshold. Various types are employed including VASI, REIL, MALS, MALSF, MALSR, SSALS, SSALF, SSALR, ALSF, and ODALS, which can incorporate different colored lights, pulsating lights, or sequenced lights.

ARTCC (Air Route Traffic Control Center)
A facility that provides air traffic control service to aircraft operating on IFR flight plans within controlled airspace – especially during the en route phase of flight.

ASR (Airport Surveillance Radar)
A type of instrument approach that usually provides only horizontal guidance to the pilot.

ATC (Air Traffic Control)
The people in control towers who arrange takeoffs, landings and other aircraft activity through their area.

ATCT (Airport Traffic Control Tower)
A facility that uses air/ground communications, visual signaling and other devices to provide ATC services to aircraft operating in the vicinity of an airport or on the movement area.

ATIS (Automatic Terminal Information Service)
A radio frequency associated with an airport and its operation. ATIS provides a continuous loop recording providing local weather and other information regarding airport operations. ATIS frequencies are designated on an aeronautical chart with the other airport data.

CAVU
Acronnym for Ceiling And Visibility Unlimited. Considered perfect flying weather with no major clouds and no major haze. CAVU does not consider wind.

CDI (Course Deviation Indicator)
Part of a VOR navigation system that shows how far off a desired course the aircraft is flying.

Ceiling
The height between the earth's surface and the lowest layer of cloud that is reported as *broken*, *overcast*, or *obscuration* and not classified as *thin* or *partial*.

Class G Airpsace (Uncontrolled Airspace)
The airspace not designated as Class A, B, C, D or E.

Combined Center /RAPCON (CERAP)
A facility that combines the functions of an ARTCC and a radar approach control facility.

Commuter
An air carrier operator that carries passengers on at least five round trips per week on at least one route between two or more points. A commuter operates aircraft that has 30 or fewer passenger seats and a payload capability of no more than 7,500 pounds.

CTAF (Common Traffic Advisory Frequency)
A frequency designed to carry out airport advisory practices while operating to or from an airport without an operating control tower.

Delay
Delays occur when any action is taken by a controller that prevents an aircraft from proceeding normally to its destination for an interval of at least fifteen 15 minutes.

Departures
The number of aircraft takeoffs actually performed by domestic and international aircraft.

ADF (Automatic Direction Finder)
A radio that can automatically determine the direction to an NDB or commercial AM radio station.

DG (Directional Gyro)
A device similar to a compass that uses a gyroscope to provide directional information.

DH (Decision Height)
The point on an ILS glide slope when a pilot must decide whether the minimum requirements to continue the approach are met or whether a missed approach procedure must be executed. Note that DH is given both as altitude and height above ground in parentheses. There are three categories of ILS approaches, each with its own minimum decision height. The DH for Category I (2400 feet minimum visibility) is shown on Approach Plates and is typically 200 feet.

Displaced Threshold
A location on a runway, identified with painted markings on paved runways, which indicates the point where a landing aircraft clears all obstructions.

DME (Distance Measuring Equipment)
A radio transmitter associated with a VOR or ILS that enables a NAV radio to determine the distance in nautical miles from the VOR. Given the distance and bearing (or radial) from the VOR, a position fix can be established.

Domestic Operations
Flight operations within and between the 50 states of the United States, Washington, DC, Puerto Rico and the United States Virgin Islands and Canadian transborder operations.

FAF (Final Approach Fix)
A point on an instrument approach where final descent for landing begins. It is typically located at the outer marker beacon (if there is one), between four and seven miles from the runway threshold.

FL (Flight Level)
A level of constant atmospheric pressure related to a reference datum of 29.92 inches of mercury. Each is shown in three digits that represent hundreds of feet.

Flare
The point where an aircraft floats above the runway just before touchdown.

Flight Plan
Specified information relating to the intended flight of an aircraft that is filed with an FSS or an ATC facility.

FSS (Flight Service Station)
Air traffic facilities that provide pilot briefing, enroute communications and VFR search and rescue services, assist lost aircraft and aircraft in emergency situations, relay ATC clearances, originate Notices to Airmen, broadcast aviation weather and NAS information, receive and process IFR flight plans, and monitor NAVAIDs. In addition, at selected locations, FSSs provide Enroute Flight Advisory Service (Flight Watch), take weather observations, issue airport advisories, and advise Customs and Immigration of transborder flights.

GA (General Aviation)
The part of civil aviation that encompasses most aspects of aviation except large aircraft commercial operators.

GPS (Global Position System)
The Global Positioning System consists of a constellation of 24 satellites which transmit a very accurate, high-resolution time signal. A GPS receiver can resolve the signal from three or more satellites to a latitude/longitude position and from five or more satellites to altitude.

GS (Glideslope)
The vertical guidance component of an ILS.

HIRL (High Intensity Runway Lights)
A system of lights for illuminating the outline of a runway during periods of darkness or reduced visibility. Runway lights are classified as low (LIRL), medium (MIRL), or high (HIRL) intensity. Runway edge lights are white except for the final 2000' of instrument approach runways where they are amber. As you approach a runway, the lights that mark the beginning of the runway are green and the lights which mark the end of the runway are red.

Hours Flown
The time from the moment an aircraft leaves the ground until it touches the ground again.

HSI (Horizontal Situation Indicator)
Combines the functions of a VOR and a DGIAC

IFF (Identify Friend or Foe)
See Transponder

IFR (Instrument Flight Rules)
Further training after a pilot's license to let pilots fly in harsher weather. This does not include thunderstorms, etc., but flying in clouds is allowed. This doesn't only refer to flying by instruments alone, but also to understand the Air Traffic Control system.

IFR Aircraft/IFR Flight
An aircraft flying according to instrument flight rules.

ILS (Instrument Landing System)
A system of transmitters and lights which assist in landing an aircraft by providing a three-dimensional representation of the correct heading and glide slope. The complete system consists of a localizer for heading orientation, a glide slope transmitter for establishing the correct descent angle, and outer, middle, and inner maker beacons for determining the distance to the runway.

Incident
An occurrence other than an accident associated with the operation of an aircraft that affects or could affect the safety of operations.

Latitude
Latitude is the angular distance from the equator north or south to the geographic poles. It is measured in degrees north or south from 0-90. Lines of latitude are parallel to each other and are called parallels of latitude. A degree of latitude is equal to 60 nautical miles and a minute of latitude is equal to one nautical mile.

LDA (Landing Distance Available)
The length of a runway beyond a displaced threshold.

LIRL (Low Intensity Runway Lights)
A system of lights for illuminating the outline of a runway during periods of darkness or reduced visibility. Runway lights are classified as low (LIRL), medium (MIRL), or high (HIRL) intensity. Runway edge lights are white except for the final 2000' of instrument approach runways where they are amber. As you approach a runway, the lights that mark the beginning of the runway are green and the lights that mark the end of the runway are red.

LOC (Localizer)
The horizontal guidance component of an ILS

LOM (Locator Outer Marker)
A navigation aid, similar to a NDB, which transmits a non-directional radio signal used to locate the outer marker of an airport runway. It is designated on an aeronautical chart as a magenta donut with a name, an ID, and a frequency. Tune your ADF (Automatic Direction Finder) to the given frequency and it will display the bearing from your position to the transmitter.

Longitude
Longitude is the angular distance east or west of the prime meridian. It is measured in degrees east or west from 0-180. The prime meridian is the great circle that runs approximately through Greenwich, England. A line of longitude is a called a meridian and runs through each geographic pole. Meridians of longitude converge at the poles.

LORAN (Long RANge Navigation)
A navigation system, originally created for marine use, that uses timing differences between multiple low-frequency transmissions to provide accurate latitude/longitude position information, at best to within 50 feet

Magnetic Variation
Compasses point to the north magnetic pole, which differs from the geographic North Pole, or true north. (The lines of longitude on a chart converge at the geographic north and south poles). The angular difference between magnetic north and true north is called magnetic variation or just variation. Variation is not constant in either time or location. Although the magnetic pole moves slowly over time, variation is fixed in the flight simulator database and we do not have to be concerned with annular increase in variation. However, since the magnetic core of the earth is not uniform, the amount of variation is different all over the world. Variation is measured either east or west depending on whether it causes your compass to point east or west of true north, respectively. Connecting the points on the earth where there is no variation creates a meandering line called an agonic line. The signal transmitted by a VOR is adjusted for variation so that the radial bearing will agree with your compass.

MAP (Missed Approach Point)
The point on an instrument approach where the DH is reached and a decision must be made to either continue the approach or execute a missed approach procedure.

Miles Flown
The miles that are determined in airport-to-airport distances for each flight completed.

NAS (National Airspace Systems)
The common network of US airspace; air navigation facilities, equipment and services, airports or landing areas; aeronautical charts, information and services; rules, regulations and procedures, technical information, and human resources and material. Included are system components shared jointly with the military.

Nautical Mile
A nautical mile is equal to 6076.1 feet or 1852 meters.

NDB (Non-Directional radio Beacon)
A navigation aid that transmits a non-directional radio signal. It is designated on an aeronautical chart as a magenta donut with a name, an ID, and a frequency. Tune your ADF (Automatic Direction Finder) to the given frequency and it will display the bearing from your position to the transmitter.

OBS (Omnibearing Selector)
Part of a VOR receiver system that lets the pilot select a course to or from a VOR station

PAPI (Precision Approach Path Indicator)
PAPI uses lights similar to the VASI, but are installed in a single row of two or four lights. They can be present on either or both sides of the runway. If all the lights are white, you are too high - if all the lights are red, you are too low. If the outer lights are white and the inner lights are red, you are on the correct glide slope.

PAR (Precision Approach Radar)
A ground-radar based instrument approach that provides both horizontal and vertical guidance

Pattern
Also called "circuits" in the UK and Canada. Pilots follow a pattern when they want to land their aircraft (unless ATC instructs differently). The *downwind leg* is parallel to the runway about a half-mile away in the opposite direction they will be landing on. At the end of the downwind leg, you turn 90 degrees to the *base leg* and fly that half-mile so you're becoming near to being in line with the runway. You turn 90 degrees again, and you should be lined up for the *final leg* or *final approach*. If everything is right, you should be pointed right down the runway and ready to land. The reasons for the pattern is to so pilots can become familiar with airport conditions before landing, to space out traffic that is near the airport and to give safe maneuvering room to lose altitude while keeping the runway and airport traffic in sight.

PIC (Pilot In Command)
The pilot responsible for the operation and safety of an aircraft during flight time.

Positive Control
The separation of all air traffic within designated airspace by air traffic control.

REIL (Runway End Identifier Lights)
A system consisting of a pair synchronized flashing lights located on either side of the runway threshold. They may be either omni-directional or facing the approach area. They are used to assist in distinguishing runways surrounded by other lighting or during reduced visibility.

RMI (Radio Magnetic Indicator)
A display similar to an ADF with two pointers that could be attached to either VOR or ADF receivers.

RNAV (aRea Navigation)
A VOR/DME based system that allows a pilot to fly to an arbitrary point instead of to a point under which a VOR exists

Runway ID
The runway ID gives the approximate runway heading in degrees. Each runway has two associated IDs. For example, a runway that is oriented approximately east-west will have the IDs 9/27 indicating runway headings of 90° and 270°. Two or more runways with the same orientation are distinguished with the letters L, R, or C for Left, Right or Center, respectively.

Runway Incursion
Any occurrence at an airport involving an aircraft or object on the ground (vehicle, person, etc.) that creates collision hazards.

Separation Minimals
The minimum distances (longitudinal, lateral or vertical) by which aircraft are spaced according to air traffic control procedures.

Slip
A method of intentionally losing altitude quickly or slide into a final approach during a heavy wind.

Squawk
The number set by the pilot in the transponder to identify the aircraft to air traffic controllers.

Stall
The point at which wings fail to generate enough lift to keep the plane stable.

Sumps
Points underneath each fuel tank to test for contamination like water or other debris.

TCH (Threshold Crossing Height)
The height above the runway that an aircraft on an ILS glide slope will be as it crosses the threshold or displaced threshold.

Transponder
An airborne transmitter that responds to a ground-based signal to provide air traffic controllers with more accurate and reliable position information. A transponder may also provide the aircraft's altitude to air traffic control.

Turbojet Aircraft
An aircraft having a jet engine in which the energy of the jet operates a turbine which in turn operates the air compressor.

Turboprop Aircraft
An aircraft having a jet engine in which the energy of the jet operates a turbine that drives the propeller.

VASI (Visual Approach Slope Indicator)
VASI is a system of two or three two-color light bars, usually set on the left side of the runway, which indicate the glide slope and the touchdown point. Each light bar consists of hooded red and white lights oriented so that only one of the two colors is visible at a time. If your altitude is such that the light from both bars is red, you are too low. If they are both white, you are too high. If the closer light is white and the farther light is red, you are on the correct glide slope. A two bar system provides only one glide slope, usually 3°. A three bar system provides a second glide slope, normally ¼ degree higher.

VFR (Visual Flight Rules)
Private pilots begin as VFR certified. This generally means that they must have at least three miles of visibility, be 500 feet below clouds, 1000 feet above clouds, and/or 2000 feet next to clouds at a bare minimum. Unless the pilot has an Instrument Rating, they're required to avoid all clouds and weather.

VOR (Very high-frequency Omni-directional Range)
A VOR is a navigation aid that transmits a very high-frequency radio signal. It is designated on an aeronautical chart in blue as a compass rose with a magnetic north indicator, a name, an ID, and a frequency. Tune your NAV radio to the given frequency and adjust the indicator needle to the center of the dial. The three-digit value on the dial is your bearing either to or from the VOR and is called a radial. Your position is somewhere on this radial. If the VOR transmits a DME (Distance Measuring Equipment) signal, you also know your exact distance from the VOR in nautical miles - in other words, you have a position fix.

VPD (Vehicle / Pedestrian Deviation)
A movement by a vehicle operator or pedestrian that has not been authorized by air traffic control (includes aircraft operated by nonpilots).

Index